MOTIVATIONAL INTERVIEWING
FOR LEADERS IN THE HELPING PROFESSIONS

Applications of Motivational Interviewing
Stephen Rollnick, William R. Miller,
and Theresa B. Moyers, Series Editors
www.guilford.com/AMI

Since the publication of Miller and Rollnick's classic *Motivational Interviewing*, now in its third edition, MI has been widely adopted as a tool for facilitating change. This highly practical series includes general MI resources as well as books on specific clinical contexts, problems, and populations. Each volume presents powerful MI strategies that are grounded in research and illustrated with concrete, "how-to-do-it" examples.

Motivational Interviewing in Health Care: Helping Patients Change Behavior
Stephen Rollnick, William R. Miller, and Christopher C. Butler

Motivational Interviewing with Adolescents and Young Adults
Sylvie Naar and Mariann Suarez

Motivational Interviewing in Social Work Practice
Melinda Hohman

Motivational Interviewing in the Treatment of Anxiety
Henny A. Westra

Motivational Interviewing, Third Edition: Helping People Change
William R. Miller and Stephen Rollnick

Motivational Interviewing in Groups
Christopher C. Wagner and Karen S. Ingersoll, with Contributors

Motivational Interviewing in the Treatment
of Psychological Problems, Second Edition
Hal Arkowitz, William R. Miller, and Stephen Rollnick, Editors

Motivational Interviewing in Diabetes Care
Marc P. Steinberg and William R. Miller

Motivational Interviewing in Nutrition and Fitness
Dawn Clifford and Laura Curtis

Motivational Interviewing in Schools:
Conversations to Improve Behavior and Learning
Stephen Rollnick, Sebastian G. Kaplan, and Richard Rutschman

Motivational Interviewing with Offenders: Engagement, Rehabilitation, and Reentry
Jill D. Stinson and Michael D. Clark

Motivational Interviewing and CBT:
Combining Strategies for Maximum Effectivenss
Sylvie Naar and Steven A. Safren

Building Motivational Interviewing Skills: A Practitioner Workbook, Second Edition
David B. Rosengren

Coaching Athletes to Be Their Best: Motivational Interviewing in Sports
Stephen Rollnick, Jonathan Fader, Jeff Breckon, and Theresa B. Moyers

Motivational Interviewing for Leaders in the Helping Professions:
Facilitating Change in Organizations
Colleen Marshall and Anette Søgaard Nielsen

MOTIVATIONAL INTERVIEWING
for Leaders in the Helping Professions

Facilitating Change in Organizations

Colleen Marshall
Anette Søgaard Nielsen

Series Editor's Note by
Theresa B. Moyers

THE GUILFORD PRESS
New York London

Library of Congress Cataloging-in-Publication Data

Names: Marshall, Colleen, author. | Nielsen, Anette Søgaard, author.
Title: Motivational interviewing for leaders in the helping professions :
    facilitating change in organizations / Colleen Marshall, Anette Søgaard
    Nielsen.
Description: New York : The Guilford Press, [2020] | Series: Applications
    of motivational interviewing | Includes bibliographical references and
    index.
Identifiers: LCCN 2020025569 | ISBN 9781462543816 (paperback ; alk. paper)
    | ISBN 9781462543823 (cloth ; alk. paper) | ISBN 9781462543847 (pdf)
Subjects: LCSH: Motivational interviewing. | Employee motivation. |
    Organizational change. | Leadership. | Social service.
Classification: LCC BF637.I5 M365 2020 | DDC 158.3/9—dc23
LC record available at *https://lccn.loc.gov/2020025569*

About the Authors

Colleen Marshall, MA, LMFT, has extensive experience in clinical practice, leadership, and management, and has held executive and senior-level positions in large behavioral health organizations. She is currently Director of Behavioral Health Operations for Well, a health technology and services company, and serves as a consultant and trainer for start-up, nonprofit, and health care organizations. Ms. Marshall is a member of the Motivational Interviewing Network of Trainers (MINT), for which she has served as Chair, Treasurer, board member, and trainer of new trainers. She has helped to consult and lead large-scale motivational interviewing implementation and has been invited to speak at regional, national, and international conferences.

Anette Søgaard Nielsen, PhD, is Professor at the Institute of Clinical Research at the University of Southern Denmark. She has extensive experience in leadership and management, primarily as the leader of one of Denmark's largest treatment institutions for alcohol use disorders, and as the head of smaller research teams. Dr. Nielsen has been a member of MINT since 1997, for which she has served as a board member and trainer of new trainers. She is the author or coauthor of numerous peer-reviewed articles, chapters, books, and other publications, with a focus on evidence-based treatment of alcohol use disorders.

Series Editor's Note

The book you are holding in your hands is a welcome addition to the Applications of Motivational Interviewing series. We have been trying for many years to bring forward a book about the value of motivational interviewing (MI) for organizational leaders. We saw a natural fit for MI in complex organizations, but we also did not want a book portraying MI as a way of manipulating employees and colleagues to do things that were not in their best interest. This long-awaited book is just what we were hoping for. It comes from two outstanding MI experts who work in complex organizations and bring a wealth of information that we hope will be useful to at least two groups of readers. First, we hope this book will be helpful for those who want to develop their skills as leaders among the employees and colleagues with whom they work every day. In addition, we are excited about the possibilities for those who will use the ideas in this book to help their organizations as a whole to move forward. Get ready for a new way of thinking about leadership!

THERESA B. MOYERS

Acknowledgments

For both of us, this book has been a journey of reflecting on what true collaboration, partnership, support, and leadership look like. We would like to thank everyone who has provided this help to us. Although we cannot name everyone who has influenced us and helped us in our development as leaders, there are a few people that we want to be sure to thank. To Orville Coonce, Karen Thomsen, and Unni Bille-Brahe: You were the perfect leaders. You always believed in us, challenged us, and created the space for us to grow. Thank you for all you taught us. Many of the ideas of this book come from what you modeled. To Terri Moyers: Thank you for gently pushing us to write this book. We so appreciate your confidence in us and your support. To William Miller and Stephen Rollnick: Without your partnership and collaboration, none of this would have been possible. Your giving spirit, compassion, and brilliance have really changed the world, and certainly have changed us. Thank you for introducing us to motivational interviewing. To the MINT (Motivational Interviewing Network of Trainers) community: Thank you for creating the space where we always feel welcomed, accepted, inspired, and loved. We have been very lucky to be surrounded by such great role models and compassionate people. To Susan Dew: Thank you for all the editing, language guidance, and help in making our ideas clear. To Lone Vester Nielsen: Thank you for the beautiful and simple artwork. Your art has really helped make the concepts of this book come alive. And to Jim Nageotte and the staff at The Guilford Press: Thanks for all your help in editing and guiding this book. We truly have appreciated your support. Thank you all.

Colleen: I wish to express special thanks to Renee Sievert: Thank you for your friendship and collaboration. Many of the best ideas I have learned about leadership have come from your trainings and our conversations. To my husband, Greg Marshall: You are my model for the perfect partnership. You make everything possible in my life. I am so lucky to call you my husband. To my parents, Clarence J. (C. J.) and Donna Ross: Thank you for always being my biggest cheerleaders. Thank you for providing me great models of family, love, and supportive parenting. To my boys, Thomas, Jeffrey, Russell, and Daniel: You have always been and always will be my why, my motivation.

Anette: I wish to express special thanks to my husband, Peter Schøning, for supporting me and for being so patient with me. I love you. To my parents, Anne-Lise and Karl Nielsen, for believing in me always. To my son and daughter, Anders and Amalie, who have managed to grow into wonderful, considerate, and kind young people. I am so proud of you.

Finally, we will just add: It has been really fun to write this book together. We have learned of lot from each other, and the result is not just a book, but also a friendship. Thank you all, for helping us to make that happen.

Preface

We feel fortunate to be able to share with you our many years of experience in learning motivational interviewing (MI) and using it in the workplace. The aim of this book is simple. In introducing you to MI, we hope to draw your attention to a specific, not well-addressed, workplace problem. We hope that by reading this book, by thinking about the ideas shared therein, and, most important, by applying what you learn, you will be better equipped to manage a very specific problem that faces most leaders every day: *How can you best help your employees and organization embrace change?*

MI is a way of helping others strengthen their own motivation to change, of enabling them to resolve their internal ambivalence and move toward making changes in their lives, including their work lives. We illustrate how the skilled use of MI can help leaders support employees in their development and their ability to make important changes. We also describe how leaders can benefit from applying the principles of MI when implementing change across the whole organization.

MI and leadership have been the backbone of our work lives for decades. We have both served as leaders of small and large institutions in health care, social services, and helping organizations for over 20 years. We have also served as MI trainers and consultants, training and supporting helping professionals to learn and implement MI for over 15 years. This book builds on our own experiences, both as leaders of helping organizations and as MI trainers. We realized while writing this book how much our work with MI has shaped our attitudes toward employees and organizations. In particular, we realized how the spirit, processes, and strategies of MI have helped us support and engage work-places where employees want to come to work motivated to achieve their organization's mission.

In addition to building on our own experiences as supervisors, man-agers, and MI trainers, the book draws significantly on a range of dis-cussions with colleagues. As members of the Motivational Interviewing Network of Trainers (MINT), we are fortunate to have access to train-ers, researchers, practitioners, and helping professionals from all over the world, all of whom focus on the best way to increase motivation and support people in making changes in their own lives. We are grateful to be part of this community and indebted to it for the free sharing of thoughts, information, and ideas. We are aware that many of our ideas presented here derive from that robust collaboration.

The cases in this book are drawn from our own work and lives, both as leaders and MI trainers, or the work of the managers whom we have trained or supported in using MI in their leadership. The fact that these case examples tend to highlight the top leader of an organization also reflects our experience. However, we firmly believe that the exam-ples and the information shared here are relevant to leaders at all levels in an organization. As long as your role is to help an individual or a team change or grow, these ideas are valuable. You do not need to be the most senior leader to benefit from incorporating MI into your thinking and your approach. Some cases are composites that, for purposes of illustra-tion, blend a number of experiences into one narrative. Other examples are close descriptions of our experience of a specific interaction with an employee or of a specific situation, but not detailed enough to identify any of our individual workplaces or any of the staff we have had the pleasure to work with. In the book, all cases have been anonymized, and names and job titles are simply made up to ensure privacy.

Like you, we have read or sampled a number of books about lead-ership, and know that time-strapped leaders do not often read books closely from beginning to end. If you too have limited time and want to select the parts of the book of particular interest to you, here we offer a guide and a few suggestions.

We have grouped the chapters into five parts. Part I, *Beginning,* comprising Chapters 1–3, explains the foundation of MI and why MI and leadership fit together. Chapter 1 describes in detail how and why MI and modern leadership fit well together. This chapter may be helpful to you in beginning to understand the benefits of integrating MI as part of your strategy.

Chapter 2 gives a brief introduction to MI. If you are already famil-iar with the principles of MI, you may want to skip this chapter. On the other hand, if you feel you need a quick brushup on MI, you might like to read this chapter.

Chapter 3 describes situations in which MI is beneficial in leadership and those in which it is not the right choice. Leadership is more than simply supporting change in employees and organizations, and there are times when MI should not be used, and leaders should turn to other strategies. We recommend that you ponder this chapter carefully. Although MI can be really helpful, there are also a range of situations for which the use of MI is not appropriate.

The next four parts and their component chapters describe the four processes of MI.

Part II, *Engaging,* comprising Chapters 4–6, describes the process of *engaging*—the particulars of listening as a leader in an organization, determining what your staff and organization need, and engaging them in the process of considering change.

Part III, *Focusing,* comprising Chapters 7 and 8, explains how to choose the right direction in *focusing* for change.

Part IV, *Evoking,* comprising Chapters 9 and 10, details how *evoking* and strengthening the motivation to change can help your employees and organization actualize change.

In Part V, *Planning,* Chapters 11 and 12 outline the process of *planning,* and Chapter 13 guides you in developing your own plan for learning and practicing MI.

For each of the four processes of MI, we first describe the process in terms of an individual employee before setting forth how MI unfolds when you apply it to an entire organization. Then, we include an employee vignette and an organization vignette presenting the specific process we just described. Our hope is that by explaining the process and then following the explanation with a detailed example of how it is applied, you will better hear how MI might sound.

If you are particularly interested in supporting your individual staff members, you might want to pay special attention to Chapters 3, 4, 7, 9, and 11, along with the examples set forth in them. If you want to know how to implement change in your organization as a whole, then Chapters 3, 5, 6, 8, 10, and 12, and the examples in them, may be the most applicable. Whatever your particular need or interest, we still recommend that you skim through all the chapters before diving into the ones that you want to focus on most. Each chapter ends with a brief summary highlighting the most important takeaways. Following the summary in Chapters 1 and 3 and in each process chapter (4, 5, 6, 7, 8, 9, 10, 11, and 12), we provide a self-reflective exercise designed to help you apply MI to your thinking and leadership approach.*

---

*The employee vignette, organization vignette, and self-reflective exercises (for the individual and for the organization) are available in their entirety on the book's website (see the box at the end of the table of contents).

Leading management teams is a bit different from leading larger organizations. In our experience, it is important to understand how the health of the leadership team affects the application of MI. The leader needs to consider when she or he might need to build trust or other team dynamics prior to using MI. We have a chapter specifically about leadership teams. If you lead or are a part of a team, Chapter 6 may be helpful to you.

Finally, the closing chapter, Chapter 13, contains suggestions for how to learn MI and incorporate it into your leadership approach. These suggestions reinforce the lessons we hope you will derive from the self-reflective exercises in Chapters 4–12. We know that using and learning MI requires practice and feedback, and these exercises and the final chapter provide practical material to explore MI techniques.

We hope you will enjoy the book and find it helpful. We have certainly enjoyed writing it. We have also created Facebook and LinkedIn groups that you can find on the book's website (see the box at the end of the table of contents), and hope that you will join our group to share your ideas and practice examples, and to gain support from the community as you consider adopting MI as part of your leadership approach.

Contents

PART IV. EVOKING

PART V. PLANNING

APPENDICES

PART I

BEGINNING

CHAPTER 1

Why Motivational Interviewing and Leadership?

Being drawn to pick up this book suggests that you are a manager or leader. You may have a leadership title, such as supervisor or manager, or find yourself a leader simply because of your influence. You might also be someone seeking to grow into a leadership role or thinking about what it takes to be a successful leader. Regardless of your role or how you came to be attracted to this book, we hope that you have picked it up because you want to become the most effective and impactful leader you possibly can.

Becoming a successful leader consists of more than implementing what lies between the covers of this book. However, in introducing you to motivational interviewing (MI), we hope to draw your attention to a specific, not well-addressed, workplace problem. We hope that by reading this book, thinking about the ideas shared therein and, most important, applying what you learn, you will be better equipped to manage a specific problem that faces most leaders every day: *How can you best help your employees and organization embrace change?*

SUCCESSFUL LEADERSHIP

Good leadership is one of the most essential conditions for organizational success. It is increasingly recognized as key to positive employee and organizational outcomes (Gifford, Graham, Ehrhart, Davies, & Aarons, 2017; Green, Albanese, Cafri, & Aarons, 2014; Judge &

3

Piccolo, 2004). But what does it mean to be a successful leader? Being an effective leader is a journey that never truly ends, and one where you never actually arrive. There are thousands of articles, books, webinars, conferences, and consulting groups focused on the topic of successful leadership. All of them describe how important leadership is to the success of organizations, and most of them also explain what you should do to achieve that success. For instance, leaders need to have a compelling vision for why their organization does the work it does if they are to inspire and mobilize their employees (Sinek, 2009). They need to have the skills to develop a healthy team, strategy, message, and direction (Lencioni, 2012). They need to have character and the ability to model vulnerability, trust, and personal growth in order to establish a safe and innovative culture (Covey, 1989; Quinn, 2004). They need to know what actually aids in motivating employee behavior (Pink, 2009). They need to have the technical skills required to accomplish their organization's unique mission and task. They need to be able to perform the role of coach, teacher, visionary, mentor, ally, and manager. In other words: A lot is asked of leaders. We all look to our leaders to give us vision, direction, and a way forward. However, the million dollar question remains: *How* do you motivate your employees and your organization? *How* do you guide them? *How* do you help them change?

MI: A HELPFUL STRATEGY FOR LEADERS

This book discusses how the science-based behavior change approach of MI can complement your efforts to help your teams, employees, mentees, and organizations change and grow (Miller & Rollnick, 2013). In our experience in both executive-level leadership roles and direct consumer-facing behavior change services, we have found that MI has much to offer. The insights from MI have helped us guide our organizations and employees, enabling them to make the necessary changes that led to personal and organizational success. We will share some of these stories with you. We hope that if you should choose to use MI, it will bring you the same success.

Successful leadership is most often defined as the ability to ensure that the organization is achieving its mission. In health care and social services, that typically means achieving the triple aim of providing effective treatment, a good patient experience, and a reduced cost of care. Implementation of change is necessary to respond to client input, to integrate the most recent research, and to follow the most relevant efficiency improvements in the field.

Pursuing continuous quality improvement means leaders are often faced with helping others change. This could be as simple as helping a staffer complete a task he seems reluctant to take on, or as big as coaching a professional to take on a role she feels is beyond her reach and ability. The change could be as mundane as helping your organization tweak a simple process and as major as redesigning an entire clinical program. Whatever the challenge, if behavioral change is the key to the employee's and organization's success, then MI will likely be highly useful.

The ability to help your staff grow, perform at their best, and achieve success is one of your most important roles as a leader, if not your most crucial role. When leaders seek to understand, coach, and train an employee to accomplish goals and that employee fails, it is easy to become frustrated and blame the employee. Leaders may blame employees for not being the right fit, not having the necessary skills or the right character attributes, or for simply just being a pain in the neck. They then look to their human resources department for help in removing them from the organization. This approach is similar to the way clients were treated for years in the addictions and behavior change field. They were blamed for their illness, their behavior, and their failure. People tried to find ways to remove them from their communities, their programs, and their families. There had to be a better way to help people than by simply removing them from our lives. MI has helped many people provide this better way to help. Changes that were once thought impossible are now possible. We now also know that MI can help us find a better way to help our employees change as well. We certainly cannot promise you that by adding MI to your skill set you can avoid removing employees in the future. But we have found that by implementing the spirit and the communication strategies of MI in leadership, we often are able to reach better solutions than simply firing and replacing people.

What MI has added to our toolkit as leaders, and hopefully will add to yours as well, is a specific way of interacting with and believing in people. It provides a way of seeing employees through their own eyes. It helps leaders understand their staff's *stuckness* and offers practical skills to teach you how to guide a conversation toward change. Leaders are told over and over that they must listen to their employees but are rarely taught *how* to do so. The skills used in MI help you do just that: listen to understand, rather than listen to respond or to fix. We hope that by learning how to listen and by understanding what motivates people to change their behavior and what you can do to facilitate the process, you will be able to directly influence the success of your employees and your organization.

As with any method or approach, MI is no panacea. We discuss the limitations of MI, the situations in which you might consider using MI, and those for which you will want to apply an entirely different leadership approach. However, if you choose to learn and use MI with your employees, people you once believed *could* not or *would* not change will surprise you and perform at work in ways that you did not think possible before.

WHAT IS LEADERSHIP?

Before jumping into discussing when MI may be a helpful listening and change strategy for leaders, we will spend a little time on what we mean by leadership. Leadership has been described in many ways, but it typically revolves around who you are and what you do. Some describe leadership as a way of being that involves what you value and what you model. For instance, Quinn (2004) notes that "leadership is first about what we are. . . . It is not what [leaders] do, because each one of them is unique in how they pull it off. It is not about what they do; it is about who they are." Other leadership authors note, on the contrary, that although values, virtues, and mindset are very important, leadership is also about what leaders are trying to accomplish, or about what they do and what roles they play. Drucker (1967) explains that the leader's objective is "to leverage the strengths of people and make their weakness become irrelevant," and Blanchard and Miller (2004) add, "The servant leader manifests caring by knowing the potential of each of the followers, respecting their powers and skills, and listening to what is in their hearts. People cannot be led where they do not want to go. Business books say that the goal of a leader is to motivate people. However, people cannot be motivated since they are already motivated. The goal of a leader is to identify these motivations and tap into them."

In truth, it is both who you are and what you do. Blanchard and Miller (2004) describe it best: "Many believe they can become effective leaders if they only had the skills. Others believe they can become great leaders if they could just develop their character. Both are wrong. It takes skills and character." Both skills and character are also essential for the effective use of MI as well.

We discuss both of these perspectives briefly in the following sections: the roles leaders play and the values and virtues successful leaders embody. Finally, we explore how MI and leadership fit together.

LEADERSHIP DEFINED

Leaders hold organizational roles that require the performance of specific functions, which include, to name but a few:

• *Visionary.* Leaders actively communicate the vision for the organization, the "why" behind their company's existence: Why do they exist?; Why do they do what they do?; Why does what they do matter to the world?; and Why should people care? (Sinek, 2009).

- *Manager.* Leaders oversee the organization, so that it achieves its mission and gets the job done. This includes overseeing and distributing tasks and the workload. It includes responding if the quality of the work is not as good as expected. It includes making the best use of the resources available and constantly being aware of budgetary and organizational demands.

- *Supervisor.* In contrast to managing, when supervising, the leader gives feedback, guides, supports, and helps the staff become more and more skillful at their tasks.

- *Implementer.* A leader is a change facilitator. In organizations, positions, tasks, and methods change, and it is the leader's job to ensure that the organization implements those changes.

- *Dual leadership.* Leaders have a constant focus on the organization and its employees. This is often referred to as dual leadership, meaning that the leader focuses on the staff, trying to lead and support them the best she can, while at the same time keeping her eye on the organization, taking stock of how she and her employees impact the collective. For instance, a leader may want to acknowledge an employee who has done a great job and give her a raise. However, before doing so, the leader has to consider how giving just one employee a raise will affect the other staff, the budget, and how it fits with the overall strategy for salaries. Similarly, the leader may feel tempted to refrain from approaching a staff member whose work is not up to scratch, because she fears it will lead to a conflict. However, the leader has to consider what that avoidance would indicate to the rest of the organization.

Associated with these and other leader roles are a range of leadership functions and tasks. Many leadership books and papers present long checklists of tasks that leaders should perform and suggestions for how they should behave. Such a checklist might look like the following, inspired by a paper on leadership scales (Gifford et al., 2017):

- Have a profound knowledge of your organization and what it is delivering.
- Be able to develop a plan for implementation of change.
- Recognize and appreciate employees' efforts.
- Support employees.
- Answer questions about the change that is to be implemented.

- Persevere through the ups and downs of the implementation of change.
- Respond to critical issues.
- Remove obstacles.
- Establish clear standards.
- Support further learning and growth among employees.

Some of these required leadership tasks and functions are straight-forward and easy to understand, albeit not necessarily easy to perform. Others, however, may appear more diffuse and difficult to pin down like, for instance, support employees, recognize the employee's efforts, and support further learning and growth. These more diffuse tasks are not only difficult to operationalize, they are also consistently highlighted as the most important leadership functions correlated to organizational success. These rather nebulous functions have been identified as necessary for the implementation of change (Sfantou et al., 2017); important for staff job satisfaction (Pishgooie, Atashzadeh-Shoorideh, Falco-Pegueroles, & Lotfi, 2018); and essential to prevent burnout (Green, Albanese, Shapiro, & Aarons, 2014; Madathil, Heck, & Schuldberg, 2014). In essence, it seems as though the difficult parts of leadership functions and tasks are the most important and the most intractable in terms of knowing whether you are doing them well. We have found that MI can help with operationalizing many of these more vague functions.

LEADER STYLE, VALUES, AND MINDSET

Part of knowing whether you are performing these essential functions well is to know whether your intention flows from *who you are* as a leader and not just from what you are doing. Leadership is, in other words, more than performing specific tasks and functions. Equally important is what a leader values and what leadership style she models.

Overall leadership styles can be antisocial or prosocial. Features of an antisocial leadership style are aggressiveness, deceitfulness, lack of remorse, and responding aggressively to criticism—particularly from subordinates (Piotrowska, Stride, Croft, & Rowe, 2015). In contrast, leaders with a prosocial leadership style have an interest in the development and well-being of others, and are empathetic to the needs, sensitivities, and difficulties of those they lead. They tend to be supportive and friendly, fostering confidence and creativity in their employees and organizations (Colonello, Petrocchi, & Heinrichs, 2017; Ewest, 2017). They endorse high moral standards for themselves and their organization and seek to avoid causing harm to themselves or others (Boyatzis, Smith, & Blaize, 2006). They have a highly developed sense of responsibility

(Ewest, 2017), and seek to create safety and security for their organization, not least in a situation of change (Mikulincer & Shaver, 2007). The leadership style that leaders model has a direct impact on the staff and organization. When leaders act from an antisocial or self-focused perspective, they create a workplace based on fear (Gilbert & Basran, 2019), achieving compliance at best. They lack the ability to help others grow and create. However, when leaders lead from a prosocial or other-focused perspective, they are more likely to lead an organization toward positive change, personal growth, and organizational innovations (Guerrero, Padwa, Fenwick, Harris, & Aarons, 2016; Lorenzi, 2004; Swensen, Pugh, McMullan, & Kabcenell, 2013). In particular, prosocial leaders promote trust, mutual sharing, team building, creativity, and innovation (Gilbert & Basran, 2019; Øvretveit, 2008).

In addition to leadership style, what leaders value and what motivates them are also important to successfully lead a change in an organization. Leaders who successfully lead change hold different values or intentions than leaders who fail to do so. Quinn (2004) describes leaders who successfully lead some of the hardest changes as purpose centered, internally driven, focused on others, and open to those around them. These behaviors differ from the traditional conception of leadership, in which the leader is externally driven, self-focused, closed off, and comfort centered. In the externally driven conception, leaders tend to put their interests ahead of the collective. They ignore or deny the existence of signals to change, and define themselves by how they think they are perceived and how well they obtain external resources. This type of leader is neither effective nor open to change. When leaders view their role through this prism, they are unable to listen, adapt, motivate, inspire, or lead others.

In contrast, if leaders are *other focused,* they transcend their own self-interest and put the common good and welfare of others first. They gain in authenticity and transparency, nurturing trust and enriching the levels of connectivity in their teams. They are *externally open.* They move out of their comfort zone. They listen and they experiment. They seek real feedback and adapt, reaching exponentially higher levels of discovery, awareness, competence, and vision. They are *internally driven*; they examine their own hypocrisy and close the gaps between their values and behaviors. They reach for higher levels of personal security and confidence. They are *purpose centered*; they clarify what result they want to create. Full of energy, they commit, engage, and hold to an unwavering standard in pursuit of a meaningful purpose (Kirkeby, 2004; Quinn, 2004).

It is generally acknowledged that the values of integrity, honesty, and compassion are essential for successful leaders and successful organizations as well. In a *Harvard Business Review* article, Covey and

Conant (2016) discuss the connections between employee trust and organizational financial performance. They quote from *Fortune* magazine's research on the 100 Best Companies to Work For, which showed that companies with high levels of trust "beat the average annualized returns of the S&P 500 by a factor of three. . . . With trust, all things are possible—most important: continuous improvement and sustainable, measurable, tangible results in the marketplace."

What a leaders' values are and how they behave directly affect their ability to be successful and help others to be successful as well. Leaders cannot fake this (Covey, 1989). They must start by modeling and leading based on who they are and what they believe. If leaders are in the business merely to enrich themselves, viewing their employees as simply resources to be used, they have no interest in the development or growth of their employees. This mindset is known and felt throughout the entire organization. Then the relationship between leader and organization is transactional at best. On the other hand, if leaders believe in the potential of others and believe that employees are team members who have something of value to bring to the organization and have their own original thoughts to contribute, their leadership style will be reflective of this belief. Others will see that, feel that, and respond in kind.

In order to be a leader who leads others to a purpose and a cause worth working for, you must first take a hard look inside. You need to look at your own motives and values, and lead from a place that is congruent with who you are and your intentions. Successful leaders get closer and closer to closing the gap between their values and their behavior with every decision, every interaction, and every conversation. As Blanchard and Miller (2004) shares, "All genuine leadership is built on trust. There are many ways to build trust. One way is to live consistently with the values you profess."

Who leaders are—what their styles are, what their virtues are, and what they value—is critical to the success or failure of implementing changes in the organization (Aarons, Ehrhart, & Farahnak, 2014; Greenhalgh, Robert, Macfarlane, Bate, & Kyriakidou, 2004; Øvretveit, 2008).

TRANSFORMATIONAL LEADERSHIP

Transformational leadership is another way of describing the kind of leader we have in mind when we think about leaders who might also use MI to support change. Transformational leadership is described as a leader's ability to recognize the unique talents and strengths of individual employees, encourage new ways of thinking and problem solving through intellectual stimulation, create a shared sense of purpose among employees through inspirational motivation, and provide positive role modeling (Aarons, Sommerfeld, & Willging, 2011; Brimhall et al., 2016). Transformational leaders empower staff and nurture them through change, attempting to help them transcend their own motives and self-interest for the sake of others or a greater good. Researchers have found that transformational leadership stimulates staff development and creativity, which in turn increases staff openness to change (Aarons, 2006). Transformational leadership is positively associated with performance (Bass, Avolio, Jung, & Berson, 2003). Transformational leaders can be defined as leaders who "motivate others to do more than they intended and often even more than they ever thought possible." But again we must ask, *how*? *How* do transformational leaders support their employees to change and achieve more than they thought possible? *How* do they motivate employees and their organization? This is where we believe MI comes in.

THE PARTNERSHIP BETWEEN LEADERSHIP AND MI

Quinn, Covey, Blanchard, and Aarons, among others, make clear that *who* you are as a person, *what* you believe in, and *what* your values are form the bedrock for how you lead. What you value and believe in and how you view your role are clearly communicated in your actions, your decisions, and your relationships. This view of who you are and what you value is at the heart of MI as well. What the leadership gurus too often neglect, however, is to tell you how to translate who you are into practice. How can you engage and motivate your staff, and how can you help your employee and your organization to change?

MI was born out of the belief that helping people toward change starts with expressing empathy, understanding, acceptance, and respect. Helping professionals trained in MI have assisted people to lose weight, floss their teeth more, increase their exercise, decrease or stop the use of alcohol or illicit drugs, improve their overall health and reduce the symptoms of chronic disease, and more. By understanding the normal process of change and the role that ambivalence plays, by knowing how our own *righting reflex* (discussed in later chapters) gets in our way, and by specifically understanding the spirit of MI and how we can support someone's choice to move toward change, we can help people make some of the hardest changes in their lives.

As we briefly described earlier, leadership is not a technique but a way of being, a virtue (Covey, 1989; Kirkeby, 2004). Similarly, it is important to know that MI is not merely a technique. MI is not something you can just do to people. MI is not about learning how to trick people into doing what you want them to do. MI is based in one's values.

It is a way of being with people. "MI is done *with* people, not *to* people" (Miller & Rollnick, 2013).

WHAT IS THE GOAL OF MI?

If your goal when using MI is not about trying to get people to do what you want, then what is your goal? What are you trying to do? In a nutshell, you are trying to help your employee, through a collaborative conversation, to resolve whatever is keeping them or the organization stuck. You are trying to increase their own reasons to change, enhance their beliefs that they can change, and explore their ideas on how they might change. You are trying to support your staff's autonomy in deciding whether or not they are willing to make the changes needed. You are not trying to trick them into doing something *they do not want* to do or *do not believe* they can do. You are not speaking passionately to try to convince them that you believe in them and that they can do it. You are not cheerleading your way toward change.

You are supporting people and the organization in becoming ready, willing, and able to manage the change before them. This does not mean necessarily that they *will* change. They may actually choose to do something entirely different than make the change you believe is needed. Indeed, some staff may decide to find another role or even to leave your organization. But by having an open, compassionate conversation about the change and how employees view a particular struggle or issue, you are inviting them to make a decision and feel ready to move forward with that decision. With MI you are more likely to see success and see your employees make the changes necessary for their and your organization's success. You are more likely to see improved job performance and employee engagement. You are also more likely to help someone choose to stay in your organization, choose to improve, and ultimately succeed.

Our intention behind the book is simple. We hope that by learning how to use MI in your work as a leader you will be able to solve a problem leaders face every day. How do I best support my employees and help them make changes that are best for them and for the organization?

SUMMARY

As a leader, one of your most critical and demanding tasks is to guide and lead behavior change among the staff and the overall organization. Research has shown that prosocial leadership is essential for the successful implementation of this behavior change. MI is a particular type of conversation aimed at strengthening a person's own motivation and commitment to change. You may find MI helpful as leader, both in relation to individuals, and when you are in dialogue with the entire organization. The spirit of MI supplements the literature on successful leadership.

SELF-REFLECTIVE EXERCISES

Throughout this book we offer exercises to help give you a clearer sense of MI. They're designed to help you decide whether MI is something you would like to use in your work—and if so, how. Each exercise builds on the previous one and, through these exercises, by the end of the book you will have sampled all parts of MI.

Some of these exercises relate to the individual, and others relate to the organization. You can choose to use all of them or just the ones directly relevant to how you hope to implement MI in your own work. You can also download the exercises in their entirety on the book's website (see the box at the end of the table of contents).

SELF-REFLECTIVE EXERCISE. OBSERVE YOUR THINKING

We would like you to reflect on your thinking the next time an employee who is considering a change comes to you, or the next time you interact with an employee you believe needs to change something. It could be that he needs to change how he interacts in a particular situation, or change how he manages or improves on something, or change a process. Just notice your own thinking when someone you work with is facing change.

Try to notice your thoughts in the moment, but also after the interaction has ended, take a few minutes to reflect on your automatic responses. Write down your thoughts so that you can come back to them at the end of this book.

- What did you notice?
- What were your thoughts about the person who approached you?
- What did you understand this person's dilemma to be? Why was the person stuck?
- How much did you attempt to understand and express understanding before moving to a solution or giving advice?
- What did you think was being asked of you? What did you feel you needed to do in that moment?

- Can you explain the person's *stuckness?*
- Why is this change important to the person? How confident does the person feel in carrying out this change?
- How helpful to the person's own growth did you feel your interaction was?
- What, if anything, might you have done differently?

CHAPTER 2

What Is Motivational Interviewing?

MI is a particular way of talking to individuals about behavior change, or, to be more precise, MI is a collaborative conversation aimed at strengthening a person's own motivation for and commitment to change (Miller & Rollnick, 2013). Research and clinicians' experience have demonstrated that there is much a helping professional can do to influence someone's motivation to change problematic behavior. The good news is that motivation for change is not a static entity; it is something leaders can impact. You just need to know how.

THE RIGHTING REFLEX

A key understanding is that people are typically ambivalent when confronting change. This means that they have simultaneous conflicting attitudes about something. They have reasons to change and reasons to stay the same. When leaders, for example, miss this point and argue with their employees rather than seeking to understand, they actually make things much harder. Studies of professional behavior and its impact on patients have shown that motivation cannot be forced on patients (Miller, Benefield, & Tonigan, 1993). When professionals seek to help patients improve their lives by blaming them for their problematic behavior or by trying to persuade them to change, they actually produce the opposite result. People tend to defend themselves against blame, resist persuasion, and persist with their problematic behavior. This reaction is completely natural. If a person blames, seeks to persuade, or attacks someone else, the person on the receiving end will react defensively for self-protection.

Recall the last time someone tried to change you in any of these ways: telling you that you ought to do something, giving you all the reasons why you should, trying to scare you or simply lecturing you. What was your instinctive response?

Attempts to persuade, convince, or even to pressure are often the first strategies that leaders try when they notice that employees, team members, or colleagues are behaving in ways they consider annoying, worrying, unhealthy, or just plain wrong. Leaders may use these strategies for what they think to be the best of reasons. They really wish to help and truly believe that what they are doing is best for the person. When leaders try to persuade a person about the need for change, it is because they are trying to prevent him from going down the wrong path. In MI, this tendency to react by arguing, explaining, and persuading when faced with individuals who exhibit behavior that you think is troubling or misguided is called the *righting reflex*. You want to take what is wrong or troubling and make it *right*. The good news is that the righting reflex is based on the best of intentions. It is simply a natural reaction of well-meaning people who want to help. The bad news is that attempts to persuade, argue, or push an individual who has not asked for advice are rarely an effective strategy for change. In fact, this strategy most often fails. If you are marshaling all the reasons why the person should or could change, or trying to convince or persuade her, a typical reaction from the individual is to list all the good reasons for acting as she does. In other words, the ambivalence implicit in the individual's mind is now out in the open. You present the arguments for change; the individual presents the arguments for the status quo (not changing or staying the same). The status quo arguments may even grow stronger or be articulated with more conviction than intended because the person feels threatened. The more you argue for change, and the more the individual digs in her heels, the less likely it is that she will actually consider making a change. She is more likely to stiffen her resolve to stay the same. You might think about this situation in terms of two lawyers in a courtroom. If you are adopting the role of the prosecutor arguing that the defendant should change, the only recourse left to the defense attorney is to defend and argue that the defendant cannot or should not change. Understanding ambivalence means realizing that your employee is already arguing both sides of the case in her own mind. She is both the prosecutor and the defense. Your role is to help the person debate the issue with herself and resolve her ambivalence so that she is able to move forward.

MI SPIRIT

Besides being aware of your own righting reflex and how it influences your employees' motivation to change, it is also important to know how

MI has informed the ways in which leaders engage employees and define their own role in the process of change. The way you interact with your employee, your belief about your role, and your intention in the conversation is called the *MI spirit*, another term for the foundation or backbone of MI. When we talk about the spirit, we mean the attitude you bring to an encounter with other people: how you meet them, the motives behind your meeting, and how you listen. In order to inspire, motivate, and support an employee's growth, leaders need to be trustworthy, listen with empathy and non-judgment, and be able to understand the employee's perspective.

Leaders need to act with compassion, meaning that they put aside their own aspirations and focus on what is best for the employee. They approach the employee as a partner seeking a collaborative conversation, grounded in acceptance and informed with the belief that each person has her own ideas of what is right for her and of how she may or may not make the change she is facing. This attitude of collaboration, compassion, acceptance, and evocation (evoking of ideas and solutions from the person), pictured in Figure 2.1, is what sums up the spirit of MI.

If you are rooted in the MI spirit, you believe that your employee is the expert on himself and on what is best for him, and you also believe that you are an equal expert, although your expertise pertains not to what is best for him, but instead to how to walk through ambivalence. The spirit of MI is the most important ingredient of MI and what keeps

FIGURE 2.1. The spirit of MI. From Miller and Rollnick (2013). Copyright © The Guilford Press. Reprinted by permission.

it from being little more than a collection of manipulative techniques. The spirit of MI is also the key as to why MI fits well with true leadership.

Understanding your underlying motives and checking them against the spirit of MI are critical to both the success of using MI and to establishing the trusting relationship you wish to have with your staff. The philosophy behind MI is clear: When you help people change, you do so for the sole benefit of the individual you are trying to help, not for your own ends. This is the definition of compassion from an MI perspective. If leaders' motives are based on their own personal success and goals, it will be difficult to use MI effectively and create the necessary compassionate and accepting climate. It is important to reflect on the components of the MI spirit (collaboration, compassion, acceptance, and evocation) before you choose to use MI in your organization or with your employees. Can you be partners with your employees? Can you embrace total acceptance of them? Can you accept their autonomy and choices, and express empathy with their points of view? Can you show compassion and honesty? Can you act solely in their best interests? Do you believe it is important to *evoke* your employees' own ideas on how to change? Can you hold to the MI spirit? If you reflect on these questions and the answer is no, then MI is likely not a tool that will be helpful for you. However, when you reflect on these questions, you might find yourself saying, "It depends" or "Sometimes." In later chapters, we come back to this idea of when leaders might choose to use MI, and when they do not.

IMPORTANCE, CONFIDENCE, READINESS
(READY, WILLING, AND ABLE)

Understanding your righting reflex and your intentions when talking with someone facing change is a good place to start. However, understanding the factors that influence an employee's readiness to change is equally important. Being able to recognize the signs of readiness equips you to meet the individual in the most constructive way. There are several considerations that affect whether an employee chooses to plan and actually perform the change. For instance, the importance of the change will greatly impact the employee's motivation to change. If the outcome matters to him and the reasons for changing outweigh the reasons for staying the same, he is more likely to decide to change. However, even if the change is important to him, he may lack confidence and not believe that he *can* change. The employee's doubt about his ability could be due to many reasons. For instance, he may lack confidence because of financial stressors or lack of knowledge or skill, or his belief that he wouldn't be able to follow through on the new behavior long enough to benefit.

If he really does not know *how* to or does not even believe that he *can*, he might believe he won't be able to change even if he knew it would be best. Importance and confidence are both necessary to being ready to change.

Even if the employee feels that the change is important and that he is confident he can carry it out, he may still believe the timing is not right. He may not be ready. He may need to change something else first. He may instead decide to wait a bit, or perhaps even postpone the change indefinitely. Leaders need to be aware that there are many reasons for not moving forward, and to help guide the process they need to understand what they are hearing from the employee's perspective.

THE GUIDING STYLE

MI is both a person-centered and directive communication style. Being person-centered means always having the interests of the other person in mind, and focusing on understanding the individual's perspectives, concerns, values, and wishes. Understanding another person's perspective is often called being empathetic. *Empathy* is probably the most crucial element in a helping relationship in general, and is the most critical element in conversations about ambivalence and change in particular (Moyers & Miller, 2013). Empathy is also an important, if not the most important, quality of a successful leader. Empathy communicates to the other, "I understand." It connects to the emotion or meaning behind how the other sees the situation. It also allows you to consider the situation from the other person's point of view. As important as the ability to express empathy is, understanding another individual's concerns, anxieties, values, and wishes does not necessarily equip you to free her from her ambivalence. MI offers a guiding communication style that moves the conversation from simply understanding the employee's viewpoint to a communication process wherein the goal is to help the employee resolve her ambivalence and come to a decision. We call this style the *guiding style. Guiding* means that you have one foot in a *following mode*—following the employee wherever she wishes to take the conversation—and the other foot in the *directing mode*—you direct the course of the conversation toward a specific focus. The guiding style gently pivots from where your employee is, what she finds important to focus on, to directing, or guiding, the conversation toward the processes designed to help your employee move forward.

An MI conversation has a focus or a target, and that target will help you in using the guiding style. We discuss how to find the target of your conversation when we describe the focusing process in later chapters. In many situations, there is an obvious best choice for the focus. MI was designed as a form of treatment for alcohol-dependent individuals, so helping the individual consider changing his drinking behavior was an obvious goal for the conversations. Addiction counseling focused on everything the individual mentioned that might point toward decreasing or stopping drinking or deciding to abandon the unhealthy behaviors that contribute to his drinking. As in kindling a fire, the therapist gently blows on the small hints that point in the direction of a change in drinking habits. The therapist aims to foster any hints in the direction of change given by the client, while refraining from attempts to confront or persuade. Listening, offering empathic understanding, and cultivating small hints in the direction of change often make the individual stop in his tracks, think hard about what he is able to do and what is in his own best interest, and help him progress toward change. Often, listening and reflecting back to the individual what he is saying and thinking helps the individual make a decision and commit to changing. In essence, MI helps the person talk himself into change by hearing himself say out loud his own reasons for and confidence about changing.

CHANGE TALK

What are those *hints* in the conversation that the leader is listening for? What are you trying to develop within or make more visible to the individual? You listen for so-called *change talk* (Miller & Rollnick, 2013). You acknowledge all the spoken and unspoken signs that point in the direction of change. When you hear these statements, you make them vivid to the employee, letting him hear what he is saying. Change talk comes in many forms but can be seen as having two subsets, referred to collectively with the acronym *DARN CAT*. They are *preparatory change talk* (desire, ability, reasons, and need) and *mobilizing or commitment talk* (commitment, activation, and taking steps). We discuss this language and how you can make it grow in more detail when we describe the *evoking* process in later chapters. Understanding the statements about why your employee wants to change, why she thinks she can, and the reasons she has for changing helps you listen for and look for opportunities to strengthen this language. We know from over 3,000 research studies that it is the presence of this language and your ability to help develop, deepen, and expand it that increases the likelihood that your employee will actually commit to change.

To guide the process, you may also connect what your employee is telling you about his values and hopes. When someone considers what is most important to him in life, such as his values, and holds his values up against his current behavior and current choices, he often becomes strongly motivated to decide to make a change in his current behavior. When you connect your employee's values to his current dilemma, you put together a fuller picture of what is important to him, one he may not recognize when thinking about the situation on his own. Guiding the conversation in this way, you offer him a safe platform for thinking and talking aloud about whether to change and a way to bring his thoughts into alignment with his values and aspirations for his life going forward. One key point is to remember that the arguments for change should always come from the employee himself. The leader is only reflecting back what the person is sharing so he can hear it himself.

Research has demonstrated that MI can help individuals who feel stuck in ambivalence and therefore have a low motivation to change (Witkiewitz, Hartzler, & Donovan, 2010). When an individual feels completely ready or is in fact already changing, strategies such as practical advice, supervision, and coaching are more appropriate than MI. But when an employee is opposed to change, avoiding it at all costs, or if she feels forced to change, how likely do you think it is that she will engage in the new behavior in a fruitful way? Instead of trying to persuade or force her, MI provides a platform for trying to understand what is happening and for helping the employee to hear her own conflicting thoughts more clearly. It offers a process by which she may resolve her ambivalence and move toward a decision.

Feeling stuck or ambivalent is often the same as feeling uncertain. It is unpleasant for adults to feel uncertain. Often in the workplace employees believe they are supposed to show confidence and strength and might find it hard to admit to a leader that they feel uncertain. Helping employees feel safe in talking about how they feel, knowing how to guide them through this uncertainty, and knowing what specific techniques might help are all useful in helping your employee to become unstuck.

The performance of MI is typically described in terms of three elements or components: the spirit, the techniques or strategies of MI, and the four processes (engaging, focusing, evoking, and planning). The spirit describes your attitude, your values, and how you approach other individuals. The techniques describe how you communicate. The four processes, starting with engaging, overlap; each subsequent process builds upon the one presented before (see Figure 2.2). In Chapters 4–12 we discuss all three elements in detail in the context of using MI with individual employees as well as with an entire organization. We also review how utilizing all of the three main components of MI can help you as a leader.

DOES MI WORK?: THE EVIDENCE

MI has been the target of extensive research that has demonstrated its usefulness. MI is evidence-based, and its effects have been studied

FIGURE 2.2. Four processes of MI. From Miller and Rollnick (2013). Copyright © The Guilford Press. Reprinted by permission.

in randomized controlled trials and used to support multiple types of behavior change. Both randomized controlled trials and meta-analyses have demonstrated that MI is an effective strategy for helping individuals to switch from unhealthy behavior or resolve ambivalence and get unstuck (Burke et al., 2003; Hettema, Steele, & Miller, 2005; Lundahl, Kunz, Brownell, Tollefson, & Burke, 2010; Rubak, Sandbaek, Lauritzen, & Christensen, 2005).

Although MI originated in the addiction field, it is now used in much broader settings and with a much broader range of problems. MI is, for instance, also effective for enhancing general health-promoting behaviors (Lundahl et al., 2010; Rollnick, Miller, & Butler, 2007); for enriching educators' interactions with students (Reinke, Herman, & Sprick, 2011; Rollnick, Kaplan, & Rutschman, 2016); for improving outcomes for people who have been caught up in the criminal justice system (Stinson & Clark, 2017); for adding to the impact of human service programs (Hohman, 2015); and for improving communication with adolescents (Naar-King & Suarez, 2010).

MI IN ORGANIZATIONS

MI is also useful for leaders who are implementing organizational change. Although the research in this particular field is still limited, the interest in MI in leadership and MI in organizations has increased in recent years. Introducing MI to the business world has, however, also been a sensitive issue. Leadership requires a consideration of multiple agendas and not just a consideration of the employee's best interests. Although MI can offer a great deal in relation to person-centered leadership and good listening skills, it also has the potential for misuse as a tool for manipulating others. The agendas of the organization, of the leader, and of each employee need to be present and taken into consideration when implementing MI. MI in leadership requires that leaders remain aware of their own agendas, while prioritizing the wants, needs, readiness, and values of the individual being led.

Certain aspects of MI are essentially little more than good communication strategies that, even when not entirely consistent with MI, are generally a good thing. However, if leaders use the strategic or technical communication strategies of MI to manipulate the behavior of others, it ceases to be MI and is no longer beneficial. That leaves us with the question: When should leaders choose to use MI, and when should they refrain from using it? We will focus on this question in the next chapter.

SUMMARY

Ambivalence about change is normal. When encountering ambivalence, you may feel tempted to push or persuade. MI is an alternative to seeking to thrust motivation upon an individual or an entire organization. MI is aimed at strengthening a person's *own* motivation and commitment to change. It has a specific focus on change language, as used by the individual, and a method to cultivate the change language and make it grow. There are three main components of MI: the spirit, the four processes, and the strategies or techniques. The most important of these components is the spirit of MI.

CHAPTER 3

When to Use Motivational Interviewing in Leadership

There are many strands of MI that a leader could incorporate in any situation. Listening to understand, expressing empathy, understanding the change process, identifying ambivalence, and using active listening skills such as *OARS* (see Chapter 4) are elements of MI that a leader can always turn to. *When* to use the strategic parts of MI, the evoking and guiding strategies, is a more complex decision. When using the strategies of MI, you must be certain that the situation is an appropriate one, that you have the right mindset, and that you are the right person to engage in an MI conversation with the employee. In addition, there are ethical questions that arise immediately. In this chapter we explore how you make the decision about when to use MI.

EMPLOYEE EXPERIENCE AND LEADERSHIP COMMUNICATION STYLES

There are times when MI is in no way indicated, as, for instance, when the reason a change is not happening is that the employee has not yet acquired the requisite skills. The use of MI depends on context and situation. If an employee is new to a job, you may have to be clear and directive when you tell him how to perform a specific task. A new nurse, for instance, who is starting work in a detox unit, needs to be informed about the intake procedures. He needs to be told what symptoms and signs to look out for in patients. He needs to be told what information he should give the doctor so she can decide whether she should also see the patient. And he needs to learn how to handle and document the use of medication.

However, once the nurse has more experience, your task becomes increasingly one of guidance and support: guiding him in solving more complicated situations and supporting him in making the right decisions. Typically, this is the point at which the use of MI may be a good choice for you. When the nurse is more experienced, he will tend to consult his supervisor for guidance himself, rather than waiting for the supervisor to provide instructions. When he consults his supervisor about resolving dilemmas or how to solve specific tasks, this situation may or may not call for MI. If the employee is asking for specific information, MI is rarely appropriate. But if you are keen to support his clinical decision making and his belief in his own competencies, MI may well be a good strategy for you to use.

Finally, once the nurse is sufficiently experienced in the role, the leader may wish to delegate responsibility for a task to him. The nurse is now an expert. Delegating may involve leadership support, and it may involve your encouraging his motivation for taking on the task; hence, MI may also be appropriate when seeking to delegate.

When approaching a change-related conversation with a staffer, there are four situation-based leadership *styles* to choose from:

- The *directive leadership style* is used entirely on the leader's initiative. It involves giving clear information. It focuses on instructing the employee on how to act or how to solve a task. It is the style that leaders use when a task is new to the employee, or when the leader is informing staff that a task has to be performed in a new way, or when the employee is already motivated to perform the task.

- The *supportive leadership style* is used in conversations that may come about on either the employee's or the leader's initiative. The supporting leadership style is used when the employee does not know how to perform a specific task or feels somewhat uncertain about the task or her role. The conversation is not about motivation at all, but about skills and competencies. MI may or may not form part of the conversation, depending on the situation.

- The *guiding leadership style* is used when the employee feels uncertain about her task or performance and consults you as a leader. The conversation often comes about on the employee's initiative. It may focus on the aims of the task or on the employee's motivation. MI is often a useful tool for the leader in such conversations.

• The *delegating leadership style* is used with employees who have the competencies to work independently. The employee has only a minimal need for guidance or for being led. Instead, the focus is on the employee's continuous learning and growth and on her alignment with the organization's vision and mission. MI may often be appropriate to use in the delegating leadership style.

In daily life, you use a mixture of these styles, and often within the same conversation. Even experienced employees will every now and then be new to a task. For example, a manager, Lisa, consulted Donna, a leader of a not-for-profit social service agency, about her discomfort around hiring people. Lisa felt that, frustratingly, she was continually hiring the wrong person for a position. She sensed that she did not always ask the questions she wanted to in the interviews because she was nervous, and ended up hiring people that she was not convinced were a good fit for her team or the job. Listening to her, it became clear to Donna that Lisa had not had any prior training on hiring practices. Lisa had not attended training about how to assess competencies, or even about how to think about what competencies, skills, and overall culture-fit measures she wanted to use when assessing candidates. Donna could have continued the conversation by focusing on what Lisa felt would help her improve her interviewing success (*guiding style*), but Donna wondered whether it would be more helpful to provide Lisa with resources, training, and examples (*directive style*). Donna decided to use these styles and asked, "Would it be helpful if we spent some time going over hiring practices, interviewing assessments, and candidate selection processes? And maybe even complete the next interviews together to put all of it into practice?" Lisa decided that she would rather be given this specific information than pursue talking about her discomfort with interviewing.

Knowing which leadership communication style is called for in different situations is contingent upon the ability to assess the nature of the change needed. Does the employee simply need to learn something new (*directive style*)? Or does she have some experience with the task but is still somewhat uncertain about how to apply it in all situations (*supportive style*)? Or does she know how to complete the task but struggles with confidence in her own abilities and looks to you for the answers (*guiding style*)? Or does she need more authority to make decisions and clarity of ownership for this area (*delegating style*)? The answers to each of these questions will help you decide which communication style the situation calls for and whether MI might help. The goal does not change. You are always looking at how to best support your employees and help them thrive. Knowing what style, approach, or skill is necessary in the given situation is the art of leadership.

MINDSET AND BELIEFS

The decision about whether to use MI, however, is not only dependent on the situation and on the employee's level of experience. You also need to self-reflect on your own mindset and beliefs.

We've briefly discussed how your leadership mindset and your values influence your effectiveness as a leader. A key mindset is the belief that the employee you are helping *can* change. Believing someone *can* change is not the same thing as believing they *will* change. Whether employees make the change depends on them and whether they believe this change is more important to them than other priorities. However, holding the belief that they *can* change is critical to being open in an MI conversation. The research is clear that your beliefs directly affect the outcomes associated with a person's success in changing or improving (Leake & King, 1997; Rosenthal & Jacobson, 1992). Your beliefs become self-fulfilling prophecies, and the employee can sense them. These beliefs govern how you interact with the person, consciously or unconsciously. Donna, the leader of a social service agency, worked with a supervisor, Ed, who explained to her that there were members of his team who had already reached their potential, while others had a long trajectory of growth in front of them. This confining belief directly influenced how Ed viewed and evaluated the growth and success of each person. The employees whom he believed had a lot of growth ahead of them were the ones he saw as more successful than the employees whom he felt had reached their limit. The truth was that both groups were capable of growth, but Ed's ability to provide coaching and feedback and his evaluation of their performance were influenced by his declared assessment of their growth potential. This echoes research findings related to teachers and their interactions with students. In these studies, the teachers were told that some (randomly chosen) students were exceptional and that others (also randomly chosen) did not qualify for this label. The teachers' interactions with the students and their overall assessment of student progress and success turned out to be directly related to the random label that the students had received—making the labels the self-fulfilling prophecies—regardless of an individual student's actual potential (Rosenthal & Jacobson, 1992). Ed believed that some of the employees lacked the capacity to grow and, as a result, he was not providing the environment that would make their growth possible. Exactly the same has been demonstrated in treatment for behavior change (Leake & King, 1997). If *you* do not believe the person you are talking to can make the change set out before her—you are certain that she lacks the capacity to make this change—then MI is unlikely to be helpful or effective.

Maintaining the belief that people can change is hard, because it is not always obvious at first how that change might come about. You may even tell yourself that it is not helpful for the employee to develop false hopes and unfair to set the employee up for failure. But, after working with people who have made dramatic changes in their lives, we have seen for ourselves how ideas and solutions that were not immediately obvious become clear, enabled by the processes of MI. Changes that we may have thought impossible in the past become achievable. Time and time again we have seen individuals choosing a different life and changing lifelong patterns in ways that others would not have thought possible. We have seen a youth emerge from five generations of family gang involvement, leave the gang, go on to college, and create a different life for himself. We have seen someone who used illicit drugs for over 20 years stop using, change her social network and her life situation, and find stable employment. We have also seen remarkable change occur in the work-place: employees who were negative, stubborn, unpopular, and hostile to management for years transform into constructive, empathic, and posi-tive colleagues. And managers who struggled to enhance their team's performance or to create a culture of compassion, support, and account-ability have made the necessary changes in their leadership approach, their mode of supervision, and their reporting to create thriving and successful teams and employees.

In the counseling field, we typically ask this question of the staff: "Do you believe the person in front of you is capable of change?" If the answer is no, then the staff member should not work with that client. The client should be transferred to another provider who does believe that he has it in him to change. We would make the same recommenda-tion to you. If you do not believe that this particular person can change, you should transfer his coaching to someone else who does. Many orga-nizations hire outside coaches to help with these types of situations; or maybe you have, or could create, an internal mentoring/coaching pro-gram that might help.

MATCHING THE STRENGTHS
OF EMPLOYEES TO THEIR ROLES

Albert Einstein once said, "Everybody is a genius. But if you judge a fish by its ability to climb a tree, it will live its whole life believing that it is stupid." So what do you do if you believe the "fish" in front of you is better off on the swimming team than having to learn to climb a tree? What if asking an employee to consider a change fails in terms of matching their strengths to their roles? In that situation, you may rightly choose not to use MI at first and instead have an hon-est, empathetic conversation about the employee's job fit. After giving your employees feedback, you might then switch to MI to find out what they make of your feedback. Evaluating employees' strengths and working on finding the right role for them is almost always a win–win for the employee and the organization. Leaders have no desire to keep people in roles in which they are struggling and not maximizing their talents, even if you believe they could make the changes needed. In discussing compassionate leadership, Jeff Weiner, CEO of LinkedIn, concluded, "It is not compassionate to the employee, other employees or to the organization to leave someone in a role that they are struggling with. They lose their self-confidence and sense of self. They become a shadow of themself. It affects their team and their family. The most compassionate thing you can do is to transition them out as gracefully as possible" (D'Onfro, 2015). If part of compassion is to relieve suffering, then providing honest feedback and making decisions about the person's role are compassionate acts. We agree. We do not believe that MI is always the approach of first resort. Sometimes having the integrity to be honest and having a compassionate and empathic conversation about performance and position are equally important, and often more appropriate.

NOT ENOUGH TIME TO CHANGE

Another reason why you might choose not to use MI and opt instead for a candid and direct conversation is that you simply do not have the time for the person to consider, decide, and make the change desired. Given organizational goals, demands, and time frames, there may be insufficient time to give the person the training needed to change. For example, a research team might hire clinicians to perform an intervention. The clinicians are trained in a model, and subsequently tested to see if they have become proficient enough to deliver the intervention in the way intended. If a clinician has not reached the required level of proficiency in the time frame given, she cannot remain on the research team. It is highly likely that given more time and supervision, the clinician could master the approach, but within this particular setting and the time frame established, she is unable to learn it quickly enough.

When thinking about your mindset before entering into an MI conversation, you want to reflect on these questions. Do you believe this person can change? Do you have enough time for change to occur? Is the issue at hand a question of strengths not matching the role? To be able to be effective with MI, you must be able to suspend judgment, listen empathetically, and believe in the possibility of change. Even if you do not yet know how the change will come about, maintaining the belief that change is possible is critical to the MI conversation being genuine, authentic, and effective.

WHEN THE FOCUS IS A PERFORMANCE ISSUE

It may be tempting to use MI when the topic of discussion is an employee performance issue. However, in such situations, MI may not be an appropriate approach. If you use MI to address a situation in which your employee actually cannot make her own choices, you may send the wrong message by indicating that she has a voice in the matter. Opting for a direct and targeted conversation about her performance is likely more helpful to both her and you. You may also need to explain the parameters within which an MI conversation can proceed. Being candid about the framework within which you are able to be unbiased makes it clear to the employee specifically where you can truly support her in whatever choice she makes. For example, if the employee wants to talk about her performance and has received disciplinary measures, you might say, "I would love to talk with you about your performance and hear your ideas and help in any way I can. I do though need to remind you that the expectation is that your team performance should increase by at least 10% over the next 3 months. I can't change that expectation, but am happy to talk about any ideas you have or ways in which I can help you achieve that."

You are also unlikely to use MI if your focus is on progressive discipline. You may need to start off by being kind, gentle, and clear. In general, when there are performance concerns, it is always most helpful to be clear and direct. You want to be sure you give the employee the feedback needed to make the necessary improvements to be successful. MI would risk getting in the way of that initially. You might, however, depending on the outcome of the conversation, switch to having an MI conversation about the employee's own thoughts on how he or she might improve. This is similar to what you might expect of a consultation with your doctor. As a patient, you want the feedback on your health status to be clear and honest. For most people, it is unsettling not to know whether they have been given the full picture. However, once you have received satisfactory feedback, you can talk with your doctor about what you can do to improve your health. The point at which you are reflecting on the feedback, and then deciding what you are prepared or not prepared to do to improve your health, is a natural starting place for the doctor to use an MI approach.

The same is true for employees receiving job performance feedback. For instance, if an employee, who has been struggling with productivity issues, wants to talk with you about his performance, you may need to clarify the parameters of the conversation. You know that there is a time limit to the period in which his performance has to improve. You know that if he does not meet his targets, the next steps are disciplinary actions that may lead to his removal from the position. However, within the time frame available and with the clear expectation of what the level of productivity should be, there is abundant opportunity for choice and creativity. You may share this parameter with the employee and keep the conversation focused on ways to improve. You can also share the options available if the expectation is not met. What would his preference be? He can leave the organization, look for a new role in the organization that is a better fit for his talents, or he can wait to be terminated. This might sound uncaring, but being clear and sharing the truth helps the employee understand the limits of your role and his own options. Inadequate performance is not an option you can support when you are in a leadership role. But you can help the employee identify ways in which he can achieve the set expectations or transfer to another role that is a better match for his strengths.

ETHICAL CONSIDERATIONS

The most important aspect of MI is that it is a gentle, yet powerful way of communicating with people who are experiencing ambivalence. It is important that you use MI with care, and consider the ethical dilemmas you face when choosing to use it. In particular, you need to be aware that leaders often have interests other than those of their employees and exert a form of power over them. This power differential can be a reason not to use MI.

If you choose to engage in MI conversations, you must be clear that you are doing so because you believe the target you are guiding toward serves the employee's best interests. With MI, you focus on and evoke change in a specific direction. This means you gently steer the conversation in one direction, which can influence someone's decision about change. The *evoking process,* in which you sensitively reveal to the employee her own desire and preference for change can resolve ambivalence and stimulate her own motivation for change. Since this communication strategy may increase the likelihood for actual change, and since the direction of change is predetermined by you, deliberately using MI should always be based on the employee's best interests.

The question then arises: Who is to decide what is in the best interests of the employee? How do you know if you should steer the conversation in a specific direction? How can you be sure you shouldn't be neutral instead? When therapists use MI with clients in social service settings or in physical, mental, or behavioral health areas, it may be obvious what kind of change is in the client's best interests. For instance, if the therapist is talking with someone who is actively using methamphetamines and facing possible jail time, guiding the client in the direction of changing methamphetamine use is quite clearly in the person's best interests.

If he makes this change, it will likely benefit him. Although the change may also have a positive impact on his community, the focus for the conversation is not on the communal benefit, but rather on how the change will likely benefit him. Contrast this conversation to the situation in which a counselor is asked for advice on whether or not an adult client should return to graduate school, or a family therapist is asked whether a woman should have another child. In such situations, it is not clear what is in the person's best interests. If it is not clear, you should stay in *equipoise* (be neutral) until the person herself is clearly leaning in one direction. You need to focus on solving the dilemma as such and counter ambivalence. In *equipoise,* you reflect on and listen to both sides of the decision equally without displaying any particular focus on, or interest in, either side. It is important that you understand that there is power in your guiding.

It may sound relatively easy to decide between equipoise and directional MI when working with clients or patients. But how about in the workplace? Let's start with an example. You remember Donna, the leader of a social service agency. She supervised Anna, who needed to train her team in a new clinical approach. The company had determined that this approach was the best method for use with clients and decided to implement the approach companywide. Anna, however, struggled because she was not sure she completely agreed with the company decision and thought other approaches were more effective with some clients. Implementing the new approach was not optional—so failing to implement it was not on the table if Anna wanted to continue in her current role. To resolve her ambivalence, Anna discussed her struggles and concerns with Donna. Donna wanted Anna to be successful, and she also wanted Anna to stay with the company. Anna was a good supervisor and regularly provided support that helped others succeed. If she were to leave, it would have a negative effect on Anna's team, Donna's team, Donna personally, and the company as a whole. Donna was highly motivated to help Anna resolve her ambivalence in a way that would lead to her staying in her position and teaching her staff the new approach as required. Donna did not want Anna to find a way around implementing the approach, because she also believed the approach was best for the company and her clients. Donna could easily have chosen to have an MI conversation with Anna about her struggle, but she knew that she would have a strong bias in favor of the outcome she wanted. Therefore, Donna decided to refer Anna to a third party (a coach external to the organization) to help her decide what she wanted to do. In other words, it was not obvious which outcome would be in Anna's interest. A conflict arose because it was obviously in Donna's interest that Anna should decide to implement the new approach. Donna was not the right person to have this MI conversation with Anna.

MI is built on trust. If you use the strategic parts of MI to guide someone like Anna into a decision that benefited only you and the company, and not Anna, it might work the first and even the second time, but in the long run it would become clear that you were manipulating instead of helping the person decide what was best for her. When your focus is on your own interests and not those of your employees, trust is lost. This situation is similar to the relationship between customers and salespeople. Customers know that salespeople gain or lose depending on the customer's decision. Salespeople cannot be 100% focused on the best interests of the customer. Knowing this leaves customers feeling that they cannot completely trust the salesperson, even if she sincerely wants what is best for them. Before you use MI, you need to be clear that your motivation is grounded in the effort to help your employees resolve their own ambivalence and not in anything else. Even if you end up benefiting from the employees' decision to change, you should not enter into an MI conversation with the intention of benefiting yourself.

WHO IS TO BENEFIT?

As the leaders and staff of an organization we are all interconnected, and it is often hard to determine who benefits from change. Sometimes a staff member's change can have positive repercussions for herself, the team, the leader, and the company. At other times a person's change can affect himself positively, and yet the team, the leader, and the company negatively. At still other times, a person's change could affect her and her team positively, and yet still hurt the company. It is not always easy to figure out who benefits from a given change, and in which situations you should steer a conversation.

As a guideline, if change is in the interest of the employee, MI is appropriate. If change is clearly *not* in the interest of the employee, MI is not appropriate. Further, the more you as a leader personally gain from the staff member's acceptance of change, the less proper is it to use MI, especially if the employee loses by the change. In Table 3.1, we present the scenarios in a matrix. Specific examples of each scenario appear in Appendix A.

An appropriate MI situation is one in which the leader does not benefit from any decision or change the employee makes. MI should not be used if the leader personally has an interest in the employee's change, unless the employee also has an interest in changing. When the employee benefits personally from the change but the leader benefits from the employee not changing, a conflict of interests arises, and it is highly likely that MI is not appropriate. Here are some pointers to consider when your employee's priorities differ from your own:

TABLE 3.1. Leader's Benefit from Change versus Employee's Benefit from Change: When Is MI the Appropriate Choice?

	Leader benefits from change.	Leader is not affected by change.	Leader benefits from the status quo.
Employee benefits from change.	MI may be appropriate—with due care taken.[a]	MI is appropriate.	MI may be appropriate—with due care taken.[a]
Employee neither benefits nor loses from change.	MI is not appropriate.[b]	MI is appropriate.	MI may be appropriate—with due care taken.[a]
Employee loses from change.	MI is not appropriate.	MI is not appropriate.	MI may be appropriate—with due care taken.[a]

[a]Use with caution—you have a bias. Ensure that you are focused *solely* on the benefit to the employee.
[b]You are the only one to benefit and have a strong bias.

• *If you benefit from change, but the employee benefits from the status quo, MI is not appropriate.* For example, John, a therapist, is asked to see more clients and already has a full caseload. He will receive no further remuneration for this change, just extra work, whereas you will get a bonus if he takes on the extra work. MI would not be appropriate in this situation.

• *If you are not affected by the employee's change, there may be no dilemma for you. MI may be appropriate. You can remain unbiased and able to focus solely on what is best for the employee.* For example, Sarah, a nurse, considers applying for another role on your team. She is a great nurse in her current position, but you know that she will also be great in the other position. Your own workload is not affected by her decision.

• *If the employee benefits from the change and you personally lose from change, it presents a challenge. MI may not be appropriate.* For example, Karen, a nurse, would like to attend a training course and learn to work with the geriatric population. You know that this change might lead to her applying for a new job, since your organization serves the youth population only. Karen will benefit from developing her clinical expertise, but you may lose her to another organization. It will be hard to find a replacement, and you will have to help cover shifts if Karen leaves. Your workload will double, because you will have to continue

your current responsibilities as well as taking on Karen's until you find
a replacement.

- *When you personally benefit and the employee neither benefits
nor loses, this may be a situation in which MI is not appropriate.* For
example, Helen, a doctor, is struggling with the implementation of a new
electronic health record. As far as her current work is concerned and
until she has mastered the new system, this change fails to add any new
value. You will benefit from the new system because you will have easy
access to reports, it will lighten your burden of overseeing the clinic's
quality and productivity, and it may even lead to you receiving a bonus
for doing this part of your job better. Over time, the new system may
possibly be helpful to Helen's work with her patients, but this improvement may take a year or more and is not guaranteed.

THE INTERESTS OF THE ORGANIZATION

Just as you reflect on whether you benefit from an employee's change
or decision, you also need to consider whether the organization benefits. You need to understand that you as a leader are influenced by the
organization's interests, just as you can be influenced by your personal
interests. A leader's primary job is to serve the organization: to ensure
that it functions, grows, flourishes, delivers high-quality services, and
stays within its budget. Most leaders are aware that fundamental to a
well-functioning organization are employees who thrive and enjoy their
work. Focusing on helping staff feel valued and thrive is an important
part of a leader's job, because caring for the staff is also about caring for
the organization. Often an employee's change is aligned with what the
organization wants. However, when the employee's needs conflict with
those of the organization, you must tread carefully. MI is not likely to be
an appropriate tool in this situation.

Typically when organizational change is needed, it is necessary for
employees to change in some way. The employee may need to learn a
new skill or implement a new procedure. The employee may also benefit personally from learning these new things. In situations where the
employee's change benefits both the organization and the employee, MI
may be a useful communication strategy for the leader.

The leader's dilemma arises, however, when a change is in the
interest of the organization, but does not benefit the employee. Since
your primary goal is to serve the organization, you have to balance
concern for the organization with concern for the employee. It is easier
to conclude that MI is inappropriate if you benefit personally from an
employee's change, but in situations with conflicting interests between

an organization and an employee, it is more complicated to work out whether or not you can or should use MI to increase the likelihood of change. In Table 3.2 we present some scenarios in a matrix. Specific examples of each scenario appear in Appendix B.

Here are some pointers to consider when weighing the conflicting priorities of the organization and the employee:

• *If the organization benefits from change, but the employee benefits from the status quo, MI may not be appropriate, but if it is used, then use only with due care.* For example, John, a therapist, is asked to see more clients and already has a full caseload. He will receive no further remuneration for this change, just increased work. MI might not be appropriate in this situation. However, if the company will close, with John and his colleagues losing their jobs, unless they increase their workload, MI may be a helpful communication strategy for the leader to help motivate the staff to work harder—at least for a period—and a means by which to elicit ideas on how to ease the workload while still seeing more clients.

• *If the organization is not affected by the employee's change, there are no dilemmas for the leader, and MI is appropriate. The leader (who represents the organization) can remain unbiased, focusing only on what is best for the employee.* For example, Sarah, a nurse, considers applying for another role in the organization. She is a great nurse in her current position, and the organization has no problems with hiring new nurses and has a vacant position that she is interested in.

• *If the employee benefits from the change and the organization loses from it, the situation is a vexed one. It may be a challenge for the leader to remain unbiased, and MI may not be appropriate.* For example, Karen, a nurse, would like to attend a training course and learn to work with the geriatric population. The organization serves the youth population only. Karen will benefit from developing her clinical expertise, but the organization receives no benefit from this training and will lose money and productivity time by allowing Karen to take the course. This change, which focuses on Karen's interests, would be very problematical for a leader to support, because the organization's interests are in conflict with it.

• *When the organization benefits and the employee neither benefits nor loses, this may be a situation in which MI is appropriate and helpful, but only if used with due care. Similarly, MI might be appropriate if the employee loses from a change in the short run, but benefits in the long run from putting the organization's interests above her own*

TABLE 3.2. Organizational Benefit from Change versus Employee's Benefit from Change: When Is MI the Appropriate Choice?

	Organization benefits from change.	Organization is not affected by either change or the status quo.	Organization benefits from the status quo.
Employee benefits from change.	MI may be appropriate.[a]	MI is appropriate.	MI may be appropriate.[a]
Employee neither benefits nor loses from change.	MI is appropriate.	MI is likely appropriate.	MI may be appropriate.
Employee loses from change.	MI is probably not appropriate.	MI is probably not appropriate.	MI may be appropriate.[b]

[a]Use with caution—your primary goal as a leader is to serve the organization. In any MI conversation, be sure that you are focused on the employee's benefit only.

[b]There may not be any reason for using MI if both parties lose from change. The decision may seem clear to not change. However, should you choose to use MI, use it with care since the organization benefits from the status quo.

needs. For example, Helen, a doctor, is struggling with the implementation of a new electronic health record. For her current work and until she has mastered the new system, this change only adds stress and no new value. The organization would benefit greatly from the use of the new record, because it will have access to better reporting and outcome tracking, and all staff groups and the hospital board look forward to receiving this knowledge. Over time this better reporting and outcome tracking may possibly be helpful to Helen's work with her patients, but it may take a year or more.

In summary, MI is not appropriate in all situations. As a rule of thumb, MI can be used if the change is in the interests of both the organization and the employee and is neutral with regard to your own interests as a leader. If the interests of the organization and those of the employee collide, MI may be appropriate, but only if great care is exercised, and not if the employee directly loses from change. We can think of times when we have had conversations with talented employees we did not want to lose, but also knew that leaving was in their best interest if they were to achieve their professional goals. We were able to put aside our organization's goals in support of those employees, but this is extremely hard and rare. Knowing who is to benefit from the conversation is critical to knowing when MI could be helpful and when, ethically, MI should not be used.

QUESTIONS FOR SELF-REFLECTION

It should now be obvious that as leaders our remit is broad, and MI is not always the approach we should use. If you find yourself needing to do any of the five following tasks, it is likely you will hold off on using MI for awhile, or for the remainder of the interaction. However, stepping back from MI does not mean that you step back from the MI spirit. You can always keep the MI mindset, and continue to practice compassionate leadership and empathetic listening.

1. Discussing job performance that is not meeting expectations.
2. Making the organization's visions, goals, and services known.
3. Teaching or training a skill.
4. Correcting an employee's undermining approach in relation to the job, colleagues, or the organization.
5. Handling salary or hiring negotiations.

Besides highlighting such specific situations, we offer a set of questions you can use to self-evaluate whether you are capable of being unbiased in your conversation and of making apt use of MI:

- "Am I open to the person choosing either for or against change?"
- "Will I benefit directly or indirectly from the employee's decision?"
- "Will the organization benefit or gain from the employee's change?"
- "Will there be indirect or direct benefits or losses for anyone other than the person I am focused on?"
- "Do I believe that this person can make the change if he decides to?"
- "Do we have enough time for the person to make the change?"
- "Does the person have the right role, or are her strengths better served in a different role altogether?"

Now, after having discussed at some length when—and when not to—use MI, the following chapters will introduce you to using MI as a leader, step by step.

SUMMARY

A leader generally has a great deal of power in guiding an employee. In addition, MI is a powerful conversation style. Hence, using MI compels you to exercise ethical judgment. MI should be the choice of conversation style when the focus is on the interests of the employee. And MI *may* be the right choice when the goal of the organization is at the forefront. However, you should also always bear in mind that MI is just one of several conversation styles that leaders use, and that there are situations in which strategies other than MI are more appropriate. Your mindset, time frames, and employee strengths are all factors to consider before using MI.

VIGNETTES

Throughout this book, in addition to the brief examples given, we include two full stories illustrating the use of MI in workplace settings. We will regularly revisit these stories as we expand and describe the four processes of MI. The stories will unfold after each process chapter, specifically highlighting the elements described therein. The employee vignette continues after Chapters 4, 7, 9, and 11, and the organization vignette continues after Chapters 5, 8, 10, and 12. Also, the employee and organization vignettes are presented in their entirety and are available to download on the book's website (see the box at the end of the table of contents).

Here is a brief description of the two vignettes that we will later expand upon.

Employee Vignette. The Conversation with Susan

Ashley, a leader of a large behavioral health care organization, was asked by a supervisor, Jim, to meet with one of his employees, Susan. Susan was in the early stage (4 months in) of learning a new counselor role and was struggling. The job had very specific productivity expectations, and she was not meeting them. To be successful, Susan had to enroll at least 20 new people a month into her services, while also continuing to provide counseling to clients who were already enrolled. Jim asked Ashley to meet with both of them because he knew Susan had the ability to do this job, but felt that her confidence was simply too low and that Susan was incorrectly evaluating her progress.

Ashley decided that MI might be a useful communication strategy to help Susan, Jim, and herself understand why Susan felt so stuck. She thought that MI could help Susan think about what she wanted and why it was important to her and then help her make a decision to move forward. Ashley knew that her role could be both helpful and harmful.

It might be helpful because she had the authority to set the parameters around when Susan would face company-related consequences if she did not improve. Ashley, as the ultimate authority, could tell Susan that her job was not currently at risk and how long she had to turn around her low productivity. Her role, however, also represented a potential threat. If Susan felt that the new job was not a good fit for her and wanted to leave the position, it might be a challenge for her to be honest with someone in Ashley's role. Susan would have to be willing to take a large risk and trust that Ashley would understand. She might fear that Ashley would fire her before she was ready to leave and that telling her about her struggle might hurt her reputation in the company. Ashley was also aware that she was not personally invested in Susan's decision to stay or leave. She knew that if Susan chose to stay and improve, the result would be increased services offered by her team; and if Susan decided to leave, she would be making a decision that Ashley might have to make anyway if she did not improve. So Ashley could stay neutral and allow Susan to decide on her own, within the context of the company time frame, whether she wanted to do what it took to improve or to leave.

Organization Vignette. Improving Client Outcomes

Marie was a leader of a large outpatient alcohol treatment agency. One of her main roles was to monitor the quality and effectiveness of services. This task is not an easy one since research has demonstrated that the quality of treatment for alcohol use disorders varies widely (Levy Merrick, Garnick, Horgan, & Hodgkin, 2002; McLellan, Carise, & Kleber, 2003). Providers, researchers, and leaders have been debating how to evaluate, monitor, and improve treatment quality for decades (McLellan et al., 2005).

Marie led a team of 60 staff members (doctors, nurses, social workers, and administrative support), and the management group. The staff were well trained in delivering the organization's selected evidence-based approach: MI, cognitive-behavioral therapy, and/or family therapy. Collaboration and teamwork were essential because staff members regularly covered for each other, and the management had oversight of all the clinics. As the head of the management group, Marie was responsible for financial performance and the quality of all treatment options. Her chief consultant had overall responsibility for the content of the treatment courses, and three managers were responsible for the operations of the three departments. Although alcohol treatment is typically delivered by a multidisciplinary team, much of the intervention is provided by a single therapist, and that work directly impacts the success of the rest of the team's interventions. Because there are many people involved in the care of an individual client, the implementation of new strategies and routines is often challenging and difficult to assess.

Marie, the chief consultant, and the management group decided to review the outcomes of treatment to determine if the agency was fulfilling its mission. A yearlong monitoring exercise of all treatment programs revealed two common quality problems for all the clinics: during their first 6 months of treatment, patients dropped out at high rate, and relatively few clients reduced their drinking to below the recommended level for sensible drinking (a maximum of 21 standard units per week) during the treatment course (Nielsen & Nielsen, 2015). Marie and her team knew they needed to find a way to motivate the whole organization to work together to reduce early dropout and improve the outcome of treatment.

SELF-REFLECTIVE EXERCISE. OBSERVE YOUR ACTIONS

Print out your calendar for the past 2 weeks. If you cannot print your calendar, then write down the various meetings or interactions you had. Consider the many ways in which you interacted with your employees. Now, keeping in mind the different leadership styles you can choose to use, write down the style you chose from the following list next to each interaction.

> Directive style
> Supportive style
> Guiding style
> Delegating style

Reflect on the following questions, and write down your answers:

- Do you find that you adapt your style based on the person or the situation?
- When do you use each style, and why?
- Now, looking back, when might you have used a different style?
- When might you have used MI?
- Was there ambivalence in the situations you encountered?

To move forward with the rest of the exercises, we would like you to select a person and an organization facing a change with whom and with which you would be ready to try some of the MI processes.

Select a Person Facing a Change

Select a person who is stuck or is facing a change. We suggest picking someone you feel fairly comfortable with (and one who is not your biggest challenge). We would like you to consider working with this person to try the MI processes as you continue to read this book. Below, we will describe each process and offer exercises you can use every step of the way.

Considering what you know about the person who is facing change, try answering the following questions. For now, don't go back to the person to ask her these questions; just see if you know the answers based on the interactions you have already had. Please write down your answers; we will ask you to come back to this list of questions later to find out if your understanding changes as you try MI with this person.

Employee Facing Change Questions

- What is the person's dilemma? Why is she stuck? Can you describe her ambivalence?
- How does this ambivalence affect her? How does she feel about this change and the situation?
- What does this mean to her? What is she trying to communicate about her stuckness and situation?
- What reasons does she have for making this change?
- Why is she considering making this change?
- How does she feel about her ability to carry out the change if she had decided to make it?
- How urgent does she feel making this change is?
- What, if anything, is she considering, or does she think would help, in making this change?

Select an Organizational Change

Select an organizational change that you are leading in your organization. As you continue reading this book, you will learn how to use MI with your organization with the help of exercises that are focused on organizational change.

For now, considering what you know about the organization facing change, answer the following questions. Don't go back to your group to ask these questions; just see if you know the answers based on the interactions you have already had. Please write your answers down; we will ask you to come back to this list of questions and find out if your understanding changes as you try MI.

Organizational Change Questions

- What is the organization's dilemma? Why are different groups of employees stuck? Can you describe their ambivalence?
- How do different groups within your organization feel about this change? Which groups are for the change? Which groups are against the change? Why do they feel differently?
- How does this change affect the different groups? How do they feel about this change and situation?
- What does this change mean for them? What are they trying to communicate about their stuckness and situation?
- What reasons do the organization and each group within it have for making this change?
- Why are you and they considering making this change?
- How do your organization and different groups feel about their ability to carry out the change if they had decided to make it?
- How urgent do they feel it is to make this change?

PART II

ENGAGING

CHAPTER 4

Listening to Your Employee

Next time you are in a conversation, ask yourself: *Am I really listening?* Am I trying to understand what this person is saying? Or am I doing something else? Am I waiting for the person to stop talking so I can have a turn to be heard? Am I thinking about what I need to do later today? Just note it, without judging yourself. Observe what is happening. Are you really listening? This is where change and MI begin. It begins with listening in order to understand.

Leaders generally believe they are listening. I (C. M.) remember sitting on the couch next to my husband and telling him about something that happened that day. He was facing the TV, watching a baseball game, and saying things like "umm," "oh," "huh." I stopped and said, "You are not listening to me." He turned to me and repeated every word I had uttered. I continued, "That is not listening, that's merely repeating." (In his defense, you might ask why I wanted to talk while he was watching his game. Context matters too.) The goal of listening is to understand what the other person is communicating and experiencing, not just to hear words. To truly listen is to grasp the meaning of what is being said.

The Chinese symbol for listening helps explain what listening means. It combines the symbols for eyes, ears, heart, and undivided attention. Listening is more than just hearing the words (as depicted in Figure 4.1). Listening means that you are using all your senses and your own thinking to facilitate your understanding. It is a more engaged and focused process than simply hearing. Thomas Gordon (1970) calls it *active listening.* Just as there are ways to improve your ability to listen, which we will discuss shortly, there are also particular kinds of responses that may get in the way. Gordon describes these common responses as

47

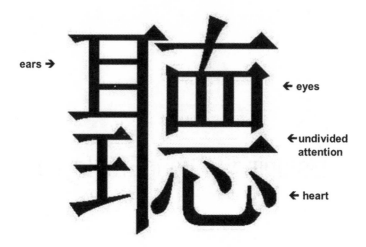

ears ➔

← eyes

←undivided
attention

← heart

FIGURE 4.1. The Chinese symbol for *listen*.

roadblocks, typical reactions from a listener that get in the way of effective communication. Such listener responses include ordering, directing, commanding, warning, cautioning, threatening, giving advice, making suggestions, providing solutions, persuading with logic, arguing, lecturing, dictating, disagreeing, judging, criticizing, blaming, shaming, ridiculing, labeling, or distracting with humor, to name but a few.

When you react to what is being said with these types of responses, you impede the speaker's exploration of his own thoughts, thereby limiting what he shares. This is not to say that some of the roadblocks should never be used. There may, of course, be situations that call for one of them. But if the goal is to *listen and understand,* the roadblocks get in the way of that intention. They make listening harder, because they change the conversation's focus from what the speaker is interested in sharing to what the listener wants to explore.

In contrast to using roadblocks, you can support the listening process by conveying understanding—by offering a guess about what the person wants to express. Reflecting back to the other person what you are hearing encourages him to continue, and helps you better determine what the speaker actually means. Communication is a multistep process, and confusion or misunderstanding may occur at any point, as illustrated in Figure 4.2.

When we listen to someone, we all use our own life experience to interpret what we are hearing. The speaker may also contribute to misunderstanding if the words or emotion expressed fail to convey what she actually means. In the picture shown in the figure, the speaker is trying

FIGURE 4.2. What an employee says and what you hear are not always the same thing.

to express an IDEA (in capitals), and the listener interprets the speech as an idea (in small letters). Although the listener is trying hard to understand, he does not always quite get it. Such misunderstandings may be avoided if you, the listener, reflect back to the other person what you believe she is trying to say. Reflecting gives the speaker the opportunity to clarify, and the listener a chance to improve his understanding.

ENGAGING

In MI, this important first process of listening to understand is called *engaging*. Engaging refers to both involving the other person in the topic and the conversation and the process of building a relationship grounded in trust and empathy, in which the listener seeks to understand without judging what the other person is trying to say. The process starts with listening, but it goes further by engaging the employee in the process by trying to show her that she can trust the leader enough to tell the leader more. The aim of this process is to understand the situation from the employee's perspective. The leader may not agree with her thinking, but that does not matter. Whether the leader agrees or not, to understand is to listen and to reflect this understanding back to the person so that she feels understood. Active listening in MI means trying to grasp what is being said, while letting the other person know what you understand—without judging, giving advice, or imposing any other kind of roadblock.

THE RIGHTING REFLEX

One of the reasons it is so hard to simply listen is that leaders often feel that listening is not enough. Leaders tend to feel that they should also react to, respond to, or fix whatever is laid before them. They believe that their role is to solve problems, provide advice, or give an employee direction. The impulse to help by trying to solve the problem is known as the *righting reflex*, which we introduced in Chapter 2.

Trying to fix or solve the problem or dilemma for your employee is something completely different than listening to understand. The good thing about the righting reflex, the desire to fix the problem or make it right, is that it most often comes from a place of caring and compassion. The not-so-good thing about the righting reflex is that it stops you from listening and implies that you are the one to come up with solutions. You assume that your answers are needed and are even the best for the person. The problem is, you are not the employee and you do not know what is best for her. She is the only one who knows that. When leaders solve the problem, come up with the solution, offer advice, or express their own opinions about the problem, they send the message that they do not believe that the employee is capable of solving the problem herself. Instead, they seem to be signaling that the leader is the person in charge and that their ideas are the most important. The righting reflex gets in the way of understanding the employee's own view of the situation and misses the opportunity to help her resolve her own issue. If you wish to support people's growth, then giving advice, instead of giving the person the opportunity to work through the process and come up with her own plan, reduces the employee's confidence and increases her dependence on you.

We find that leaders often struggle with this concept. They believe that their righting reflex is an obvious strength, because their responsibility is to have an employee perform a task or role. Giving advice and solving problems is part of their role. They often share that sometimes the employee does not know what to do or what is best in the specific work situation. We understand their dilemma. There is a balancing act that leaders, like you, constantly juggle. There is a time to teach, tell, and show, and there is a time to support your employee's exploration and growth, guiding her through an MI process that enables her to come up with her own answers. The leadership styles (directive, supportive, guiding, and delegating) described in Chapter 3 provide guidance in deciding when you might profitably consider resisting your righting reflex and instead choose to have an MI conversation. Sometimes the employee's experience level will make it clear to you that this is the time to train rather than to help him find his own solution. We are certainly not saying that, as a leader, your ideas or direction are never needed. We explore an MI consistent model for providing information or advice in

Chapter 11. This model, termed *elicit–provide–elicit (E-P-E)*, starts by first *asking permission* to provide advice or information, eliciting the employee's ideas, then sharing your own ideas, and ending again with eliciting the employee reaction. We are, however, arguing that when you provide advice or a solution, you are simply dealing with the immediate issue and missing a larger opportunity to help your employee build his own confidence and improve his skills so that later he will feel able to solve other problems on his own.

When people feel they are thriving and matter to the company and their leader, they are more likely to stay in their organizations and actively work to support the success of the company's mission. Daniel Pink (2009) describes this belief as the key to understanding what motivates employees. He points out that research has demonstrated that we have three innate psychological needs—competence, autonomy, and relatedness. "When those needs are satisfied, we're motivated, productive and happy. . . . Human beings have an innate inner drive to be autonomous, self-determined, and connected to one another. . . . And when that drive is liberated, people achieve more and live richer lives." Thus, if the number one goal of leaders is to achieve their mission and meet their "bottom line," engaging and developing the staff and reducing staff turnover in the process are essential to achieving that goal.

Often, when we are teaching MI to leaders, we ask them to write down what behaviors they are looking for in their staff. We suggest that you take a minute to do that as well. Ask yourself, what behaviors or qualities you are trying to generate in your team or with your employees. Typical responses we hear include creativity, initiative, independence, passion, openness to feedback, accountability, and the ability to find solutions. Next, we would ask you to write down what you are already doing to cultivate these behaviors. What do you specifically do to generate these desired behaviors or qualities? When we ask this question in training situations, it always sparks good discussions. We regularly hear responses like "I really want them to take the initiative, but they are always waiting for me to make decisions," or "I would love it if they could solve problems without me, but there is a line of staff outside my door all day waiting for my ideas. They don't think for themselves." When we hear comments like these, we are led to assume that when staff members bring their challenges, dilemmas, and struggles to the leader, the leader's response is to solve the problem rather than help employees come up with their own solutions and answers. Employees do not become better at their jobs if leaders always react with their righting reflex and constantly offer solutions.

Of course, not responding to the righting reflex takes faith. It means believing in the person and believing that he can solve his problem. Part of expressing empathy and using MI effectively is trusting in the belief that employees do indeed have their own ideas and solutions and that if listened to and guided in a conversation, they will make the best choices for themselves, and as a result be more successful.

It is, of course, not always wrong for leaders to solve problems. There are times where leaders *will* want to share their input, provide answers, and point people in a particular direction, and for good reasons. But often the employee is more expert about his own life and situation than the leader is, and has the capability of coming up with answers and solutions. His ideas are likely to be even more effective than the leader's—precisely because he came up with them. So, he is more likely to buy into the solution, and do whatever it takes to implement it. After all, it was his idea to begin with.

SKILLS THAT HELP LEADERS LISTEN

What skills are helpful if your intention is to engage and truly listen to understand? The good news is that these skills are ones that you likely already know and use, such as Open-ended questions, Affirmations, Reflections, and Summaries. In MI, these skills are often referred to by the acronym *OARS*. OARS are commonly used skills in counseling to encourage exploration and discussion with individuals. OARS are not unique to MI. They are often taught as ways to improve listening skills in many counseling approaches and in good management strategies as well. There are many books describing listening skills, and we suggest that you consult them if you are interested. William R. Miller (2018) has recently written a short book on listening, *Listening Well: The Art of Empathic Understanding*. This would be a great place to start. For our purposes here, however, we'll briefly describe each skill.

Open-Ended Questions

Thomas Gordon's roadblocks, described earlier, also include questions as barriers to conversation, because they steer it in a direction set by the listener, and thus curtail what the speaker is encouraged to share. However, open-ended questions are also important tools for understanding what an employee means. Questions, and in particular open-ended questions, assist you in figuring out what is important to the employee in a given situation, what she values, and what she thinks is possible. You want to keep in mind, though, that too many questions, and specifically lots of closed-ended questions, can turn a conversation into an interrogation rather than a setting for exploration. If you respond to what you hear with a barrage of questions, it may feel like you are assessing your employee. If that happens, questions no longer serve as a pathway to understanding.

If you wish to listen to understand, it is often better to ask an open-ended question rather than a closed-ended one. Closed-ended questions tend to limit the employee response. Examples of closed-ended questions are: "Did you inform your team?"; "How many staff are working on this?"; "When will this be completed?" Closed-ended questions typically only lead to a "yes" or "no" or a specific answer. In contrast, open-ended questions allow the person to share her thoughts freely. Open-ended questions include, for example: "How might this impact your team?"; "What are your ideas on how to share this with others?"; "What is your plan?" When you ask open-ended questions, you will more often get an elaboration of the person's beliefs and thoughts. Asking open-ended questions is a strong first step in the engaging process.

Affirmations

Providing an *affirmation* is another skill leaders may use when listening in order to engage the employee. Affirmations are reflections or statements that recognize and acknowledge the employee's strengths, values, or efforts. Such acknowledgments are intended to encourage the person as well as being a way of registering understanding. It is important to remember that affirming does not mean that you are judging the person or taking a paternalistic or authoritarian approach in relation to approving her behavior. Instead you are drawing attention to a strength or value of the employee or an effort that the employee has made. Examples of affirmations are "I can tell you have really been working hard on this"; "It's clear that you're passionate about your team and our work"; "You are resilient. You never give up on anything." Affirmations can infuse optimism and understanding by building strength and confidence. Leaders should bear in mind that affirmations from them have a strong impact on the employee and add to her sense of feeling recognized, appreciated, trusted, and seen.

There is a great deal of variation in terms of what is considered an affirmation by different cultures and individuals, and you should of course keep this in mind. Also, giving a lot or too many affirmations can be counterproductive as well. Affirmations have to be genuine, and part of being genuine means they need to match what you as a leader really feel and believe. Affirmations should be honest, and not just a kind of cheerleading. If you are the type of leader who gives affirmations sparingly, there still can be power in the rarity of the statement. If, on the other hand, you naturally provide affirmations regularly, your frequency might be higher, but just as honest and sincere. Also the employees themselves may respond differently or desire different degrees of affirmation. Some might appreciate being affirmed regularly, while others prefer affirmation less often. What is important to keep in mind is that an affirmation only works if the recipient feels affirmed. It is like the saying that beauty is in the eye of the beholder: affirmations are in the heart or ear of the recipient.

Reflections

Reflections are at the heart of empathetic listening. The ability to form reflections is the most important skill to practice if your goal is to understand and to convey understanding. To reflect something is to cast it back—as when light is reflected in a mirror. However, *reflect* also connotes thinking or considering—as when you reflect on a certain topic. In an MI conversation, reflections draw upon both meanings of the word. When you form a reflection, you formulate your interpretation of what has been said and offer it back to the person. Reflections are statements that you provide in response to your employee's sharing. The statement describes what you think the person means, and the reflection is a way of checking out whether you really get it.

When forming reflections, you are making a guess at what you think the employee means so as to get closer to understanding what she actually means. When creating reflections, you consider not only the words uttered, but also all the other nonverbal information you notice. You are seeking to show your understanding of what the other person thinks, is experiencing, and is feeling. Reflections are an effective way of showing that you are listening carefully, and the typical reaction to a well-put reflection is that the other person continues to describe what is on her mind. A good rule of thumb is to offer at least three reflections for every question asked. Some examples follow:

Reflection Example A

EMPLOYEE: (*with head down and in lowered tones*) I don't think I'm going to make the deadline, and want to know what you want me to do about that. I've really tried; my team and I have worked overtime on this, but I just don't see us finishing before the deadline, and I thought you would want to know sooner rather than later.

LEADER REFLECTION: The task is really important to you, and you and your team have done everything you could think of. You're just stuck right now, and not sure what to do about the deadline.

EMPLOYEE: Yeah, we are so stuck. I can't see a way out right now, but I sure wish I could.

LEADER REFLECTION: It's clear you want to. Tell me more about why you feel so stuck right now.

Reflection Example B

EMPLOYEE: (*rushing into your office, speaking rapidly and smiling*) I think we have a new project that would be great for our team. Do you have a minute?

LEADER REFLECTION: Sure. I can see your excitement and would love to hear more.

EMPLOYEE: I know you don't want our team to take on more, but I think you'll change your mind when you hear about this amazing opportunity.

LEADER REFLECTION: You're hoping that I'll share your enthusiasm so your team will be able to get to work on this new project. Tell me more about why you think your team should take this on, and how you see it in relation to everything else you have on your plate.

Note that the reflections are not formulated as questions. Instead, reflections are statements. They may *feel* like a tentative question since they invite the employee to tell you more, but reflections aim to mirror what has just been said or expressed. Reflections are a lot like the summaries that we describe next in detail, but in contrast to the summaries, a reflection is typically only one or two sentences long. You might define a reflection as a very short summary.

Summaries

If a reflection is a short summary, we can describe *summaries* as longer reflections. Summaries are a set of statements put together to connect thoughts or to condense a quantity of information down to the main points or themes. They are a way of making sure you understand the main ideas and are often used to encapsulate the totality of what you have understood so far. It is also a way to help the employee sum up his main points. Summaries may also facilitate rounding off one part of a conversation and transitioning to the next step or next topic. Examples of summaries are:

Summary Example A

EMPLOYEE: I have been working with my team members on improving our documentation. They are really frustrated with the process. They don't seem to see the importance of this. I'm not sure what I am doing wrong, but they aren't getting the message and fail to see the need for improvements. I know that this documentation issue is not new, and I suspect they simply aren't taking it seriously because it has gone on for so long. They don't think the company even cares whether documentation improves. They are waiting it out, and hoping I'll eventually let it drop. I'm not really sure what to do next other than just carry on nagging them. I hate being someone's nagging mother.

LEADER SUMMARY: Let me see if I've got it all. You are really concerned about the documentation quality. You've tried a number of things but with no result, and you are wondering what else you might do to get your team to take this seriously and make changes. Is that right? Did I miss anything?

Summary Example B

EMPLOYEE: I am sick and tired of being the only one on the team who volunteers to help out when someone calls in sick, and the team needs coverage. I can't keep on doing this. It means I miss time at home, and my family resents my having to work so many extra shifts and missing out on family time. I am not the only person available, and it wouldn't be such a burden if others pitched in, but no one else seems willing to volunteer. I'm tempted to simply not respond to requests in the future, but that's not the right team approach either, and I want to be a team player. I am just so frustrated and feel put upon.

LEADER SUMMARY: You are helping out a lot, and are frustrated that others aren't willing to do their bit. You want to be a team player, but aren't feeling that the balance is fair right now. You are hoping the team dynamic will change. Is that right?

EMPATHY

OARS are the technical side of MI, so to speak. They are the basic tools you use. But as we have indicated several times, the backbone of MI is your intention when talking with one employee or groups of individuals in your organization. Part of this intention is grounded in *empathy*. Empathy is at the heart of listening and MI. By truly listening, by expressing your best guess as to what the employee feels and means, and by trying as hard as you can to understand and express empathy, you are building the foundation that underlies engaging the person in the change process. Reflections in particular suggest empathy and an attitude of understanding. When we reflect and do not judge, we express empathy, and are saying to the other person, "I get it. I accept this as your reality, and I am trying to see the situation from your point of view. I accept you without judgment."

Empathy is not to be confused with sympathy, in which you feel sorry for someone or for his struggle. Rather, empathy is about how you look at a situation together, trying to see it through another person's eyes and grasping his experience. Demonstrating empathy is about stepping into the other's person's shoes for a moment, to feel and understand what that is like.

For example, Donna, a leader in a not-for-profit social service agency, whom we discussed in Chapter 3, asked an employee, Laura, to cover a meeting. Covering this meeting meant that Laura had to stand up in front of a group of people for about an hour and talk about the division. Because Laura always wanted to be helpful and do a good job, she accepted the task. Shortly after asking Laura to run the meeting, another employee came in and shared with Donna that Laura was in her office shaking with anxiety and looked about to be sick. When Donna asked Laura what was wrong, she explained that she was afraid of speaking to large groups of people, but understood that her help was needed and figured that she would be able to manage it. Talking to groups or crowds is not a problem for Donna. It is something she does very regularly, and in fact enjoys. But by stopping for a moment, and understanding Laura's perspective, how the task actually felt for her, and the fear and anxiety it produced and not judging her for it, Donna was able to facilitate a conversation that led to Laura working on her public-speaking ability as part of her professional development plan. Laura came up with her own ideas on how she could work toward the goal of covering meetings in the future, but in the short term, Donna found another employee to help out. Imagine if Donna had judged Laura's fear, laughed at or teased her, or pushed her to cover that particular meeting anyway, rather than understanding her experience. Laura would likely not have represented the division well, done a good job, or decided to work toward improving her public speaking ability. By accepting her experience for what it was, Laura was able to work toward being able to speak in front of large groups. She ended up being really good at it.

Empathy is not about feeling the same way as the employee. Nor do you have to have experienced the same situation in order to show empathy. It simply means that you allow yourself to feel, see, and understand the situation from the employee's viewpoint, and show the employee that you understand. It allows you to recognize why something may be a struggle for the person, telling her that you see that, that you get why she feels stuck, and that you understand rather than judge her experience. In other words, you use the MI spirit of acceptance and compassion. This spirit is what guides the skills of MI.

UNDERSTANDING AMBIVALENCE

When an employee shares a problem, more often than not you will hear *ambivalence*. Ambivalence is feeling two ways about something at the same time. The ambivalent person is typically simultaneously arguing both for and against change. If ambivalence is not present, then MI is likely not the leadership approach to use. But if it is present, MI may be a particularly helpful communication strategy. It can support your ability to understand what is being said and to refrain from responding to just one part of the *stuckness*. Employees, like anyone who feels torn between two ideas, feel stuck when they are ambivalent. The employee will feel ready to change or make a decision when she can see that the benefits of changing outweigh the benefits of staying the same, and when she feels confident that she can make the change.

Understanding the many ways ambivalence can occur will help you empathize with your employee's experience. Appreciating that ambivalence is a normal part of the change process can help you refrain from judging the person, and from trying to fix it for her, and instead focus on the goal of listening to understand and then moving through the process accordingly.

IMPORTANCE

Because ambivalence can look different in different situations, it is important to think about what affects ambivalence. When your employee is sharing his struggle or situation, you may ask yourself how *important* this is to him, and in what ways does it conflict with other issues that are also important. For instance, recently I (C. M.) was talking with Jane, a social worker, about her performance and her desire to progress to a higher level in the organization. To move up, she would have to attend training in project management and oversight of budgets and business processes. This meant she would have to take classes on the weekends, which would cost her money and take away from time with her children. To help her work out what she wanted to do, she explored possible promotion opportunities and her feelings about the impact the change would have on family time and the family budget. This was not an easy decision, because both were important to her and that made the decision hard.

It is also possible for an employee to be ambivalent because he does not know whether the potential change is important compared to other priorities. For instance, John, a nurse, described a problem he was having with productivity on his team. He was considering modifying the team's reporting structure to focus more on their billable time. He saw a need to help his staff focus on increasing the amount of time they spent on revenue-generating activities, but was concerned that time spent this way would take away from the time spent on the quality of client care. He also felt that the more they focused on quality, the more their billable time would improve. In short, he was not sure that he really needed to focus on productivity at all or make any adjustments. The conversation with John focused on his thinking about the importance of balancing the quality of work and the amount of work, and how he saw his team dealing with this issue. Both were important.

Both Jane and John were weighing the costs and benefits of making a change and their view of its importance. There will be costs attached to any change, and working through what is important to the employee is part of helping him resolve ambivalence. People will make a change when the importance of changing outweighs the importance of staying the same.

CONFIDENCE

Ambivalence may also be influenced by a person's *confidence,* or her belief that she can make the change. Psychologist Albert Bandura (1997) describes this belief as "self-efficacy." Bandura's research demonstrated that individuals have beliefs about their abilities, and that these beliefs influence the likelihood of success as much as their actual abilities do. If your employee feels that she is not able to do what she is considering doing, she may stay stuck. She may also reduce its perceived importance if she does not believe she can make the change. For example, Julie, a manager, was discussing with Donna, the leader in a not-for-profit social service agency, the fact that she felt she needed to improve her skills in using data and reports to diagnose and analyze her team performance. Julie felt that this was important because she wanted to be sure she was gauging performance accurately and providing the right training, guidance, and support to her team. But Julie was not confident that she was able to use the data in practice. She described how working with data and reports had been a struggle for her for most of her life. Julie had even taken extra statistics classes in school, but was always left confused. While she was talking, she began sharing that she was not completely sure that she needed reports, because she was already experiencing success with her team. Her confidence in her ability to use and understand reports and data to guide her team was at the center of her ambivalence. As she talked about the change with Donna, her confidence diminished, and its importance receded as well. Julie talked herself out of a possible decision to implement data as a feedback instrument.

AMBIVALENCE MAY SOUND LIKE RESISTANCE

Often, when you hear ambivalence in its many forms, you likely hear it as resistance to change. Leaders tend to miss the conflict inherent in ambivalence. As in the example of Julie, you might hear that she is resistant to changing, rather than understand that on the one hand she wants to use data and reports and sees them as important, but on the other does not feel confident she could implement them correctly. When you miss the two sides of ambivalence, you might focus on one side and, instead of listening and reflecting understanding, begin to argue for change. You might even put pressure on the person to make a decision or change. This is a common righting reflex reaction when leaders register reluctance among the staff. However, when you focus on one side, naturally the person begins to argue for the other side, because inside she already feels the pressure of both sides. So, you end up arguing, instead of listening and guiding the other person in exploring her ambivalence and allowing her to reach her own answers.

In the example with Julie, if you focused on the side of change, you might have told her that you absolutely believe that she can work with data and reports. You might also have said that you know that she is more capable than she thinks, and that you would be willing to go over the material with her. However, since Julie is ambivalent, instead of feeling heard and understood, she might feel that she was being pushed, and respond by bolstering her argument against change, insisting that she really cannot use data and reports to manage her team and does not think she needs to right now. If instead you understand that you are hearing ambivalence, and that your job is not to resolve this struggle for Julie, but rather to guide her through a process in which she can decide for herself at what point she is ready, willing, and able to use data and reports to improve performance, you would thereby reflect both her ambivalence and what she is hoping for. The conversation might sound like this:

> JULIE: Using data has always been a challenge for me. I am not so sure that the new reports are going to help me improve my team's performance. My team is doing well and improving every week, so I am not sure I need to use them. It is possible the data would help me see themes or help me direct my supervision; I am just not sure I can figure it out.
>
> MANAGER: You want to be the best support to your team that you possibly can. You know that you're successful right now, but you are wondering if your team could do even better if you found a way to use the reports and data more effectively. You are worried

that you might not be able to use the reports, but you see the importance of using data more in your management system.

JULIE: Right. I see the benefit of using data. My peers tell me how much doing so has helped them focus on the right skills with their employees, but they are better with data than I am. I wish this was easier for me.

MANAGER: You can tell that your peers are benefiting from using data, and you want that too. You are trying to figure out for yourself how best to use data so they work for you.

JULIE: I am. I would like to be able to use data; I just need to know how to read data and understand when someone is improving. Maybe if I sit in on my peers' meetings and observe how they use data . . . maybe that would give me some ideas.

By reflecting back what you understand, you also help Julie to perceive more clearly how she sees the struggle. You allow her to explore how she really feels about the situation without her having to worry about what you might think of her or her experience. Because you are not pressuring her, you are, in fact, allowing her to consider changing. This is an important first step on the route to getting unstuck.

Values

Ambivalence might also stem from values conflicts or misaligned values. Living your values is an ongoing process that is never done. For example, if you value honesty, you can never say, "Well, I've made it, I am now totally honest." Honesty involves committing to a pattern of choices, behaviors, and actions that you engage in daily. Values are often what motivate behaviors and help people make difficult changes in their lives. Your values guide your behavior, and when you probe what you really value in relation to a specific behavior or a specific change, you'll find that your values can provide the fuel that enables you to move through the process. As Roy Disney once said, "When your values are clear to you, making decisions becomes easier."

Employees strive to live according to their personal values, even in the workplace. Henry, a vice president of behavioral health, held a position that involved raising money. In this role, he faced a values conflict. In meeting with people and asking for money, he felt that he had to be less than honest with potential donors. The goal was to raise as much money as possible for a worthy cause, but the act of raising money did not fit with his overall view of himself. He felt that to be successful at fund-raising he had to be insincere, even fake. Integrity and honesty were his two most deeply held values. As a result, he was not very good in the role and did not enjoy the job. He was, however, fortunate to have a supervisor who was willing to explore this concern with him. His supervisor asked Henry to describe how his values of integrity and honesty related to his current dilemma of not doing well in his fundraising role. Henry shared how being fake or insincere made him feel uncomfortable and not very effective. His supervisor then asked him to consider how his values might help him decide what he wanted to do about his current struggle over not doing well in fund-raising. Henry shared that he did believe in the mission and cause that he was raising money for, and if he could find a way to do this in an honest way, he would be open to learning new approaches. His supervisor summarized that Henry wanted to improve his performance, wanted to raise money for a noble cause, and was interested in learning a new way to accomplish these goals that included being sincere and honest. By resolving this conflict, Henry also resolved his ambivalence in deciding to make a change in his approach and learn different ways to raise money that led to his improved performance. This is just one example of how clarification of values can resolve ambivalence. Asking a person to think about what he values, or what matters most to him, and how his values might impact how he thinks about the situation he is facing are effective ways to help him figure out the right direction to go in.

It may seem strange in a workplace context to explore someone's personal values. However, by assessing someone's values and exploring a person's key strengths, you send the signal to your staff and your organization that what someone values and what she is good at is important to you and contributes to her overall success. It is helpful for a leader to understand the employee as a whole person who has important values that guide her decisions and actions. Whether or not you explore them, the employee's values are often what fuel her behavior or decisions. Identifying the employee's values can help you understand her actions and behavior and support her growth.

Goals/Mission

As with values, goals or personal visions may equally be at the center of someone's ambivalence. Goals can be specific or more general. For instance, you might have the goal to learn how to use presentation software more effectively and also to improve your ability to lead a team. The presentation software proficiency goal is specific and time limited. You can take a course, find a mentor to teach you, or read books and learn the skills of effective software presentation that way. Being able to lead a team, however, is an ongoing goal. This goal is likely something you will continually strive toward—an ongoing pursuit.

Goals can come into conflict with other priorities and may then lead to ambivalence. For instance, I (C. M.) had an employee named Meredith whose goal was to become a trainer, in addition to performing well in her current role as a counselor. However, at the time Meredith did not have a training role in the company, and the company had other expectations for her. In order to do a good job in the position she currently filled, Meredith often had to decide between attending trainings and meetings for her current role, and trainings for a potential role as trainer. She was constantly conflicted, because she valued doing a good job as a counselor, but also wished to advance and become a trainer.

Another common conflict occurs when a company is moving in a direction that does not match the employees' vision for themselves.

The example of Henry, a vice president of behavioral health, who had to lead fund-raising efforts, illustrates this as well. The company needed to raise money to support the good work it was doing with individuals. Raising money was never something Henry had envisioned himself doing, and he would not have applied for the job had he known that this would be a core task. However, with the shift in company priorities and the role he held, fund-raising became his primary responsibility. After resolving the conflict of values, there were still improvements Henry and his supervisor felt that he needed to make to be successful. Henry felt ambivalent, because he really did not see this role as something he wanted, and consequently he didn't really want to put in the necessary work to learn what it took to be a successful fund-raiser. He ended up finding a new role more suited to his goals and strengths.

Recognizing That Ambivalence Is Important

Ambivalence is often misunderstood as lack of motivation, lack of caring, or an overall negative workplace attitude. If, instead, you as a leader can suspend your own judgment and try to hear and understand ambivalence, you will create a better situation in which to guide your employees out of their ambivalence. But first it is important to recognize ambivalence and, since it is often hidden behind a façade, this is not always easy. We often say to colleagues who are leaders that no one gets up in the morning thinking, "How can I make my boss's day horrible?" Most people want to do a good job—they want to improve and grow. A recent study found personal growth to be the number one factor in what makes work feel meaningful (Hickey, 2018). Most people also want to do meaningful, fulfilling work. But in order to do so, they need someone to listen, understand, and guide them to find ideas and solutions that work and that they can choose when they are ready, willing, and able. In other words what you hear as resistance, low motivation, or lack of caring is often ambivalence. Understanding the many ways in which ambivalence can be heard will enable you to empathize with your employee's experience. Appreciating that ambivalence is a normal part of the change process can help you refrain from judging the person and from trying to fix what's wrong for them, in order to focus on the goal of listening to understand.

ENGAGING COMES FIRST AND NEVER ENDS

It is also important for leaders to remember that none of the MI processes will be successful if a leader fails to spend enough time engaging. We all too often see leaders jump ahead in the process, trying to get to planning or action too soon and failing to see the importance of the engaging process. It is the understanding of the employee's perspective and the building of a relationship based on trust, empathy, nonjudgment, employee autonomy and support that allows that change to be possible. Engaging has to come first and be sustained throughout the conversation. It is important to reflect on whether you understand your employee enough, and whether your employee feels understood before moving to the next process.

SUMMARY

Engaging is the first and most fundamental process in MI. Listening is the most important skill when engaging with an individual. Listening is not the same as responding. *Listening* is an active discipline, involving a strong focus on reflecting back what you hear and understand to the individual, thereby ensuring that you really comprehend what has been expressed.

Employee Vignette

Let's pick up on our conversation with Susan from Chapter 3. To recap, Jim, her supervisor, asked Ashley, the head of the organization, to meet with Susan. Susan was new to her job and struggling with enrolling new clients into the program. Here is how the conversation began, focusing primarily on engaging and understanding.

> ASHLEY: So, I understand that Jim asked us to meet to see if I might be able to help. You have been trying to learn to meet the standards for this position, and it has been a struggle. Is that right?
>
> SUSAN: Yes. It has been a struggle, and I am not sure that you can

help, but I am sure open to trying anything. I really like this team, and I think the work is meaningful. I'm just seriously struggling with enrolling new people into the program.

ASHLEY: You really want this to work. (*affirm*) You are not sure what will actually help at this point, but you are open to this conversation and to giving it your best shot. (*reflection*)

SUSAN: Yeah. If you could help, I would love that.

ASHLEY: Would it be okay if we started with you describing to me how you view what is happening? (*asking permission*) How you are doing? Describe the struggle. (*open-ended question*)

SUSAN: Sure. As you know, for me to be on track at this point, I should be able to enroll at least one person a day, or five people a week, into our program. I have not been able to achieve that. Not even once. I start a conversation with a potential client about what we do and how it helps people, and the minute I think they are going to say they are not interested I just stop talking and shut down and stop the conversation. I worry so much about trying to meet the expectations that I lose sight of the person and her wants.

ASHLEY: You are feeling a lot of pressure to meet this expectation, and you can tell that this pressure is affecting your ability to actually hear your clients or care about what they want. (*reflection*)

SUSAN: I worry so much that I am going to get fired, and I don't want to leave this company. I have never failed at anything in my life, actually. I have always received good grades in school, I was a dancer and always ended up winning, and I even coach a dance team right now, and we almost always win our competitions. Even if we lose a round, we always end up winning in the end. I really don't know how to handle failing. I really never have.

ASHLEY: You are used to putting in the work and pushing through to success, so it is confusing to you that it is not happening this time. You are not sure what to make of this. (*reflection*)

SUSAN: Right. It's like I freeze. I just keep telling myself I am failing.

ASHLEY: How about the other parts of the job? Apart from enrolling new people. (*open-ended question*)

SUSAN: That is actually going very well. Once someone wants our program, I can work very easily with the person. I am able to listen and understand what the client hopes for from the program and how I might best help. It is just the first part that is so terrible.

ASHLEY: Okay, so let me make sure I understand. You are doing very well with most of the job. It is just this first part of enrolling new people that has been a struggle. You really want to sort this out, because you love your team and find the work with your clients meaningful. You are confused about why this is so hard because you are used to putting in hard work and you typically succeed in the end. (*summary*) Did I miss anything? (*open-ended question*)

SUSAN: No, that is it. I am used to sometimes not winning. I mean, I didn't place first in every dance, and my present team doesn't win every meet. I am just not used to losing every time, every day, like I am here.

ASHLEY: So small setbacks are something you expect, but not achieving the goal, ever, is what is confusing. (*reflection*)

SUSAN: Right.

ASHLEY: So you are struggling because you freeze and focus on failing. You don't like this feeling and are confused about why you are so stuck. It is really important to you to sort this out. Failure is not something you are used to or like, and you want to find a way to make this work. You like the team and find the work meaningful, and are just trying to figure out how to be successful here. (*summary*)

SUSAN: That is right.

SELF-REFLECTIVE EXERCISE. LISTEN TO YOUR EMPLOYEE

Listening with the intention of understanding rather than fixing is a main ingredient in MI. In this exercise, we would like you to try to listen and not to fix the next time you talk with the person you selected. When the person is sharing with you how he views the issue or is approaching it, try to listen to understand and reflect back to him your understanding. Practice asking the following open-ended questions and reflecting back in reflective statements your best guess as to what the person just shared, what it means to him, and how he might feel about it.

Exercise: Have a Conversation with This Person about the Change

You might decide to use all the self-reflective exercises at once in this meeting, or schedule several meetings, with each one building on the previous process. For instance, you could use this listening exercise, and then schedule another meeting to focus, have the following one to evoke, and finally hold a session to plan. Or you could combine two processes at once: listen and focus, then evoke and plan. You can decide what works best for the time you have available and the meeting structure you choose. The exercises are written to allow you to attend to one process at a time.

Check if you can explore the following questions, while always reflecting understanding when the person shares his thoughts. You can have a free-flowing conversation with the person and can use these questions as guides for the conversation.

- Ask the person if he would kindly describe the situation.
    - Reflect what you understand about what he shared. Try to include in your reflecting what this might mean to the person and/or how he is feeling about this.
- Ask the person to tell you why he is considering making a change.
    - Reflect what you understand about the *why* behind his wanting to make this change.
- Ask the person what reasons he has for making this change.
    - Reflect what you understand about why this change is important to him.
    - Ask him to elaborate. What other reasons might he have for making this change?
- Ask the person what ideas he has about how he would approach this change, if he decided to make it.
    - Reflect what you understand about what ideas he has about approaching this change.
    - Ask him to elaborate on his other ideas about how he might approach this change.
    - If he has been successful with a change like this in the past, ask what helped him with it back then.
- Ask the person how confident he is that he could make this change, if he decided to do so.
    - Reflect what you understand about his level of confidence.
- Ask the person what he imagines he might do going forward.
    - Summarize what you have heard throughout the entire conversation.

Now that you have had this conversation, stop for a moment and consider what you thought and believed previously. Review your answers to the questions in the exercise at the end of Chapter 3. What did you answer then? What did you think? And what do you know now? Then answer the following questions:

- Where were you correct in what you thought?
- How was your understanding different then as compared to now?
- What else did you learn?
- What more do you understand now about the situation and the person's ambivalence to change?

CHAPTER 5

Listening to Your Organization

In the previous chapter, we discussed how to listen to individual employees and engage them in order to understand their thoughts, values, dilemmas, and ambivalence. In this chapter, we will concentrate on the same process, but from an organizational angle: not focusing on the individual, but looking rather at the organization as a whole, as an entity that reacts to change. In other words, we will apply our knowledge of what motivates individuals to change by discussing how to use these same principles and concepts in relation to companies. Organizations, after all, are made up of a group of individuals continually facing change.

Implementing change in organizations is an important part of a leader's role. You have probably already tried to implement minor or major changes multiple times. Sometimes, no doubt, you have succeeded; at other times, you have failed. You may well have wondered why. When leaders find themselves unable to implement changes they believe to be important, it's natural to feel frustrated and confused. They realize that making changes, large or small, is complicated and a struggle. Leaders ask themselves, "Why don't my employees grasp the importance of this change? Why aren't they making it happen?" They may even begin to question their own ability to lead.

You would probably not be surprised to learn that your role as a leader is one of the most important in terms of implementing change. Leaders set the course, direction, and pace of change. We know both from research and from firsthand experience that leadership, or the lack of it, is the most influential factor in determining whether change is

69

actualized. Although leaders hold many responsibilities, such as managing budgets, attracting and hiring the right talent, or monitoring the quality of services, implementing change is a key part of a leader's remit. Only leaders can prioritize the company's time and resources and guide the organization toward those imperatives.

Leaders face the need to implement change for a variety of reasons. They may include a board decision, a reduction in funding, customer priorities, staff modifications, legislation, threats from a rival, or a new market strategy, to name but a few. But regardless of the reason, the processes involved are often the same. Surprisingly, they often mirror similar processes individuals go through when facing change.

As with employees, organizations tend to pass through certain phases that may vary in length and complexity. Understanding these phases can help you determine where to direct your attention, your interventions, and your conversations. Similarly to what we have discussed in previous chapters, supporting change processes starts with listening: to concerns, values, worries, ambivalence, and aspirations. This is also where you start with organizations. First, you listen to understand.

WHAT ARE YOU LISTENING FOR?

When you listen to people in your organization, you are likely to hear many ideas for change. Your staff might share ideas for improving services, workflows, or processes. Your leadership team might suggest taking on new services or lines of business. Or you might notice that there are problems with staff retention or satisfaction that need attention. When you listen, you will doubtless pick up on multiple ways in which your organization is thinking about evolving, and be faced with a host of decisions about their relative importance and where to begin.

It is likely that the prospect of change will initially prompt organizational ambivalence. Listening is a tool for exploring and understanding this ambivalence, specifically seeking it out so that you are able to grasp all of its aspects. Understanding how your organization feels about its own growth, abilities, challenges, and evolution is critical to knowing where best to lead your teams. Listening helps you do just that. It helps you stay aligned with the organization, the staff, and the many stakeholders invested in your services, so that you are able to make informed decisions. Without listening and understanding, leaders are simply making decisions in the dark and likely feel at a loss as to how to proceed when their ideas are either not carried out or fail to work. When you listen, you get to understand where your organization is at, what it hopes for, what it is worried about, and how it feels about its ability to change.

ORGANIZATIONAL AMBIVALENCE

One of the hardest parts about leading change in companies is deciding where to begin and how to move the staff forward. The reason for this is that people typically fail to agree. Often, when leaders start considering a new idea, they are met with opposing and contradictory opinions. Organizations, just like individuals, tend to be ambivalent about change. Teams may have different agendas, the leadership team may disagree on priorities, individuals or groups may have different beliefs about the organization's ability, and still other groups may simply find the new idea neither necessary nor as important as other priorities. Since organizational ambivalence spans a range of views regarding the importance of and confidence in making this change, the organization may become stuck and unable to move forward. Leaders may not know how to lead the team forward, because while one group argues for one direction, others argue for another. Or else different groups are not convinced the team is able to do what is needed. Or maybe the leader is simply unable to narrow down the priorities to two or three. Leaders are keenly aware that they must garner support from the employees if they are to actively participate in the implementation, but how does a leader achieve that commitment if there is such a divide of opinion or degree of disagreement? Understanding the nature of the ambivalence about the change engulfing you and your organization is an important first step in moving ahead. When you realize that people and organizations are ambivalent, you acknowledge that forcing the change through will likely not be successful, but more likely lead to resistance, conflicts, or even staff leaving your organization. Turmoil among your staff is the last thing you want; it is both costly and time consuming. Instead, leaders can turn to the processes of MI to help move the organization conversation forward, to resolve the ambivalence, to win the organization's commitment to the new plan, and then to proceed with active implementation.

For example, Allan, a vice president of a not-for-profit organization, and a director of integrated health, was leading a pilot program to improve clients' access to care. He and his leadership team regularly reviewed reports that showed that it took about 6 weeks for new clients to access services. This trend was far from the organization's quality metric for access to care being 24 hours for urgent clients and 7 days for routine appointments. On several occasion, Allan had said in staff meetings and to his directors that access to care needed to improve, but was not seeing an improvement across the organization. He had also tried to email the entire team members, letting them know what was happening and asking them to work toward improving access to care, but still did not see any change. Allan then decided that he needed to hear from his organization's leaders, and began by gathering all the directors and managers together in a meeting. At the meeting, Allan shared the data and the current performance trend and reminded the audience of the organization's quality standard. Then he asked the directors and managers to assemble in smaller groups and to discuss and answer these questions:

- "Why was this trend increasing?"
- "What do you believe are the barriers to achieving our quality standard?"

After an hour, each group reported their answers. Several people felt the issue concerned the caseload size—that each therapist had too many clients. Others believed that some clients who were given priority appointments (within 24 hours) were in no more need than other clients, and were only straining staff availability. Others believed that the staff were spending too much time in meetings, training, supervision, and documentation; and still others believed that a lengthy assessment and treatment plan process were to blame. The organization turned out to be ambivalent about several issues.

WHY IS COLLABORATIVE LEADERSHIP IMPORTANT?

MI is a collaborative approach, which means that the leader, the employees, and the whole organization work together to find the answers to organizational problems. You might wonder why this matters. "Why can't I just make decisions, give directions, and have my employees do what they are asked?"

Research, experience, and training have demonstrated over and again that collaboration works, and is indeed essential in the new, ever-changing business environment. Business schools, management journals, and business leaders all teach a collaborative leadership approach, because collaboration is simply more effective than any alternative. The Harvard Business School Leadership Training Program explains:

> As the business landscape becomes increasingly dynamic and new players enter the market, successful companies are tasked with building their capacity for agility, adaptability, and speed in order to maintain competitive advantage. Business leaders globally are responding by transitioning from a hierarchical organizational structure to more flexible, team-centric models that foster collaboration, information sharing, and empowerment. We call this the responsive organization. With this shift, companies have realized improved productivity, better employee engagement, and increased revenues. (Harvard Extension School, 2019)

Many of the problems facing leaders in today's market are unique and complex, and it is the diversity of opinion, people, and skills within organizations that makes it possible to solve these very complicated issues. It is our experience that when leaders adopt the spirit of MI, specifically empathy and collaboration, they are able to guide their teams from a no-solution situation to a place of meaningful and successful change.

WHY INVOLVE THE STAFF IN THINKING ABOUT ORGANIZATIONAL CHANGE?

As a leader, you can, of course, rely on yourself and use your own imagination when considering new ideas. You may even think this course is easier. However, often the leader and the leadership team encompass only one perspective, which may diverge from the perspective taken by your employees who deliver services to their clients. The leaders may indeed be the first to know that something should or must improve. They might be the right people to think about *why* the organization needs to change, but they are probably not the right people to ask *how* the organization should change. Take, for instance, Arthur, a director of mental health services, who was on a leadership team that became aware that the organization was losing family therapy contracts to a rival agency, who was offering free parenting classes. Free parenting classes were attractive to new families as well as to the community referral sources (schools, doctors' offices, and faith-based organizations). Many families would attend the free classes offered by the rival organization and then sign on for services, which led to more revenue and the delivery of further services. Arthur and his team knew that they, too, were capable of offering free parenting classes, because their staff were already trained in positive parenting and they had the physical space to accommodate groups. They also knew that if they failed to offer these classes, they would continue to lose customers and referrals, and might even go out of business. So the leadership team was clear about the need to add free parenting classes to their portfolio of services. Or rather the leadership team knew that a change was needed and *why*. What they did not know was *how* best to implement the change with staff. Who should run the groups, when should they be held, and how might this change be introduced without overwhelming the already overstretched staff? The direct care staff would be better suited to answer the questions about the *how*.

Once you know that your organization needs to change and why, it makes sense to turn to your staff for thoughts about *how*. You can tell your employees about the challenges that lie ahead, explain why they are necessary, and then ask: what is the best approach? Resistance to change weakens if everybody in the organizations understands why the change is essential. As Simon Sinek (2009) explains, "If you don't know why, you can't know how." This is an important first step, but nevertheless many leaders forget that the management team had those "why" discussions. In those discussions, the team became convinced that change was needed, but when they begin to implement the changes, they forget that the staff were not involved and so may be less convinced. If staffers are merely presented with a decision without having been involved in making the decision, it is easy for them to say to themselves, "Why change? Everything is fine," and be reluctant about the change. If you present the reasons why a new idea is necessary and solicit views on how best to approach the task, you can engage staff in problem solving, take inspiration from their ideas, come up with the best ways to initiate change, and increase the probability of success. Sounds easy, right? As a leader, you already know this process can be complicated. That is why we believe that the principles of MI might be helpful to you, and may be useful to bear in mind when you intend to listen to your whole organization. How can you do that?

THE ANSWERS LIE IN THE KNOWLEDGE AND EXPERTISE OF THE ORGANIZATION

The easy answer is that your organization is not a uniform entity or a fixed box. It is a group, and perhaps a large one, of individuals. It is a group of real people with a lot of insight, skills, and knowledge. They are all experts in their particular areas. They typically feel responsible for their work, and hopefully feel proud to be part of your organization's mission. With the combination of your own and your staff's knowledge, with all their diversity of experience, views, and ideas, you will have the information you need to be able to make the best decisions. In other words, just as the ideas, solutions, and reasons related to change reside in the individual, so do the *answers lie within your organization*, even if you do not see them at first.

Just as there are roadblocks when listening to individuals, as described earlier, so too there are traps that may keep leaders from listening to understand the organization. Let us take a look at the most common traps into which leaders may fall.

THE PERSUASION TRAP: THEY JUST NEED MORE CONVINCING

Leaders sometimes believe that it is their duty to persuade the organization to change. They believe that they know what is best and simply need to convince others of the same, and it will happen. They give numerous talks and send out memos and newsletters, all explaining the changes to come. They believe, and their behavior bears this out, that if they just provide enough information, the staff will understand and will accept the need to change. We saw this in the earlier example of Allan, a director of integrated health, who tried to change the access to care trend by explaining what he was seeing to his staff in meetings and emails and asking them to improve. His efforts were met with no improvement in the access to care data. Information, advice, and attempts to persuade are roadblocks to listening (Gordon, 1970). Trying to persuade an organization to change often feels like a struggle, if not a battle, as bad as trying to convince your teenage son to clean his room. Why is this? Why does it feel like your organization is working against you? What should you do? Should you just argue more, persuade more, or provide more information?

Leaders fall into the persuasion trap with the best of intentions. They can see that change is needed and simply seek to bring it about. At first glance, it would appear easy for leaders to explain to employees what is expected of them and what they need to do. Leaders may even feel that they should have all the answers. It seems reasonable that arguing logically why this new idea is important will persuade others and motivate the organization to work to implement it.

But what typically happens when leaders try to persuade? Persuading people to change is effective sometimes, but rarely. In fact, it can actually make the change harder. Just telling employees what to do differently often produces resistance, especially if they do not know why or how. When a leader is the one arguing for or lecturing the staff about the change, she is proclaiming that she is the expert, that the staff have no choice, and that their ideas or views do not matter. The bad news is that this approach leads to the staff holding back on sharing their ideas and views, because they sense that the leader is only interested in her own. When the leader misses the opportunity to draw on the staff's fund of knowledge and wisdom, the organization ends up losing out.

THE PREMATURE FOCUS TRAP: THEY JUST NEED MORE TRAINING

Sometimes leaders may believe that the organization just needs to learn new skills in order to change. They may quickly decide to simply train the staff, believing that additional training will lead to change. They may bring in expensive trainers to teach better customer service or time management skills or a new therapeutic intervention. Again, sometimes more training might work. But often, it does not. If staff have not bought into the change, it is unlikely. Employees may dutifully attend the training, but not implement what they have learned when they are back in their offices. If they do not agree or understand why the organization needs to make the change in which they are being trained, they are likely to consider the training as just one of many tools they can choose to use as they wish.

We call this the *premature focus trap,* because the leader simply jumps into training and skill development too early. Training, or skill development, is typically helpful only when your organization's ambivalence has been resolved and the team understands how this specific training will help achieve a larger change initiative. If the staff approach training understanding the *why,* and with its implementation in mind, they are likely to be more engaged, and more creative in finding ways to overcome the barriers they will likely encounter when incorporating this new skill into their everyday work.

THE BULLY TRAP: THEY JUST NEED TO BE SCARED

Feeling frustrated and short of options, leaders might think that threatening or scaring their organization could be a way to get change to happen. They think that if the employees understand that their jobs are on the line here, they will accept change. Again, this strategy might work on rare occasions, but what is more likely to happen when people are scared is a rise in defensiveness, blame, and competition for resources. Leaders may hope that scaring the staff will lead to teams finding a way to come together and agree on a plan. What typically happens instead is leaders start justifying their own department's roles and the need to keep their teams in the company or making a case for why they or their teams cannot be sacrificed. Scaring, threatening, and bullying does not create the open, trusting environment that is essential to being able to listen, understand, resolve ambivalence, and identify solutions that will work.

If you notice that you have fallen into any of these common traps, embrace this opportunity to stop to reflect on and assess your strategy. You can ask yourself how well your approach is working. Are your teams motivated? Are they part of the approach and solution? Do you understand how your organization or different groups within it view this change? Have you taken on board their reasons and their ideas about how to change? Are they part of the answer? Instead of compelling people by using your knowledge or expertise to convince them, or by threatening your staff, or by providing more training, you might instead try to really listen to what is going on in the organization. What do you hear?

LISTENING: A PARTNERSHIP

When listening to your organization, your aim is to understand its ambivalence and how different groups in the organization view issues.

Your intention is to build a relationship that goes from being a wrestling match, in which you are forcing employees to change, to a free-flowing dance, in which they choose to actively participate in the implementation. It may sound silly to talk about dancing with your organization, but we are sure that if you have experienced a time when you and your staff were aligned and collaboratively working toward change, you know exactly what we mean. It is fun to be a leader when you and your team are working together. It is like being the conductor of a symphony orchestra: you gently lead the violins, the flutes, the horns, and the cellos, calling forth from them their very best. Performing together, you *all* create a symphony. You, as the conductor, cannot do this on your own—you need the orchestra musicians, or no music is produced. If you are not there, the groups may play their own parts, but lack the direction to perform a whole symphony. Together, you make music. When you listen and guide, using MI, you too can produce amazing music and change.

THE IMPORTANCE OF FEELING SAFE

If you wish your staff to not only contribute ideas for change, but also to bring their ambivalence, reluctance, and perceptions of barriers and even resistance against change to your attention, they need to feel safe. They have to believe that you really do want to know and care about their point of view. They need to trust that you value their input and to know that if they take the risk of sharing this input, it will not be to their detriment. For instance, let's say your staff know that that they have not found a way to shorten the wait time for a first appointment, and they know that this change is critical to a new quality initiative to increase access to care. If the staff worry that sharing this information means that you will fire the team or the team leader because you have no faith in their being up to this challenge, they will withhold observations that might have enabled you to see the barrier. This is not to say that you never *will* need to fire someone. You might have to fire an employee for a number of reasons, including a lack of resources or not adjusting to workload, or even because he does not function in the organization or is not ready or willing to change. Making tough decisions like firing someone is part of a leader's job, and it is important to be clear about that. A leader who avoids this responsibility is just as hard to trust as the leader who does not listen to the staff's proposals, ideas, and suggestions. But when leaders listen to their organization, they need to make it clear that it is safe for the staff to express concerns and point out barriers to change without the fear of being punished. They need to believe that the leader is prepared to work with them to solve problems, deal with concerns, and remove barriers.

It is, of course, important for a leader to be clear about the boundaries for staff involvement. This is analogous to using MI with individuals: There is no point in exploring ideas and thoughts if a decision has already been made or the outcome cannot be influenced. However, such situations are in fact rare. In most situations, listening will not only help you better understand the situation, it will also help you engage your employees in identifying solutions. When your employees are actively involved, they are significantly more likely to comply with the decision and be more creative in carrying out the solutions and adapting when the plan needs modifications. If employees do not feel that they are part of the solution or that their ideas are taken into account, they will implement the change, but hold it at arm's length and not take ownership of it. When you are able to guide your organization through ambivalence, you help your employees enter into a place of readiness and willingness to make the change, so they can embrace the solution wholeheartedly.

HOW CAN YOU LISTEN TO THE
STAFF AND INVITE THEIR INVOLVEMENT?

There are many ways to invite staff to share their thoughts. Strategies for collaborating with your staff often depend on the size of your organization and how it is structured. For instance, you may inform employees—through emails, talks, or newsletters or in meetings—about the problem that needs to be solved. In these verbal and written forums, you can carefully explain the reasons why something needs to be changed. Once the staff understand the *why,* you can suggest how they might share their proposals, concerns, and ideas. You can then clarify the time frame within which a decision needs to be made, and ask for their thoughts on how to approach the change and what needs to be protected in the process.

When we (C. M. and A. S. N) have been able to solve dilemmas using this process, we have had good feedback. To give one example, Carol was the leader of a drug and alcohol agency that was asked to provide home-based services for pregnant women who were continuing to use alcohol while pregnant. Several possible teams and groups could provide this new service. She knew that she wanted to find the best solution and include the staff in the decision making about how to proceed. She made it clear to the staff that she needed their input, explaining that they knew best which team would be able to take on the delivery of this new service, and also knew how to combine this new responsibility with significant existing demands. She shared that their input, concerns, and proposals were all necessary for her to make the right decision and to ensure that the organization continued to deliver good, customer-centered quality services. She also explained that she needed to make this decision by the end of the month. She used every opportunity to gather input. She reminded her staff during meetings and via newsletters that she needed to hear their thoughts, and when she met them in the kitchen or break room, she would ask them about their current thinking. She always ended the conversations, meetings, and discussions by briefly summarizing what she had heard, and reflecting it back to them before moving on. When, together with the rest of the management group, she finally made the decision about how best to proceed, she briefed them again on why including home-based services for pregnant women was important to the company mission, describing what she had heard and learned during the previous month, and then explaining her ultimate decision. She acknowledged that there had been conflicting views and even worries about increasing the workload of teams that were already stretched, and also explained the specific reasons why she found that it was in the organization's overall best interest to choose one particular team and process instead of another. She communicated her final decision during meetings and via newsletters and minutes from management meetings. In other words, she did what most of the staff expected, in that she took on the responsibility of choosing the best way to proceed, but did so on informed grounds. She resolved her own and the organization's ambivalence by eliciting thoughts from the staff. You might add that the ambivalence of the organization was resolved by listening to the whole. In listening, she paid particular attention to thoughts highlighting the importance of successful change, while still recognizing possible barriers, and, most crucially, related the decision to the overall goal, core mission, and values of the organization.

CREATE STRUCTURED PLATFORMS FOR LISTENING

As you have read, listening is an active, not a passive, sport. It requires creating the space, time, and culture that conveys that open communication is important, valued, and necessary. There are many ways to listen, but what they all have in common is starting with creating the format and the space. A systematic structure for how to listen to your organization can be helpful. You may even consider forming an internal team within the company that regularly creates opportunities for discussion and input, similar to the implementation of a quality-assurance team (or the audit team described in the organization vignette example at the end of this chapter) or the like. If you have the opportunity, you should be active in it yourself. Listening to the organization is not something that can be delegated to others.

Another platform for listening to and engaging with your whole organization may be that of asking for input from the entire staff. You could systematically ask for thoughts, views, and other input that can be discussed during management meetings. For example, Carol, whom we previously discussed, arranged an annual 2-day leadership meeting. During this annual meeting, the leadership team focused on the organization and discussed what needed to improve, both in relation to the services and treatment offered, but also in relation to infrastructure and operational processes, collaboration between teams, collaboration between managers, and other practical problems. The meeting took place at an off-site location where the management team stayed overnight, dined together and—on top of having enough time to thoroughly discuss all the topics on the agenda—also had the opportunity to get to know one another. The staff knew that this 2-day meeting took place every year in May, and everyone was encouraged to hand in topics, questions, and areas of concern they wished attending leaders to discuss and consider. Careful, detailed minutes were always taken of the meetings, in which *all* the topics raised by the staff were recorded, in addition to issues introduced by the leadership team. The minutes also carefully chronicled team discussions and the final agreed-upon conclusions. Following the meeting, the minutes were sent out to the entire staff in the organization. In the early years, relatively few topics for the meeting were suggested by the staff, but soon everyone realized that the leadership really did take to heart and discuss all of their topics, questions, and ideas. The staff began to feel that the leadership team took their questions, proposals, and ideas seriously, discussed them, and reflected their thoughts back to them. Most important, since the 2-day meetings took place every year, they soon became a well-trusted part of the routine for listening to and engaging with the organization.

Again, listening is not just about hearing what is said, it is also about showing what you understand from what you heard. To create an atmosphere of trust, it is important not only to hear staff voices, but also to reflect back what you have learned. As mentioned in Chapter 4, reflecting back is a way of preventing misunderstandings. It is, however, also a strategic method for guiding your organization toward change, as we discuss in the next chapters.

HOW DO YOU LISTEN TO YOUR ORGANIZATION IF IT IS LARGE?

There is, of course, an upper limit to how many employees you can listen to in face-to-face conversations. If the organization is really large, you may need to listen to your organization *by proxy* or make use of structured ways of collecting thoughts from the staff.

Listening *by proxy* means, for example, asking your management team to listen, or creating groups of employee (or customer) representatives who have been asked to brainstorm and explore with you. You may not hear all of the staff's thoughts, but you can hear enough to understand dilemmas, to identify barriers to change, and to highlight resources that can be drawn upon and cultivated to implement change. Listening by proxy is most helpful if it is also a transparent process. You can make the process transparent by letting it be known with whom you are meeting and what topics you will be discussing and encouraging the staff to tell their colleagues who will represent them what are their concerns or thoughts. You can be continually feeding back to the organization what you learned and how individual employees can share further thoughts.

Another way to listen to a large company could be by electronic means. You may decide to ask all staff members for their ideas, even when it is a large group. You can get their ideas, for instance, by means of a survey. If you decide to go down that route, it is still important that you give feedback on what you learned from the survey. Feedback means not just presenting the results to the staff, but also reflecting on what you learned from the information that was offered and how you interpreted it. You can also use these opportunities to communicate and clarify any misunderstandings.

We also believe there are a lot of solutions currently being created that will allow for more technology-enabled collaboration. Ibarra and Hansen (2011) describe how Marc Benioff, the CEO of Salesforce.com, was able to listen to and engage his entire organization in a strategy meeting using Chatter, a Facebook-inspired application for companies that allows users to keep track of their colleagues and customers and share information and ideas. Benioff was able to stream his leadership strategy meeting and discussion in real time to all employees, while simultaneously sharing his own thoughts and reactions on Chatter. Benioff described what happened when the employees started sharing their thoughts in response to the discussion, as follows: "Suddenly, the meeting went from a select group participating to the entire company participating." "We felt the empowerment in the room," recalls Steve Gillmore, the head of technical media strategy. Ibarra and Hansen explain that "in the end the dialogue lasted for weeks beyond the actual meeting. More important, by fostering a discussion across the entire organization, Benioff has been able to better align the whole workforce around its mission. The event served as a catalyst for the creation of a more open and empowered culture at the company." If your goal is collaboration and your intention is to engage and listen to your organization, we are confident that you will also find creative ways, like Benioff, to include as many voices as you can.

THE IMPORTANCE OF BEING A ROLE MODEL

When leaders model in their approach an interest in hearing from the entire staff, along with the message that all ideas or thoughts are welcome, they also model the values of inclusion and acceptance. It is our experience that when we actively seek our employees' ideas and views, our management team starts to do the same, and this attitude spreads throughout the organization like wildfire. The very act of modeling a caring attitude, or one of listening, and where input is taken seriously, means that these values become management values throughout the organization, no matter how large. In most areas, the staff share their thoughts with their leaders who, in turn, share their team's ideas with their leaders, until they finally reach the executives or the decision makers of the company. When people know that they are part of a company in which the sharing of ideas is valued, they will share and, more important, they will take ownership for their work and the mission of the organization. They will be engaged.

SUMMARY

Listening to an organization is like listening to individuals. Organizations *are* groups of individuals. In order to be able to listen to and engage with the organization, you may have to build an infrastructure for how to listen. Reflecting back to the organization what you hear and how you understand what you hear is just as important as the listening itself.

Organization Vignette

Recall that Marie was leading her alcohol treatment team and organization in finding a way to improve the quality of treatment. Let's see how the engaging process looked.

Based on a review of the past year's data, Marie and the leadership team knew that the organization needed to improve its overall quality on two fronts: the premature client dropout rate and the outcomes of treatment. The staff were highly motivated to provide the best care to their clients. However, tracking data was also a demanding task that the staff felt was simply a waste of time and detracted from their more important priority, the time spent with their clients. In particular, some long-term staff did not believe that documentation, tracking data, and using data for treatment planning would, in fact, improve the quality of the treatment. In contrast, newer staff felt that collecting data was a natural part of treatment delivery and were more open to ensuring that data were accurate and complete. The newer staff felt they needed the data in order to perform their work. The leadership team realized they needed to understand this staff ambivalence.

The leadership team arranged a 1-day meeting for all staff members. Carefully planned and scheduled, the meeting was to be held at a location external to the organization. The meeting announcement was sent to all staff members and, in addition to a short description of the organization's mission, it included this agenda.

Staff Meeting

Focus: Developing the Quality of Our Treatment Service

Venue: Hope Conference Center

8:30–9:00 A.M.   Breakfast

9:00–10:00 A.M.   Marie (CEO): Update on the status of the current outcome of our service. What do we know?

10:00–10:15 A.M. Break

10:15–12:00 P.M. Discussion in small groups. What outcome should we aim for?

12:00–1:00 P.M.   Lunch

1:00–2:00 P.M.   General discussion on future goals

2:00–3:00 P.M.   Planning: How will we reach those goals?

At the meeting, Marie started by describing the organization's mission. She reminded her staff that each and every employee's absolute focus was to help clients solve their problems with alcohol and live a life of abstinence or controlled drinking. Marie presented the latest figures on the outcomes of treatment. The figures showed that 30% of clients dropped out of treatment within the first 3 months, and only 50% of the clients who initiated treatment reached an acceptable treatment goal (i.e., abstinence or controlled drinking) after 6 months. Marie also showed figures illustrating that most clients dropped out during the first weeks of treatment.

Marie continued explaining that improving these treatment outcomes could only happen if clients actually stayed in treatment and the organization found new ways to engage clients in their own care. She explained that the leadership team had decided to take this full day away from client services to address this critical question. They knew that they needed the knowledge, expertise, and wisdom of the entire staff in order to reach the goal of preventing premature client dropout and improved client success.

She then divided the staff into eight groups of six, representing all the professional groups, and asked them to consider and discuss what the organization should focus on and what was needed to improve to decrease client dropout. She also asked them to consider, once they knew what they wanted to focus on, what would be a reasonable target or success metric for the organization to achieve. For instance, if the goal was to increase client engagement in their treatment, what percentage of clients remaining in treatment for at least 3 months should be the target? What needed to change in order to meet that goal? What needed to be improved? The groups were asked to discuss these issues over a 2-hour period. After lunch, each group was asked to present their discussions and conclusions to the entire team.

Marie took thorough notes and requested that during each group presentation all the others simply listen and ask questions to clarify what they did not understand. She made clear that this was not the time to debate or argue with the offerings. As Marie continued to take notes, she also asked her staff to elaborate on and share their thoughts. She would occasionally reflect on or summarize what she was hearing to be sure that she and everyone else in the room also understood. When everyone had finished sharing, Marie gave the following summary:

> "OK, let me know if I get this right. Some of you believe that we need to focus on how the agency engages clients from the time of their first approach to the agency, suggesting that we need to improve our staff's engaging skills and customer service skills, generally. Others suggest that involving the clients' significant others and families may be helpful. Some of you also are concerned that spending time on documentation may, in fact, not be helpful in improving treatment outcomes and might take us away from our client care. Collectively, we agreed that tracking data is an important issue that we should all be aware of. Nobody wants to spend time on documentation for its own sake. The overall conclusion reveals that you are all concerned about delivering effective and good treatment to all clients in need, and that you are willing to work assiduously to that end, but that our task now is to find out what our primary focus should be and how to address it."

Everyone nodded and agreed. Finally, Marie thanked the groups for all their thoughts. She shared that she saw that everyone appeared to want to move forward and work on making these improvements. Since the ambivalence about making the change was resolved, and the staff agreed that there needed to be improvement in the client dropout rate (the goal), they were now motivated to move on. It was time to start planning. Marie described how she would take the responsibility for securing the process to move on. She shared that she would create an audit team within the agency that would lead the future work of improving services. She reported that the audit team would consist of representatives from all the professional groups (nurses, social workers, doctors, etc.) at all four clinics, and from management. The audit team would be given the authority to regularly review the quality of services, including monitoring the dropout rates reports, and the authority to establish quality circles (i.e., small working groups consisting of staff only) to develop suggestions and plans for quality improvement. Finally, she asked staff members to consider volunteering for the audit team and shared how they could apply to join. Marie stressed that she knew that they had the knowledge and understanding that could ensure that the quality improvement process would focus on the right areas and prevent the organization from turning into a documentation bureaucracy.

SELF-REFLECTIVE EXERCISE. LISTEN TO YOUR ORGANIZATION

Listening to your whole organization is a main ingredient in using MI within organizations. The next time your team is facing a change, we would like you to use this exercise to try to listen only to understand, and not try to solve the problem.

Invite your team members to share their thoughts about an upcoming change. For this exercise, bring your group together in an in-person meeting. We know that the size of your organization might prevent you from having everyone in it attend. For now, that is okay because you are trying and learning these concepts. Later you might consider the other examples we have given on how to engage more employees in your organization.

You might decide to use all the self-reflective exercises at once in this meeting or schedule several meetings to build on the previous process. For instance, you could use this meeting as a listening exercise, schedule the next leadership meeting on focusing, have the following one on evoking, and hold the final session on planning. Or you could combine two processes at once, such as listen and focus, then evoke and plan. You can decide what works best for the time you have available and meeting structure you choose. The exercises consist of written responses to allow you to focus on one process at a time.

Once your team is assembled, share with them the change you are considering or facing. Then ask the members of the group to share their thoughts. You can have a free-flowing conversation and use the questions below as guides. You might want to write their answers on a whiteboard to show that you have understood, or you might choose to reflect back and summarize the themes.

When asking the questions, be sure to hear from several people and different groups to get a range of perspectives. Try to hear from people that represent different roles (i.e., a nurse, a doctor, a social worker). Also, consider the group members' typical responses to change and try to hear from people who are eager to try new things and from people who typically resist any change. Your goal is to hear from as many attending as you can to elicit the various viewpoints of the collective.

- Ask the group members to describe how they view this change.
  - Write down or reflect what you understand. Try to include in your reflecting what this might mean for the person and/or how he is feeling about this change.
- Ask the groups to tell you why the organization should consider making this change.
  - Write down or reflect what you understand about the *why* behind their wanting to make this change.
- Ask the groups what the organization should protect, or not change, if it did decide to make this change.
  - Write down or reflect what you understand.
- Ask the groups what reasons they have for making this change.
  - Reflect what you understand about why this change is important to them.
  - Ask them to elaborate. What other reasons might they have for making this change?
- Ask the groups what ideas they have about how they would approach this change if the organization decided to make it.
  - Reflect what you understand about what ideas they have about approaching this change.
  - Ask them to elaborate on what other ideas they have had about how they might approach this change.
- Ask how confident they are that the organization would be successful in making this change if it decided to do so.
  - Reflect what you understand about their level of confidence.
- Summarize what you have heard throughout the entire conversation, and propose to the group what you think might be the next steps.
  - Ask the group to comment on your proposal.

Now that you have had this conversation, reflect back on Exercise 2 (in Chapter 3), in which you asked yourself some of these questions before proceeding to this exercise.

- Where were you correct in what you thought?
- How was your understanding different then as compared to now?
- What else did you learn?
- What more do you understand now about the situation and organization's ambivalence to change?

CHAPTER 6

Leadership Teams

Leadership or management teams add a new dimension to how to guide change in organizations, because the teams have their own personalities, characteristics, and group dynamics. A leadership or management team consists of a group of colleagues who are relatively equal (although one—maybe you as the leader—is higher in the organizational structure). The members have similar job tasks and similar levels of responsibility. Just like individuals and organizations, management teams can be ambivalent about change, and MI can be helpful.

DYNAMICS THAT AFFECT TEAMS

A leadership or management team is a group of often dedicated and powerful team members, who need to work together and support one another. Together they have a strong influence on how the organization develops. Often, a leadership or management team is the first forum in which organizational change is discussed. It is worth spending a little time on the dynamics that may affect the effectiveness of such a team.

We have already discussed the importance of trust, and the need for a leader to be trustworthy. *Trust* is also the primary element that is critical to the health of leadership teams. In order for the team to function well, the members must be able to rely on and support not only the leader, but also one another. As Lencioni (2012) puts it, "The kind of trust that is necessary to build a great team is . . . when everyone on a team knows that everyone else is vulnerable . . . and that no one is going to hide his or her weaknesses or mistakes." A healthy team accepts and respects that all members are vulnerable and make mistakes and, based on this knowledge, all members dare to take risks, admit their mistakes, and ask for help. They trust one another. If a team is dysfunctional owing to lack of mutual trust, the team members do not wish to show weakness, vulnerability, or emotions or share ideas. In dysfunctional teams what you see may not be classic ambivalence, but signs of a lack of trust. What may *look like* ambivalence, or the lack of confidence in their ability, might actually be a management team dynamic that needs attention. If the team does not believe that each member will embrace the decision about change, support one another, work hard to accomplish the goal, and ask for help along away, they may argue against the change, because they simply do not trust one another. Brown (2018) similarly stresses this point by saying, "Trust is the glue that holds teams and organizations together."

The tricky thing with establishing trust is that someone has to go first—and it should be the leader who takes the initiative. When you as the leader do so, it is helpful to say out loud to your team members that only they can decide if they are willing to take the risk and trust one another and you. This is similar to an MI conversation in which it may be helpful to deliberately stress to the ambivalent person that the decision to change is his alone. Supporting their autonomy and letting them know that this is a choice only they can make help support the team's ability to make the decision to trust. It is also why it is important for you as the leader to go first—that is, you demonstrate that when you are faced with uncertainty and risk, you still choose to trust the team, even though you cannot be sure of the outcome.

Lencioni (2002) mentions two other team dysfunctions—*fear of conflict* and *lack of commitment*—that may come into play when a team is facing change. For instance, when team members do not engage in debate or discussion about the ideas raised, but rather agree in order to avoid conflict, they end up not truly committing to the decision. In the team meeting, they may acknowledge that the change should happen, but if they are not committed, as soon as they leave the meeting they tell their staff or their peers why the change is not needed and fail to put the necessary energy into making it happen. Given these operating dynamics, it is no surprise that two additional team dysfunctions (*avoidance of accountability* and *inattention to results*) arise. Team members do not hold each other accountable for the decision and the change, and the results therefore fall short.

To support organizational change, the leader and the team must first trust each other, be willing to look at all sides and disagree, reach a decision, and hold each other accountable. Sherry, a director of training, presented to her team a new training project that she wanted to implement. She explained that she believed that this project could improve staff morale and decrease client no-shows, resulting in an increase in revenue. She was also confident that her trainers could deliver the training well and hoped the other directors would support her idea and encourage their staff to participate wholeheartedly. She asked the team to approve her beginning this new initiative, and she also asked for a large percentage of the division budget to implement it. However, this project had never been done before in the company's setting, and the data supporting whether it would work were limited. After a robust discussion and debate, the team decided to trust Sherry and support her proposal. Allison, the leader and final decision maker, had to decide if she could risk the investment. There was a chance this initiative would be beneficial to the organization, and there was a chance it would fail. Sherry was risking her reputation to try something new, the team was risking being wrong by supporting the idea and wasting valuable staff time and money, and Allison was risking the company budget and her reputation if she decided to support a new idea that had not been tried before. Allison had to trust her team's decision and Sherry in order to say yes. And even more important, Allison and the team had to trust Sherry and one another if the project became hard to implement and new problems arose. They had to be willing to commit to the decision and work together to overcome obstacles and achieve the ultimate goals: improved staff morale, lower client no-shows, and increased revenue.

We can't stress enough that when a team is not healthy and lacks trust, fears conflicts, or is unable to hold team members accountable, the team and organization lack the necessary requirements for managing the uncertainty and fear that comes with change. Without this kind of trust, leadership teams struggle to accomplish their mission and strategic goals and perform at their highest potential.

Take, for example, Josh, a vice president of behavior health, who led a team of directors who supported the clinical work for a large non-profit. Josh pulled his team together because the organization was beginning training on a new electronic health record-keeping system, and he wanted to think through how best to support the clinics and staff in the training. Josh knew that some programs were better than others when it came to adapting to new technology. The team included some members who were new to their roles and others who had years of experience. Trust among the team members was not yet fully developed.

In the discussion, several directors shared their concern that the training would overwhelm the staff and that the team did not have enough workers to provide on-site support to each clinic. Some directors worried that some staffers would have trouble learning the new system. Team members disagreed on the best way to roll out the training. One group believed that it should be rolled out slowly, one clinic at a time, and that the next clinic not receive training until it was fully implemented in the first one. Others thought that all the clinics should be trained simultaneously.

After much debate, it was decided that all the clinics should be trained at once, and that the directors would support their programs with additional support from IT. Josh left the meeting believing that everyone had shared their thoughts and had supported moving in this direction. However, in individual supervision with each director later in the week, Josh learned that many directors actually did not agree with the decision. They felt that the other directors were not able to support their programs because they lacked technological savvy and their technical abilities were varied. They thought that in principle the idea of training all the clinics at the same time was good, but in reality it would lead to disaster. Josh asked why they had not mentioned this problem during their discussion. Several directors responded that their peers would have acted defensively to that kind of feedback. By telling Josh now, they hoped he would be able to do something about it.

The lack of candor and trust in this group left Josh facing an uphill battle with almost all his initiatives. Had the members of group trusted one another, they would have been able to say things like:

- "I do think this is best, but my ability to learn technology is limited, so I will need more support than the other directors."
- "I hear that we as a group agree with this, but can we talk about what gets in our way, like several of us in this room are better than others with new computer systems."
- "Ann, I am glad to hear that you support this. I wonder if we could talk about what support you might need, because I know new computer systems are sometimes a struggle for you."

In other words, once trust is established in a group, members can allow themselves to become vulnerable, for example, by raising their own shortcomings and asking for help. They are not afraid of conflict and are able to disagree and debate, because they feel supported and respected by their team. They are then able to share their own strengths and challenges honestly without the fear of being judged. Team members can maximize their resources and strategies to develop a plan together, which they can commit and hold each other accountable to, that will lead to overall organization success.

MI can help create a culture of trust and acceptance when the leadership team embraces the spirit of MI and actively works to understand the team members and the employees. Trust is built when the leadership team actively reflects what it understands the organization and employees believe and collaboratively includes others in discussing and developing solutions. However, MI is designed to help resolve ambivalence, and if what you are actually experiencing is a dysfunctional team, then using other strategies to help resolve team dynamics is indicated first. Understanding that you are facing a team problem, rather than facing a team that is ambivalent about change, is important. Rather than listening to resolve the ambivalence, you may actually need to stop the change process altogether, focusing instead on spending time building the health of the team.

Moving a team to optimal functioning starts with the leader. You must not only be a role model, you also need to set the expectation that the health and dynamics of the team matter and that they are part of the strategy for the team's work together. This means spending time and money on the team itself; for example, with initiatives like going off-site for team-building retreats or hiring outside coaches or consultants to observe (and advise on) the ways in which the leader and the team could improve in their interactions.

An organization must pay special attention to its leadership group, and devote time, money, and energy to working on the relationships and dynamics themselves, aside from other organization initiatives and strategies. Spending time, energy, and money on inculcating an atmosphere of trust is essential if your goal is to help your leadership team and organization reach their optimal level of performance. You may wonder if all the effort spent on developing leadership teams and cultures is really worthwhile. Brown (2018) shares the story of Stefan Larsson, CEO of the Ralph Lauren Corporation, who is credited for turning around the iconic American company Old Navy. Larsson focused his efforts on changing the dynamics of his leadership team and organization, which led to a culture built on trust; this approach completely changed the brand reputation, and sales grew from $3 billion to $17 billion. Larsson shared, "Once we removed the fear of failure and the fear of being judged, we started to outlearn and outperform our best competitors" (quoted in Brown, 2018). The health of a leadership team is key to overall organizational health. When a leadership team is healthy and grounded in trust, it can accomplish far more than a team riddled with doubt and suspicion.

FOCUSING ON THE HEALTH OF THE TEAM

Instilling trust into your team enables a level of engagement that becomes necessary when you need to effect significant changes. Leaders often say that they do not have the time or resources to spend on the team itself. This is analogous to the response we hear from clinicians when they move too quickly through the engaging process of MI. When leaders do not spend enough time engaging (i.e., neglect to focus on the team's dynamics), they end up frustrated because the team does not make the necessary changes. The health of the team is the foundation and is essential to the organization's performance. The truth is, without spending enough time on the health of the team and on engaging, nothing will work.

Angela, a vice president of a social service agency, was part of an organization that was going through significant change. Angela knew firsthand that the leadership team was not functioning well. She also knew that if the team dynamics did not improve, its members were not going to be able to accomplish the aggressive goals in front of them. Angela shared her concerns with the CEO, John. John explained that the team simply did not have the time to focus on how the members worked together because everyone was so busy on other strategic goals. As a result, many of the strategic initiatives were not accomplished; the dysfunction of the team was obvious to the rest of the organization and undermined its effectiveness. What John failed to realize was that the health of the team was a necessary component to reaching those strategic goals. If he and the team could have taken the time to work through the lack of trust and fear of conflict that they were steeped in, they could have led the organization through the changes successfully.

HOW DO YOU KNOW IT'S THE HEALTH OF THE TEAM AND NOT AMBIVALENCE?

How do you know if the resistance to change you are seeing in the team is about negative team dynamics and not ambivalence? Or that the ambivalence is actually a result of team dysfunction? We suggest that you look to the decision-making process and conflicts within the team. What does the discussion sound like when the team is considering the change? Are members challenging the idea itself or challenging one another? Are team members not talking at all?

Just as a good marriage often involves a couple knowing how to communicate and handle conflict, assessing the level of health and trust in a management team often comes down to assessing how the members discuss, debate, and commit to a change. If they are not able to look at both sides of the change, not able to express out loud their worries about their own and their staff limitations, and not able to ask other team members to consider their limitations, that means the level of trust is low. In our experience, a healthy team can look at an idea, share differing opinions on the idea's importance, and deliberately invite disagreement to be sure that nothing is missed. The members then discuss whether they are confident that they can carry out the change and realistically look at their strengths and challenges.

Donna, the head of a not-for-profit social service agency, was part of a management team in which there was a high degree of trust. She recalls that this team discussed implementing a new training initiative and rolling it out to the organization. After a lot of discussion about the idea and agreeing that it was important, the team turned to what needed to be included in the training, and ran into difficulty. One member said that the training needed to be easy and brief, and then expanded on later. Another person said that the training needed to be thorough and longer, so it could be delivered correctly the first time. Still another person mentioned that the team's last two training initiatives did not go well, because the training was overcomplicated and the team noticed that it was not moving in the direction of implementing the training. The members started to argue their points even louder. Donna asked them to consider why their past initiatives were not as successful as they had hoped, and what they learned from them. Each person became self-reflective. One person said, "I don't think we had the balance of easy and complicated right last time. I know I personally push for things to be easy so we see results, and that often means that the more difficult things are not trained well and people are left confused." Another person shared, "I agree we did not have the balance right, and I am just the opposite. I want people to understand it all so they are not confused, but they then are left being overwhelmed and not knowing where to begin." Then Donna shared, "I tend to argue too strongly against taking a lot of time to train, because I worry about productivity and failing to meet our targets, and thus disappointing the board. Limited time makes it hard for us to accomplish the goals of the training." She continued, "So we have all the elements we need for a good decision here. We are aware of our own biases, and we have competing viewpoints. I believe if we discuss some more, we will figure this out so we get the right balance." This conversation was loud and emotional. Stopping and reflecting took energy, commitment, and patience. However, the team members did this difficult work because they understood that it was essential that they function well together if they wanted to succeed. They trusted one another and were able to argue, because they felt safe.

LISTENING TO YOUR TEAM IN PRACTICE

The nice thing about working with a leadership team is that you can directly model and even discuss how you would like the group to operate. This means that you can model how to listen, how to reflect, how to resist the righting reflex, and how to evoke and pay attention to change talk.

We have found it helpful to go over with our leadership or management teams the concepts of the righting reflex, ambivalence, and reflecting understanding. Often explaining these concepts helps teams understand the change process and identify when their own actions can be helpful and when they are not. The knowledge of the process can help them understand how change happens and how they can support each other. Chris Wagner and Karen Ingersoll (2012) describe how they use this idea in clinical groups. They explain, "It is important to define early on the general nature and Spirit of the group, to emphasize the idea of supporting one another, without pressure, focusing on positives rather than negatives and on the many possibilities for change . . . the only rule is that all members must decide for themselves what to change if anything." The process is similar with teams. You may even consider training your entire team in MI concepts and skills, so the members know how to use them with their own staff and in your leadership discussions. However, if you prefer you could also just focus on the main points of change. You could explain how to focus to understand ambivalence, how to support members in deciding, and how to expand the many possibilities for change. We typically host a day of training for supervisors, in which we discuss many of the principles in this book and practice using OARS in the context of supervision or management scenarios. We find that a training session is the most useful way to orient our team and our organization to the use of MI in leadership. We continue the practice and implementation by modeling it in our own meetings and supervisions. Often, we coach other leaders on the use of MI as well to help them master the approach and use it with their employees.

WHEN DOES THE LEADER SHARE?

Another point to consider as a leader is determining when you should join in the team discussion. Leaders can easily deplete a discussion by joining in too soon. Sometimes groups think that when leaders share ideas, they are not actually sharing, but rather saying what they want to happen, and their input shuts down the conversation.

Donna, the leader we mentioned earlier, noticed this once in her team. She asked team members to discuss whether or not they wanted to add a new technology to the continuum of care. This new technology would allow the care managers to use telehealth to connect with their clients, send regular reminders for appointments, send clients regular scales to monitor symptoms like anxiety and depression, and provide access to online learning about behavioral health topics. In Donna's mind, this technology would complement services and improve patient outcomes. She asked them to review the technology and report back on what they thought about adding it to services. One director shared, "This really only works if clients have access to the Internet and have mobile devices, and many of our clients do not have either." Another director shared, "I think it would add to the services, but I do not think the staff will implement it. They are already overwhelmed, and it would end up just being a waste of funds." Donna, thinking the team was brainstorming, decided to share her thoughts too. She explained, "I see a lot of value in adding this. I have ideas on how to overcome the access to Internet issue. I also think if we as the leadership team are clear and consistent with the care managers they would implement it and implement it well. We would just have to be dedicated to carrying it through." When she finished, the directors just nodded. No one else added any other thoughts. Donna, realizing that the conversation had stopped, asked for feedback on what had just happened. The room was quiet for a minute, and then one director, who had not yet shared, said, "If you have decided that we should do it that is fine, we will make it happen. But if you are asking for our input, we really don't see it working yet." Had Donna, instead, reflected the groups' feelings and asked for thoughts on how the new technology might work or what the value might be if the group decided to carry it forward, she likely would have received a different response. She unintentionally shut down the conversation by sharing her thoughts too soon, and without explaining that they were just thoughts and not a decision.

You might reflect on *when* you share. You might ask yourself, does it add to or shut down the discussion? What do you notice? When is it ideal for you to join in and share your ideas too, especially if the members of the group disagree, and when might it be better for you to guide the group toward questions to consider? When might it be bestto reflect an understanding of the group's points of disagreement or agreement, and ideas for solutions?

There is no clear right answer to these questions, but as a leader it is important to be aware of the potential pitfalls of offering your own opinion prematurely. We have tried many approaches ourselves. Sometimes we reflect only what the group is sharing and ask pointed questions to have the group reflect even more. At other times, we have given our own point of view to add to the discussion, then asked the person holding an opposite opinion to share what he thinks about what we shared. In any case, if the leader is doing all the talking, then it is likely not a productive discussion and likely not resolving group ambivalence.

SUMMARY

Listening to teams is in many ways similar to listening to individuals and listening to organizations. However, be aware that what you hear may be team problems and not ambivalence. Lack of trust in one another may hinder sharing thoughts about ambivalence and committing to change.

SELF-REFLECTIVE EXERCISE. LISTEN TO YOUR TEAM

Listening to and understanding what is happening with your team is different from listening to an individual or your whole organization. You may be listening to ambivalence, and you may also notice that team relationships or the health of the team is actually what might need attention.

In this exercise, the next time your team is facing a change, we would like you to try to listen to understand if your team is facing a team dynamic issue or is expressing ambivalence. Knowing which one your team is facing can help you know whether MI might then be helpful, or whether focusing on developing the team might be more prudent.

Invite your team members to share their thoughts about an upcoming change. For this exercise, bring them together in an in-person meeting.

Once they are assembled, share with them the change you are considering or facing. Then ask the members to share their thoughts. As you are guiding and reflecting your understanding of the team feelings and thoughts, also focus on and notice the team dynamic.

- Ask the group members to describe how they see this change.
  - Do they seem to be able to openly discuss their hopes and concerns? Are they able to challenge each other's views?
  - Is there debate and discussion, or are people simply nodding and agreeing and not engaging? Does it seem that the team is actively considering this idea and owning the decision?
- Ask the group members to tell you why the organization should consider making this change.
  - Invite all group members to share. How are team members considering each other's thoughts? Do you notice a level of trust and respect among the members, or might you notice competition or even distrust or hidden agendas or politics?
- Ask the group members what ideas they have about how they would approach this change if the organization decided to make it.
  - Are the members willing to share where they might need help?
- Ask how confident the members are that they would be successful in making this change if they decided to do so.
  - Reflect what you understand about their level of confidence.
  - Ask the team if there is anything that makes it concerned about moving forward? Is the team willing to discuss challenges the team

as a whole or each member personally might face, or to encourage other team members to reflect on their own personal or the team's ability?

Now that you have had this conversation, reflect back on this chapter, in which you learned something about your team health.

- What would you say your team is facing right now? Is this a normal feeling of ambivalence toward change, or are there team dynamics that might need your time and attention?
- What tells you that your team is doing well? What tells you that the team trusts and respects each member, is willing to engage in conflict and debate, and is willing to commit to a group decision?
- What tells you that this team is willing to hold each member accountable to this decision to achieve optimal results? Is this team wholeheartedly ready to face this change together?
- What have you learned that might mean that your team has some relationship concerns that might need attention prior to beginning your change?
- What else have you noticed about your team when you focus on the team's health and relationship concerns and not simply on the change itself?

PART III

FOCUSING

CHAPTER 7

Focusing with Your Employee

Once you have a sense of what your employee or your organization is thinking, experiencing, and sharing, you can start to think about where you might guide the focus of the conversation. *Focusing* is the second important process in MI. It is important to remember that you do not want to focus too soon. It is easy to want to jump ahead in a conversation and rush to try to solve the problem. This is your righting reflex at work. You need to remember, however, that your goal right now is not to find a solution but to understand, and maybe take one step forward. If you focus prematurely, you are likely to miss the most important issue. We imagine that you can think of times when you rushed to solve a problem, only to discover that you were working on the wrong problem, or had misunderstood the issue from the beginning. This can also happen in conversations. You want to be sure that you understand the ambivalence that is present before moving to focusing.

WHEN TO FOCUS

How do you know that you understand enough to focus? This question is not easy to answer because there is always more to understand. But in general, it is the feeling that you understand the issue in depth, not merely on the surface, and that the employee feels understood. We typically ask ourselves: Do I understand why she is stuck, why that matters to her, what she is hoping for, what she might already have tried, and what has kept her in this stuck place? You do not put these questions directly to the employee. Instead, reflect to yourself, "Do I understand?"

And when you reflect your understanding back to your employee, does she indicate that you are getting it?

You might also ask yourself a series of "whys" to check if you are taking in the depth of what your employee is sharing. For instance, let's say a manager tells you that he is struggling to schedule his team's safety drills. He has tried to get this item on his schedule several times and failed. How could you respond—specifically, what would be the appropriate focus for your response and the ensuing conversation with him?

You might think: this is easy—we just need to focus on whether he wants to move forward with practicing safety drills with his team. That may be right, but if you do not first pause to understand his concern and why he feels stuck and why it has been hard for him, you might miss the more important point altogether. It might not be about finding the time. It might be that he feels drills are pointless exercises that take away valuable patient time. Or he may fear that people on his staff would be reluctant to do the drills, and he wants them to like and respect him. Or he might fear that the drills fail to address the real safety concerns that worry him and his staff, and he is not sure how to handle their questions when he is asked what to do in those specific situations.

The only way you and your employee will know what to focus on is by first getting to grips with the depth of his ambivalence and reluctance. You might ask yourself, why is scheduling safety drills important to him? Let's say the answer is that he knows safety drills are important, because they help everyone feel safe, and he wants his team to feel safe. Why does he want everyone to feel safe? He might say, because if they do not feel safe they will be hindered in providing effective care. Why is safety so crucial to care? Because without everyone believing that safety is paramount and acting in ways that address it, someone could get hurt. So the appropriate focus may not be scheduling drills at all. It might instead be how to get the staff to embrace the need for constant attention to safety.

Remember that engaging is always the first part of the process, and it never ends. You are continually listening to understand. However, once you have understood the issue and your employee feels understood, then you will transition from just focusing on the feeling of being stuck to moving a step forward. Just as you do not want to focus prematurely, you also do not want to give all your attention to engaging. Although it may be tempting to explore all the reasons why change is so difficult to achieve, doing so typically just cements the sense of *stuckness*.

In the process of listening and engaging, you need to remain aware that your goal to understand should not lead you to spend too much time on the problem. Rather, your aim should be to understand where the person is now, so that you can guide him forward. MI calls for us to focus on the present and on the future. It is not about exploring the past or uncovering deep truths about the issue. It is about understanding where the employee is right now, and then focusing on where the employee wants to go.

FINDING A FOCUS

Focusing, like the rest of MI, is a collaborative process. This means, in short, that the employee and the leader need to agree on what the conversation should be about. A collaborative focus gives you permission to gently bring the conversation back to that focus throughout the remainder of the process.

Finding the right focus is key to helping your employee come up with her own ideas and solutions to her dilemma. Finding it requires listening and reflecting back to your employee what you hear as the main topic or target and obtaining her agreement to continue. When we train managers in using MI in management, we often hear comments like "I think the focus for this conversation should be X [e.g., peer relationships]." Then the manager starts the conversation with this focus, and soon gets stuck. When we ask why she thinks they are stuck, the manager typically responds by saying, "I don't really think that the focus should be X [peer relationships]; I think that my employee is actually struggling with Y [e.g., role confusion], but I don't want to tell her what her focus should be." We then suggest that she check it out with the employee, and sure enough, Y [role confusion] is really what is on that person's mind and is what she hopes to talk about. The manager knew this all along, but was afraid to offer it as an option for fear of not letting the employee decide.

You may fear that you might be judging, analyzing, or imposing a focus on the person when checking out whether she agrees with what you think the focus might be. However, the only way to discover if the focus is yours alone and not also the employee's is by asking your employee. If she says, "No, that really is not it," then you know and can revert to trying to understand. However, if you are truly trying to understand (i.e., not trying to talk the person into thinking about the issue from your perspective), then it is likely that what you think she means is what she actually means.

Let's return to Donna, the social service agency head, who supervised a new manager, Jody. Jody was trying to help a counselor improve the quality of his care by coaching his recorded client sessions. Jody explained to Donna that she was trying to help the counselor by modeling the new approach, pointing out areas in which he was being successful, and identifying areas in which he was not using the new method correctly. Jody felt that the counselor was not really making improvements and was not seriously interested in learning the approach at all. When

Donna asked Jody what her conversation with her counselor had focused on, she replied that it had been on applying the learning. Donna asked, "If I understand you correctly, you think the concern is that he does not want to learn the approach, not that he cannot learn the approach." Jody agreed that she felt her concern was about the counselor's unwillingness, not his ability. Donna asked why that was not the focus of their conversations. Jody shared, "I don't want to offend him by implying that I don't think he's trying." Donna asked, "Do you think he is trying?" Jody said, "No." So they talked about how Jody could introduce the issue of the counselor's ambivalence about learning to use this new approach in their next supervision. Because Jody was focusing her conversations with the counselor on the wrong issue, her supervision was not helping improve his performance. As long as the counselor's ambivalence (which looked like resistance) went unaddressed, he would likely make small adjustments to please Jody, but not embrace this new change fully.

So often focusing involves using your intuition and saying what you really think is going on and not just what you consider polite, while at the same being open to the fact that you may not completely understand yet.

Having a target is one of the main differences between MI and just good empathetic listening. Without a target behavior, a target decision, or a target change, the conversation is not MI. If you do not know what the change at the heart of the conversation is, you won't know in which direction to guide it, and what part of the conversation is communicating change, or is change language. Having a clear target is necessary for the third and fourth processes, which we discuss in later chapters.

In some situations, the focus is immediately clear. A manager may ask you to help him improve his ability to hold his team to specific goals. Your focus is clearly the manager's performance in relation to holding his staff to these goals. At other times, though, the focus may not be so clear. There may be many issues that you could choose to focus on, or there could be no clear focus at all, or you and the employee might be thinking about what to focus on in different ways.

HOW DO YOU CHOOSE WHAT TO FOCUS ON?

When there are many issues you could focus on, you may need to take time to discuss everything that has come up in the engaging process. You could explore what you hear as the themes or issues that your employee is facing. You know that you cannot focus on all of them at the same time, so you want to help your employee guide you as to which would be the most helpful to start with. You can always make time to address the other issues as well, but you want to be clear about where you will begin.

If there are many issues to focus on, you may simply say so out loud:

"There are a lot of things we could start with. For instance, you want to focus on how to motivate your team and improve morale. You are also wondering about your overall management style, and whether it is effective for this group of people. You also mentioned having considered different cross-functional teams you might want to start, to help engage your employees in achieving team goals. I'm wondering which of these topics is the most important to you right now. Which one would be most helpful to focus our time on, or is there something else more pressing?"

You want to put all the different concerns or issues on the table and work with your employee to select the best place to begin. This might take some time, because it may not be clear to the employee either. She may feel that they are all important or equally important. You should continue to use reflective listening to help the employee work through where she would like to start. If she really is not sure, you can always offer a topic that you think might be the best to start with and see if the employee is okay with starting there. You could say, "You're not sure what is most important. I wonder whether if we start with your overall management approach, it might also help you think about staff morale and cross-functional teams. What do you think? Do you think we might start there?"

WHAT IF THE TOPIC REMAINS UNCLEAR?

Similarly, if the topic is unclear, or you do not see a clear target behavior to focus on, you might have to guess your way forward and ask the employee to make some guesses as well. The suggestions that arise may be general ones, but should be specific enough for it to be clear whether you are working toward a change. For instance, a manager may say that she wants to work on improving her leadership abilities, because she feels conflicted about how she is performing and whether she is improving. This is a very general topic and may mean anything. However, you can guide the conversation toward making changes to improve her overall leadership abilities and away from staying the same and making no change in her leadership approach. Yet, the focus can be more specific. It could be that the manager wants help in feeling more comfortable in having difficult or critical conversations with employees. She may find herself avoiding difficult conversations even though she knows they are important, and notices that the situation only gets worse when they are avoided. She avoids these conversations because she does not feel that she handles them effectively and dislikes the uncomfortable feelings that occur before and during them. Here you can hear the desire for, and guide her toward, a conversation about change that will help her handle difficult conversations in a more comfortable way. Listening for it, you will hear both the part of the conversation that argues for making the change of practicing having difficult conversations and the other part that is against making this change.

If, once you have listened to the manager's dilemma, the engaging process still leaves you not really sure about what the focus should be, guesses are the next step. You might say something like "I wonder whether, if we focused on—it would help you with this concern?"; "If you had to pick a main focus for our conversation to help you address this concern, what might that be?"; or "If you had to bottom-line this issue to one topic, what do you think that topic might be?" The conversation could sound like this:

> MANAGER: I wonder if we focus on you delegating more, if that would help you think about how to manage all your tasks?
>
> EMPLOYEE: No, I am not sure about that. I don't think I have trouble with delegating. I think I have more trouble with saying no or not taking on more things because I like to be helpful.
>
> MANAGER: Then would it make sense to talk about how you might say no more?
>
> EMPLOYEE: Maybe. I think that is part of it, but I wonder if it is also me not wanting to disappoint people and needing to find a way to be able to say no, because it is the right thing to do and not because I want to please people.
>
> MANAGER: So if you were to pick the main focus for our conversation, would it be "how to say no"?
>
> EMPLOYEE: Yeah. That sounds right.

Remember, it is okay to be wrong. If you guess wrong, or if the employee does not find a given topic helpful, she will let you know, and you can continue to explore until you are able to identify a focus together. You don't want to focus on the wrong issue, and you want to be sure to prioritize what is most important to the employee.

WHAT IF YOU THINK DIFFERENTLY ABOUT THE FOCUS?

There are still other times where you and the employee might think differently about the focus. MI is a collaborative process, which means that you are also part of it. Sometimes, the employee might say that he would like to discuss one area, while you remain convinced that there is another area that might be more relevant. For instance, a manager might say that he wants to focus on delivering constructive feedback to his teams because at the moment he does not think his feedback is being well received. You might believe instead that the focus should be on his relationship with the team and how he is setting up the overall supervisor/employee expectations and structure. This is not to say that your focus is correct. It is not to say that the employee's is right. What you need to think about instead is that you are each seeing it from your own perspective, and that you want to talk through both options. You might say something like, "You wish to focus on how you deliver feedback. I am also wondering if focusing on the overall relationship you have with your employees might be a helpful focus, too. What do you think?" If the manager still wants to prioritize his view, you would make that your focus. You may find later that the topic you thought was important will come up anyway. In MI, your goal is to help the staff resolve *their* ambivalence and come up with *their* own ideas and solutions to their concerns. You do not want to push your agenda or your own way of thinking on them. So, in a situation in which you think differently about the focus, you want to share your thoughts, have the employee consider them, but follow the employee's lead.

CHANGE OF FOCUS

Once you have found a focus, the gentle guiding of your conversation toward that target continues throughout the remainder of the process. You may need to come back to focusing as you move forward through the processes, because a different priority becomes clearer. When this happens, it is important that you are resolute about shifting focus. You might say something like "It sounds like focusing on X is more important than focusing on Y right now. What do you think?" Once the focus is clear to both the employee and yourself, you can guide the conversation toward the evoking process. Just like engaging, focusing never ends. All the processes build on the previous ones. You continue to listen to understand and to engage, and now focus, or refocus, as needed, to help steer the conversation in the direction of the chosen target behavior, decision, or change.

TARGET BEHAVIOR OR TARGET DECISION?

Sometimes the focus is not about a specific behavior or change. Sometimes the focus for the conversation may be on helping your employee

with a decision he has to make. It is important to understand the difference. When the focus is on making a decision, your guiding will be
around helping him to decide. As an example, Eric, a counselor, is trying
to decide whether he should apply for a position as a clinical supervisor. You may have your own thoughts as to whether he is ready for
this position, but for now you will hold those thoughts unless he asks
for your advice. If he wants to think it through with you, you would
look at the pros and cons of applying for the position. You would not
lean in one direction or the other, but instead think about the overall
process of making this decision and what Eric feels he needs to know in
order to be able to decide. The situation is different when the focus is
on a specific behavior; when you focus on a specific behavior, you guide
the conversation toward achieving a specific change. You know that not
changing is an option and changing is an option, and the employee gets
to decide which choice to make. However, if it is in the interests of the
employee, you gently guide and evoke the change language that shows
a leaning toward changing. Take, for instance, the situation in which
Eric instead wants to talk about whether to improve his skills in project
management. You know this change would benefit him if he made it. In
the conversation, you will focus on his thoughts on making this change,
on how he feels about learning and improving in project management.
But you will also pay particular attention to why he feels that it is important to improve his project management skills, what he believes about
his abilities to do so, and his ideas about the prospect. You deliberately
explore and evoke the side of change. In contrast, if you are talking with
Eric about whether or not he wants to apply for the clinical supervisor
position, you would not guide him in the direction of applying, asking
him all the reasons he has for applying or how he feels about his ability
to do that job. You would instead guide him in the direction of thinking
about what he needs to be able to make this decision. What is important
to consider in making this decision? What information might he need?
How has he approached difficult decisions like this in the past? Because
your focus is on a decision and not a behavior, your guidance is adapted
to that end.

Understanding whether your focus is a target behavior or target
decision making helps us choose the most helpful approach when thinking about the next process, the evoking process.

SETTING UP THE FOCUS AT THE BEGINNING

Sometimes, you may enter a conversation with a clear focus. For example, when you are completing a performance evaluation, it is natural to
move to an action plan or goal-setting part of the evaluation. This is an

ideal place to use MI. After having a collaborative conversation with an employee about how he assesses and how you view his performance, you typically advance toward what you both believe the next new goals for him should be over the upcoming evaluation period: what he would like to work on or improve and what you would like to see him improve. The focus would then be clear. The conversation is about how he wants to grow in his role: what he hopes to learn, try, and improve. You keep the focus on his growth, as he talks about his hopes and anxieties or worries about these new goals. There is no need to develop a focus because you have a clear topic from the start, his growth goals.

MI IN COMBINATION WITH FEEDBACK ON PERFORMANCE

If there is a performance issue that you've noticed with an employee, MI in a slightly modified form might be helpful. If you set up your relationship from the beginning with the understanding that you are there to help the employee succeed, seeing your job as helping her achieve her goals and believing that she can, when it's time to give constructive feedback, the employee will receive it with the confidence that you are giving it precisely because you care and want her to succeed. Not giving the feedback would not only be unhelpful, it would also damage the trust upon which you have built this relationship.

It is also important to remember when giving constructive feedback to focus on one or two areas at a time. It is not uncommon for managers to sit down with an employee and list several areas that need improvement. People can typically work on one or two areas at once, but asking them to improve in multiple areas is unfair and not likely to be successful. As they improve in one area you can always add another, but if you start by listing 10 things they need to work on, the likely response will be one of frustration, lower confidence, and an absence of improvement.

Once you are clear that you want to give specific feedback about performance, you will likely start the conversation with this topic as the focus. You let the person know that you want to talk about her performance and the areas needing improvement. The goal is that your employee should know what the issue is and be given an opportunity to correct it and understand that you are there to help if you can. Be both gentle and clear when letting your employee know that there is a performance concern. We often see managers who are neither clear nor gentle. When you are not clear about your expectations, the employee leaves the conversation not really understanding what needs to be improved or may work on the wrong issue altogether. On the other hand, if you are blunt, direct, and neither kind nor compassionate, you create an environment that is not safe—and you need the employee to feel safe if she is to work on doing something new and different.

If you are going to use MI as a way of interacting with your employees, then compassion and empathy need to be at the heart of *all* your interactions. You can be kind by being clear about what you are seeing that is going well; by acknowledging or affirming the employee's positive intentions and efforts; and then also by being clear and compassionate about what needs to improve, why it is a problem, and what your expectations are about the change and when it should happen. After putting the issue on the table for discussion, you pause to listen to your employee's perspective. How does she see this issue of her performance? What thoughts does she have on what she hopes to change or improve, on how she might approach it, on how you might help, and on what the plan will be? It is likely in this situation that the focus will remain on your performance concern and may or may not include MI. Depending on how the conversation goes, and whether the employee is open to talking with you about her ideas regarding change and improvement, you could be in a position to move to an MI conversation. You might also simply continue with the performance conversation, discussing how you might help her and how you will follow up.

You might ask yourself the following questions to see if you have a clear focus:

- "Are the employee and I on the same page? Do we know what the target of this conversation is? How do I know this? Have I asked about this specifically?"
- "Is this focus the most important focus for the employee, or does there appear to be an even more important focus? How do I know this? Have I collaborated with the employee on the focus?"
- "Is this focus something that lends itself to MI? Is there ambivalence present? Or should I use a different management approach now that I know our focus?"
- "Is the employee willing and interested in talking about this focus? Is it appropriate in my role and, given my relationship with the employee, to guide her toward this focus?"
- "Am I clear about my role? Am I guiding toward a specific behavior or change that the employee is considering making, or am I guiding the employee toward making a decision, and therefore staying neutral (and not guiding) regarding any specific decision and guiding only toward what will help her make the decision?"
- "Have I explored and understood enough about the relevant concern to be sure I know the depth of the issue and have a clear focus? Do I need to engage a bit more to understand?"

SUMMARY

Focusing means deciding what the goal for the conversation should be. Focusing is also central to keeping the conversation moving in the direction of the chosen goal. Focusing is a collaborative process between the individual and the leader.

Employee Vignette

Let's return to our conversation with Susan at the end of Chapter 4. She was new to her job and struggling with enrolling new clients into the program. She felt that she was doing well in all the other parts of her job, but this part was a struggle. She also was not sure why it was so hard, because she typically succeeded in all the things she did in her life. She wanted to figure out how to move forward because she loved her team and found the work meaningful. Recall that Ashley is Susan's supervisor.

ASHLEY: Susan, I wonder what you think would be the most important thing for us to focus on? (*open-ended question*)

SUSAN: I really don't know. I just want to get better at my job and not feel this bad. And I don't want to get fired.

ASHLEY: So you are not sure where to even begin. You know you're not happy with the way things are going now but are not sure what would help. (*reflection*)

SUSAN: Well, I guess I do know that the way I am evaluating my progress is not working, because Jim keeps saying that. I keep focusing on the fact that I am failing or might get fired. I am just not sure how not to think about that, because the truth is that I am not meeting expectations.

ASHLEY: Looking at how you evaluate your progress might be a place to start? (*asking permission*)

SUSAN: I guess so. But I am not really sure.

ASHLEY: So, when you think you're failing at this it impacts your ability to enroll new clients. (*reflection*)

SUSAN: (*Nods.*)

ASHLEY: I was actually thinking the same thing. I was wondering if we could talk a little about what happens specifically when you think "I am failing," and how that affects your attempts to enroll new clients? (*asking permission*) That seems to be when you start to freeze. What do you think? (*open-ended question*)

SUSAN: Yeah. I know that when I start thinking I am failing, that is when it all goes wrong. So maybe trying to find a different way to evaluate progress might be a place to start.

ASHLEY: Okay, so let's focus a little on how you are evaluating your progress overall and how that might affect your ability to enroll new clients. If something else pops up that you think is more important, just let me know.

SUSAN: I will.

SELF-REFLECTIVE EXERCISE. FOCUS WITH YOUR EMPLOYEE

Now that you have a better understanding of why your employee feels stuck and how she is thinking about this change in terms of its importance to her and her belief in her ability to carry it out, it is time to see if you can help her focus on a specific target or topic. Remember, you want the topic to be specific enough for you and the employee to be able to hear which side is the side of change and which is the side of staying the same.

In this exercise, we would like you to try to narrow or focus your conversation. When the person is sharing with you how she views or is approaching the issue, try using some of our guiding questions to help you focus the conversation on one topic or target.

Before you have a conversation with the person, take a guess as to what you think the topic or target is and write it down. Come back to what you guessed, and check whether you were hearing a clear focus prior to the ensuing conversation.

Have a conversation with this person about the change. The conversation can be free flowing and the focus questions can be used as guides. Always remember to continue the engaging process by reflecting your understanding when the person shares her thoughts.

If the Topic Is Clear

If you think that the topic is obvious, you can simply ask your employee if the topic you have in mind is indeed the most important topic. You can use these discussion prompts as a guide to help you focus. You might say to your employee:

■ "Is X what you think is most important for us to focus our time on?"
Or

■ "I think what I am hearing is that you are wondering about X and would like us to focus on this specifically."

Or

▨ "If you had to narrow down this conversation to one topic that you would like us to focus on, what might that be?"

If the Topic Is Not Clear, or If Your Assumptions Differ From What the Employee Is Sharing

If you are not sure what the specific target is, or you think it might be something else, you can use these discussion prompts as a guide to help you focus. You might say to your employee:

"It sounds like there are a lot of things we could focus our conversation on; what do you think would be the most important priority to start with?"

"It sounds like you are not sure where to begin. I wonder whether, if we started with X and focused our conversation there, would that be a good place to start?"

"I hear that you think X is most important right now; I am also wondering if it would be helpful to focus on Y. What do you think? Where would be the best place to begin?"

Later, after you have had this conversation, reflect on the process.

▨ What do you notice?

▨ Were you hearing the main focus, or were you thinking it was something else?

▨ What happened if you thought the focus should be one thing and the employee thought it should be something else? How did you collaboratively discuss your differences?

▨ How did you know that you had the right focus?

▨ What did the employee say or do that led you to believe you had an agreed-upon target?

▨ Would you say that the focus was a collaborative process or that you decided on the focus? If you decided, why do you think that was?

CHAPTER 8

Focusing with Your Organization

Once you have a sense of what the organization is thinking, experiencing, and sharing, you can start thinking about a focus. How do you help an organization choose a focus? Again, as with individuals, it's best not to focus on solutions too soon. You may remind yourself that since a company consists of people, and that choosing a focus is all about listening to people, you can turn to Chapter 7 on focusing with individual employees for ideas. Some of those same approaches and strategies also work with organizations. However, when focusing with large groups of people, and listening to what may lead the collective in the direction of change, there are other strategies and considerations that we also find helpful.

WHEN IS IT TIME?

Timing is important in focusing with an organization, similarly to focusing with an individual. Devoting too much time to worrying about what might happen, and imagining everything that could go wrong, may cause the whole organization to feel increasingly ambivalent and despondent. It may also damage the staff's trust in their leader if they sense that the leader is avoiding hard decisions. You may believe that you need to drill deeper, gather more data, have more discussions, and analyze the company's history and all the factors leading up to where you are now in order to make a thoughtful decision. The problem with this approach is that you can spend years researching the problem and never make any progress. Your aim is to understand the current situation of

your company so you can *move forward*. A driving force in MI in organizations is an understanding of where the company is right now, while
at the same time focusing on where you collectively want to be. It helps
you and your organization look beyond why you are stuck and move
forward to what is possible.

Just as you can spend too much time researching the current state or
history of your problem, you can also jump to focus too soon or focus on
too many areas at once. The goal of engaging is to ensure that you hear
where your organization is now and where you want to go, but also to help
narrow down your conversation to the most important goal to pursue.

As an example, Joan, the chief operating officer of a health coaching practice, noticed that there was a high turnover of the coaching staff.
She initially thought, "Good, now I know our focus. We will create a
task force to improve staff retention." However, she decided to explore
this idea with her staff. She asked former and current employees for
their thoughts on why people were leaving the organization. She met
with people individually, asked her human resources team to interview
former employees, and also created a survey requesting input from the
entire coaching team. She then met with her leadership team who looked
at all of the input and ventured conjectures as to what it all meant. The
team noticed that there were several themes. Some staff felt undervalued
or not paid enough. Others did not see upward growth opportunities.
Some employees also felt unheard and not part of decisions or felt disconnected from the company's mission and that it no longer cared about
providing quality care. Others felt that their managers were weak and
ineffective. And still other employees were less than enthusiastic about
the direction in which the company was headed. To arrive at a focus,
Joan started by narrowing down this list to a single clear target. She
asked her leadership team, "Is our focus to improve retention? Or is it to
improve staff morale? Or should our conversation be aimed at improving the organization's ability to listen to its workforce? Is our target the
improvement of our organization management or of leadership training? Or is it to improve the quality of our services?" There are many
directions in which this scenario example might go, and before moving
forward, Joan, now with input from her leadership team and her organization, needed to narrow the focus to one or two areas, three at most.

It is not uncommon for leaders to want to start plans that address all
areas (salaries, staff morale, upward growth, leadership training, quality
of services, and increasing staff input and idea sharing), but by having
such broad areas of focus you end up confusing your organization's priorities. Instead, to help move the organization forward leaders need to
zero in on no more than three topics at a time. As the leadership guru Jim
Collins (2001) reminds us, "If you have more than three priorities, you
have no priorities." You can always come back and add to your goals once

one goal is achieved. For now, as you understand your current state, you want to be sure that you focus on the most important and main target.

FINDING A FOCUS

Sometimes the focus is not that obvious, and leaders are not quite sure what to prioritize. To be able to create organizational clarity, leaders need a clear message about what specifically needs staff input and attention. The focus is what guides the conversations toward that target or goal. But how do you go about choosing a focus? When working with an individual, a consideration of personal values and overall goals in life is often helpful in terms of finding a focus. Likewise, when resolving ambivalence, using the overall mission, goals, and values of the organization is also often helpful in terms of choosing which focus is the most relevant. Asking how a change will achieve your organizational mission, or better reflect its values, could help you clarify the target or focus for change.

For instance, if the company goal is to deliver high-quality treatment for as many psychiatric patients as possible, and there is currently a long wait time to access services, while the outcomes of treatment are showing only moderate improvements in patient symptoms, the organization will likely agree that a change is needed. But what sort of change is needed? Since the organization may have limited resources (time and money) available, the decision about where to spend these resources will be guided by what form of change will bring about the most improvement. There are many possibilities. To improve the quality of and access to care, the organization could train counselors on short-term effective treatments or real-time access solutions, add complementary digital health solutions, or maybe shift staff scheduling to open access models. Using the organization's mission of providing high-quality services to as many patients as possible can help guide you to which focus is the most relevant.

However, since the mission has two priorities, the question of whether to focus on accessibility or to improve quality requires an understanding of what your staff and clients believe is the most important topic with which to start. To do this, you need to share what you are hearing, and gain confirmation from your staff that you are indeed pursuing the right focus to move forward.

HOW DO YOU CHOOSE WHAT TO FOCUS ON?

When there are many areas that you could choose to focus on, you may need to spend time making a decision. Listening to the organization, understanding what is being proposed, and collecting knowledge may lead to a discussion of the many areas that may need improvement. You know that you cannot focus on all of them at the same time, and should therefore decide, in conjunction with staff, which area would be the most helpful place to start. Remember, if everything is a priority, then nothing is, and it is the leader's job to help the organization narrow down what is most important. Organizations can only improve collectively in a few areas (one, two, or three at most) at a time. You know you have clarity in your organization when everyone is able to say what the first and most important priority is, even if there are other initiatives under development. Without that kind of clarity, teams and individuals are not able to make real-time decisions when facing conflicts in priorities. They are also not able to reflect accurately about both sides of the present ambivalence. For instance, if the mission is to deliver high-quality treatment to as many psychiatric patients as possible, there are two priorities, access to care and quality of care. If they can't deliver on both quality and access, the organization needs to know from its leader which one takes precedence. Do they decide to provide more services to more people but at a lower quality, or to deliver higher-quality services but to fewer people?

Connect Change-Related Topics

One way to help narrow down the priorities and choices is to connect change-related topics. It may be the case that several topics are connected and that the overall goal is, in fact, easier to implement if several changes are set in motion at the same time. Often the leader or management team is able to make these connections, because they have a helicopter view and can see overall patterns. For example, Carol, the leader of a drug and alcohol agency, was asked by its board of directors to train and implement MI with a large group of team leaders in her organization. This group was told to implement MI with their counseling teams to improve outcomes with the vulnerable elderly population they served. Before introducing MI, Carol asked the 40 team leaders what initiatives they were currently working to implement. They had a long list: They had been asked to implement a new system for case notes; to improve services so they were focused more on the clients' goals and needs; to administer a new structure and process for admission to their services; to implement rehabilitation as a general therapeutic model; to employ a new client outcomes-monitoring system; and now to implement the use of MI to improve outcomes. "It's all too much at once," one of the team leaders exclaimed. Carol wrote all the topics on a whiteboard, while the team leaders shared their thoughts. She then reflected what she was hearing: "You are all being asked by the board to involve your clients more in their treatment and services, and it's been decided that the general strategy should be rehabilitation, indicating that the goal of the work is to engage your clients as much as possible in participating in social life, while increasing their level of functioning as much as possible too. Is this correct?" They all nodded. She continued, "Your board has also asked you to implement a new tool for case notes designed to document client needs and to monitor how the clients improve?" They affirmed that this was so. "And the board has offered your entire staff and yourselves training in MI as a strategy for communicating with your clients and as a way to help your clients communicate what they actually want and need and make their desired changes in order to function better." Everybody thought about what Carol had said for a minute. She continued reflecting, while pointing to the whiteboard and drawing a few lines between the topics. "Maybe all these initiatives support one another: Some save time that can be used to implement others; some gather information that can be used by others. Maybe it makes sense to implement all of these initiatives at the same time because they are interdependent. For instance, MI will help your staff know what your clients actually want to improve in their lives. This understanding will give your staff the information needed to improve their client notes, and to know the most important client outcomes to track and monitor, which in turn will help the client make progress toward the goal of rehabilitation." The team leaders nodded. Until now they had seen each improvement as separate and disconnected and had missed the links between them. So the real priority the board was asking the team leaders to focus on was client outcomes, and the steps to doing so were all the changes they had listed. Because Carol had spent time listening to their frustrations and created the links between the topics, she was able to put their worries to rest. This allowed the managers to let go of their anxieties, engage in the training, and actively participate in learning how MI could help. Later, when Carol was training the team leaders in how to use MI, she referenced this conversation. She had them reflect on how expressing empathy and a nonjudgmental attitude along with the use of reflective listening and the offering of summaries ensured that the professional (Carol) understood what the clients (the team leaders) really had on their minds and helped them move forward in the change process.

The Strategy Amoeba

There are other models designed to create a focus in an organization or a team that we find helpful. Lencioni (2012) describes a similar process using a *strategy amoeba*. In this process, you engage your team in a discussion wherein you list what they consider to be important priorities. You note these items, even if some are redundant or in conflict, on an amoeba shape drawn on a flip chart (see Figure 8.1).

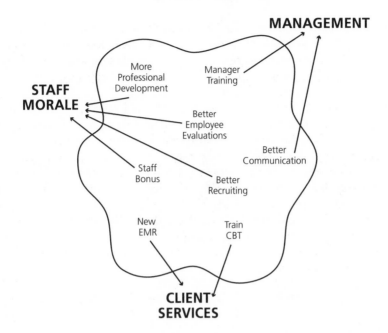

FIGURE 8.1. Strategy amoeba.

Lencioni (2012) explains that not listing the items linearly supports the creative process of finding connections. Once everything is listed, you connect items and themes until you are able to find at most three main guides for future action. Lencioni advises, "Remember, this process will always be a little messy and organic. It requires judgment, reflection, and, at times, intuitive synthesis on the part of the members of a leadership team. Nonetheless, it is a reliable process that should lead to an outcome that will resonate with the team and inspire confidence in how decisions can be made in an intentional, strategic way." In a sense, the strategy proposed by Lencioni can be regarded as a form of a visualized complex reflection.

Connect Themes via Sticky Notes

Another process that we have found helpful in combining ideas is using sticky notes. You can schedule a meeting with your whole organization or representatives from all areas of your organization. You can ask the group to help you think about a certain topic. For instance, you might have the group discuss how the organization should improve overall in client services or employee engagement. Once you have shared the topic and why it is important to discuss it in terms of the organization's over-all mission, you can ask the group to have a discussion and write down on sticky notes their points of agreement on what should be considered. You can have the group then put these sticky notes on large poster paper on the wall, as illustrated in Figure 8.2.

Once all the notes have been collected, the leader can start to combine them according to themes (pictured in Figure 8.3), making sure to check in with the group to ensure that a particular sticky note does indeed belong in that specific cluster. Remember that you want to have at most three themes for all the suggestions and that you would need to collectively decide which of the three themes is the most important. You can continue with this process until there is one main theme that summarizes each group of suggestions, as pictured in Figure 8.3; the themes turned out to be management, staff morale, and client services. Using sticky notes makes it easier to move and combine items until the main themes emerge.

FIGURE 8.2. Sticky-note focus exercise.

FIGURE 8.3. Organized sticky-note focus exercise.

Set Priorities

Finding a focus is not just about connecting themes, it is also a way of prioritizing what to do first. You and your staff know your organization best and know what takes priority. It is the leader's job, though, to listen to everyone's input, engage them in a healthy debate, and then make a decision, even if not everyone on the staff agrees. We find that the staff will follow through on whatever decision is made, even if members disagree with what you choose, as long as they feel that they were part of the decision-making process and that their thoughts and input were duly considered and appreciated.

You do not want to focus on the wrong issue, and you want to be sure to focus on what is most important to achieve the organization's mission. If you do not really know what that is, you may end up suggesting a series of changes, trying to implement them, then changing again and again without really getting to the core issue, and without really succeeding in solving the problem. For example, Carol (discussed earlier), the leader of a drug and alcohol agency, was in charge when her organization was acquired by a larger company. A few months after the merger, the board of the larger company announced that all units were required to implement a series of strategies to reduce sick leave. Loyally, Carol started working on this task with her team leaders and staff and implemented the required strategies. A couple of months later she met with one of her new leader colleagues and told him how she and her organization had started rolling out the strategies to reduce sick leave. Horrified, he looked at her and said, "No, no, don't spend time on that. Our board changes direction all the time, and it won't be long before they're asking for something different. Don't waste time on implementing their changes. Just focus on the day-to-day work that you and your unit find relevant—and wait and see if the board really sticks to their own decisions." It turned out that Carol had focused too soon on a change, and did not really understand the reasons for it or the process by which her new board made decisions. Not only did she focus too soon, but she also focused on the wrong priority for her organization. What she did not know, and her new colleague did, was that her board was not good at either listening or focusing, which led to numerous inconsistent decisions, only a few of which were ever implemented, and that the staff lost trust in the board. It was now Carol's responsibility to understand this dynamic and focus her organization on what was most important rather than on just following directives. Focusing—and prioritizing—is necessary for organizational clarity, trust, and success.

FOCUSING DOES NOT END

It is also important to remember that if a leader pauses to focus on something, the organization does so as well. Focusing takes active involvement and attention and never ends. We will talk about this fact more when we turn to planning, but for now we want to remind you that each of the four processes builds on the previous one but is never completed. Consistency is of huge importance when it comes to guiding and maintaining the organization's attention. Consistency also means repeating the *why* behind the change that is needed again and again.

When you find a focus, the gentle guiding of the process toward that target continues unendingly. It is even possible that you will need to come back to focusing as you move forward through the other two MI processes, because a different topic or priority becomes clearer. As in the situation with the individual employee, you want to be resolute about this, when it happens. You may say something to the people in your organization like, "It sounds like focusing on X is more important than focusing on Y right now. What do you all think? Please get back to me if you disagree. If I have not heard reasons for not focusing on X first before the end of next week, we will begin exploring how to move on in this new direction." Having a clear focus for the organization allows you to guide the conversation toward the evoking process.

SUMMARY

Just as with individuals, focusing in organizations means deciding on the priority of the conversation. Sometimes the focus is given and does not need to be negotiated. But more often, focusing in organizations is a shared decision-making process, similar to that with individuals. However, contrary to the process regarding individuals, it is typically the leader's task to decide on the focus on the basis of what she has learned and heard. The leader (or group of leaders) is the one that decides what should be changed. However, in order to choose the right focus and secure organizational buy-in, the leader needs to listen, understand, and engage employees in the focusing process. If multiple topics are to be considered, the values and overall goals of the organization should be the guiding stars in choosing the right focus. If the staff and management leaders identify different topics as important to focus on, there needs to be transparency about what topics need to be prioritized first and why. Leadership is also about ensuring that all parts of the organization feel respected and heard.

Organization Vignette

Let's revisit the organization example from Chapter 5. Marie's organization, a large outpatient alcohol treatment facility of which she was a leader, was focusing on improving the quality of its treatment. Let's see how she leads the focusing process.

The discussions in the audit team's meetings were concentrated on the last 6 months of data that evaluated the quality of services. In particular, the team reviewed statistics that illustrated client characteristics, dropout rates, and individual outcomes of treatment. Because there were so many ideas and ways of addressing the goal, the challenge for the audit team was to decide on where best to begin. The overall focus—the quality of services—was clear, but the question was what specific focus would help improve the quality of services the most. The audit team had to consider and review each idea one at a time to ensure that it understood why an idea might lead to the most change before it could move forward.

The data guided the discussion. The audit team reviewed what the statistics showed in terms of positive treatment outcomes. The review showed that 30% of clients dropped out of treatment after only a few sessions with a therapist. The data also showed that about 50% of the remaining clients achieved a good outcome (i.e., abstinence or controlled drinking) after 6 months. The audit team discussed the most significant barriers to staying in treatment and to reaching the desired outcome. Were there particular times where the clients seemed to drop out the most? Why might that be? What could be done to prevent the high drop-out? In a brainstorming format, the audit team collected all suggestions, including ideas from the literature, and the input from the full-day meeting with all staff members, and discussed which ideas might lead to the greatest gain for their clients and the organization.

Marie led a brainstorming discussion with the audit team and wrote all ideas on the whiteboard. She reassured those present that all ideas were welcome, would be carefully considered, and would be treated with respect. The list of ideas on the whiteboard ended up looking like Figure 8.4.

When all the topics had been written down, they were prioritized, and the team discussed their relative importance to the overall company mission. Marie outlined on the whiteboard which areas were considered most important and by whom. She elicited as many specifics as possible in order to ensure that the group understood the suggestions and were able to consider whether or not the organization should be working toward a change in particular areas. As an example, one member of the audit team said she believed that the organization should try to come across as more welcoming to new clients. Since this was a rather general aspiration and might involve doing a number of things, Marie guided the conversation by asking, "What does more welcoming look like? Is it, for instance, about the organization's marketing materials, such as its website and brochures?" Some of the team members nodded. "Or is it about making the waiting rooms nicer?" No, said the team members. "What might it be, then?" Team members suggested that every client entering the facility should always be greeted by a secretary and offered assistance. Marie wrote the proposal on the whiteboard in slightly more general terms: All clients are provided with help and assistance when entering treatment (reflecting and reframing).

Marie consistently guided the audit team toward focusing on topics that addressed the areas in which the current quality of services was not satisfactory. She did so by reflecting and reframing the conversation in a way that lead to the areas of focus being accepted by the whole team.

Written information material for patients.

MI training for staff.

Organize staff in small teams.

Establish a more welcoming atmosphere in the waiting rooms.

Reorganize treatment for withdrawal symptoms.
(focus on easy access)

Reduce waiting time.

Treatment via video conference for patients from rural areas.

More flexibility in opening hours.

Always encourage involvement of significant others.

Remember to ask for permission to coordinate
treatment with other services.

Establish an outreach team of staff.

Perform a satisfaction survey among patients every 6 months.

Evaluate the treatment plan with the patient
every 4 weeks.

FIGURE 8.4. List of ideas on a whiteboard.

In order to improve compliance with treatment, to prevent premature client dropout, and to enhance treatment outcomes (the number of clients not drinking at 3 months following the start of treatment), the audit team narrowed the selected improvement areas down to the following: acute treatment (detoxification and treatment of withdrawal symptoms); involvement of the client's significant others in treatment; providing information material to clients; and the training of staff in evidence-based treatment methods.

SELF-REFLECTIVE EXERCISE. FOCUS WITH YOUR ORGANIZATION

Now that you have a better understanding of why your organization feels stuck and how it is thinking about this change in terms of its importance and its ability to carry it out, it is time to see if you can help the organization focus on a specific target or topic. Remember, you want the topic to be specific enough for you to be able to communicate clearly with the whole organization about whether you are making progress toward improvements in this specific area.

In this exercise, we would like you to try to narrow or prioritize your conversation. In your team meeting, try using the process below to collaboratively come up with one or two areas, so you can continue your team discussion with a clear focus.

Before you start this process, venture a guess as to what you think the main change target is or should be and write it down. Come back to what you guessed and check whether you were hearing a clear focus prior to this continuing conversation.

Lead the conversation with your team about the change you have started discussing. The conversation can be free flowing, and these suggestions can be used to help guide it. Always remember to continue the engaging process by reflecting understanding to the group, either by saying back what you hear or writing down the feedback on the whiteboard or on sticky notes.

Summarize to the group what you have heard so far in terms of themes about this change.

- What does the team think about why there needs to be a change?
- Why does the team think it is important?
- Who is in agreement, and who has different views?
- Share anything else that would be important to demonstrate that you understand the current views of the team.

Write on sticky notes. Tell the group that you would like to work toward a focus to help guide all of you in making a plan. Ask the members of the group to use sticky notes to write down what they think is the main topic that you should all focus on to make a difference in the area of change they have been discussing. If they are not sure what the main topic should be, tell them that they can write down a couple of topics, but no more than three.

Share thoughts and notes. Ask each member to stand up and share her sticky note theme, saying why she thinks it is the most important focus and placing the note on the wall.

Organize and synthesize the notes. Once everyone has shared, ask the members to see if they can reduce the sticky note themes to one or two main topics. You can guide this conversation by asking them what note should be placed under what note until you have rows of notes with similar connected topics.

Guess the main topic. Have the group, yourself included, guess at a topic that might connect all the notes arranged in rows. If you are able to come up with a main theme, write it on a new sticky note, preferably in a different color, and put it above all the other notes in that row. This process might require asking the question "Is this more important than that?" to see how the group collectively prioritizes all the shared ideas.

Share the focus. Once you have one or two main focuses, share with the group that you can always come back to the other topics, one at a time, but for now you will continue the discussion by focusing on just this area. For this exercise, just continue with one focus, and then repeat the process with the second topic later if you wish.

If you cannot get consensus from the group, and there are many topics to consider, decide for the group which topic you will start with. Recount what you have heard from the group, including all sides of the discussion, and why you have chosen this topic for now.

Later, after you have had this conversation, reflect on the process.

- What do you notice?
- Were you hearing the agreed-upon main focus, or were you thinking it was something else?
- What happened if you thought the focus should be one topic, and the team or a group thought it should be something else? How did you collaboratively discuss that?
- How did you know that you had the right focus?
- What did the team say or do that led you to believe you had an agreed-upon target?
- Would you say that deciding on the focus was a collaborative process, or that you chose the focus? If you made the decision, why do you think that happened?

PART IV

EVOKING

CHAPTER 9

Evoking with Your Employee

The third process, *evoking*, is where the conversation embraces all of MI. In earlier chapters, we described the overall mindset (or "heart-set"), the spirit of MI, and the engaging and focusing processes. All of these elements of MI could easily be thought to resemble other good listening or management strategies. Up to this point, you may think that these are strategies you practice already. Where MI clearly reveals itself as a guiding approach with elements other than simply listening is in the evoking—or drawing-out—process. Knowing what and how to evoke from your employees, and why it is important, will help you guide them from a place of ambivalence and being stuck toward a decision and change.

A good place to start, when thinking about evoking, is to ask yourself where you assume the answer or solution will come from. Do you look to your own experience and expertise, or do you look to the employees themselves? Or maybe it is somewhere in between? In MI, the basic assumption is that the solutions, the ideas, and the reasons for change are already present in the employees or in the organization. By moving through all the processes discussed in the previous chapters, you have created a platform for change to happen. The intention behind evoking is to strengthen your staff's motivation for and commitment to change and to elicit their ideas about how this change will come about for them.

This takes a leap of faith at first. You may worry that unless you provide an answer your employee will struggle. You might think that it would be faster and easier just to skip the conversation and offer a solution yourself. The problem with answers coming from the leader is that they are perceived as the leader's answers, and even if the employee

131

accepts these solutions, the message being sent is that he is incapable of solving his own issues or struggles; only the leader can do that. Leaders want to support employees' growth by strengthening an employee's own skills, abilities, and confidence. If the goal of leaders is simply to solve the problem, they miss a huge opportunity to support the growth of their staff. When your employee grows, so does your team, so do you, and so does your organization.

Your goal as a leader is to fully understand what is going on with the employee; why she is stuck; what she hopes for; what she thinks is possible; and what she is ready, willing, and able to do. Once you have this basic understanding, you can shift your focus and selectively pay attention to and guide the side of the conversation that leads to change. When your staff member is ambivalent, she feels two ways about her dilemma. One side of this ambivalence is in the direction of change. The statements that you hear from your employee that point in this direction are called change language or change talk. To help your employee move forward, you will train your ear to hear this language and make attempts to strengthen her own reasons for and ideas about how she might change. We know, from over 3,000 research studies, that it is the presence of this language and our ability to help it grow, deepen, and expand, that increases the likelihood of commitment to change. Evoking is the process that focuses on expanding this language. When you hear such language, you want to spend your time there, strengthening, exploring, and deepening the importance (desire, reasons, and needs) of making the change; building her confidence (ability) that she can make this change; and assessing her readiness (commitment) to change.

PREPARATORY CHANGE LANGUAGE

Although there are many forms of *change language*, there are primarily two types: preparatory language and mobilizing or commitment language. The preparatory language includes the *DARN* part of DARN CAT that we described in a previous chapter. Preparatory change language plays a role when the employee is describing how she is already thinking about change, to some extent. She is not, as yet, committed; she is simply considering the change, and maybe even visualizing what might be different for her. When listening for change talk from an employee, you will listen for her *desire (D)*. Desire is what the employee wants, hopes for, wishes, or would like ("I want to increase my team's performance"; "I wish I could manage the team dynamics better"; "I hope I can increase the quality of my work"; "I wish I was better at detail"). You might ask questions, ask for elaboration, or reflect back what you hear: what does the employee want, what would she prefer, and what does she desire?

You also listen for language about *ability (A)*. Ability is what the employee believes she can do, is capable of, or could do if she so decided ("I know I could focus on detail if I had the time"; "I have in the past had conversations like that and they went well"; "I know that when my team is focused we can accomplish any goal"). You might reflect back or ask a question with these ideas in mind: What do you think you are capable of doing? What do you think would be possible if you decided to make this change? What have you done before that tells you that you would be successful if you did make this change?

You listen for *reasons* to change *(R)*. Reasons are the "why" the employee might make the change. Reasons often become apparent when explored by if/then statements ("If I focused on the detail, I know I would not have to redo so much work"; "I know that if I had that conversation, our relationship would be stronger"; "I know that my team wants to be seen as being the best, and if we were successful in this, we would be"). You might reflect back or ask for elaboration with the following ideas in mind: What would be gained if you made this change? What reasons do you have to make this change? What do you believe that you will get from the change that benefits you?

Finally, you listen for why the employee feels the *need (N)* to change. In feeling a need, an employee expresses her urgency about the change without her necessarily giving a specific reason ("I know I will be fired if I don't stop making all these mistakes"; "If we do not turn this around now, we won't be able to later"; "If the team does not improve now, we are likely to lose team members to other teams"; "I know I am out of time"; "I need to do this"). In order to elicit such needs, you might reflect back or ask questions like: What do you feel must happen? What needs to change now? How serious or urgent is this change?

Understanding that statements about why the employee wants to change, why she thinks she can, and what reasons she has for or why she feels the need to make this change help you identify opportunities to guide in the direction most helpful to the employee. Evoking can be as simple as strengthening, elaborating on, or eliciting more of the change language already shared by your employee.

SELECTIVE ATTENTION

Before introducing the evoking process, you listened without selective attention. Your goal was simply to listen to understand. The initiation of the evoking process does not mean that you stop engaging, listening, or focusing. Listening to understand—the engaging process—is never left behind. Now that you are adding evoking, you focus more in the direction of change, because you now have a better picture of what is going on and how the employee feels. Hopefully, the employee also feels understood. The goal of evoking is to attempt to move one step forward from just understanding to helping the employee resolve his ambivalence. Evoking involves listening for and cultivating change talk by gently encouraging it, and allowing it to grow by bringing it into the light. This is done by gently reflecting it and offering it back to the employee.

When you start being selective in what you reflect back and in what you ask your staff member to elaborate on or explore more, you are helping him move toward making a decision to change. In principle, you can be more selective from the very beginning of your conversation as long as you feel sure that the employee is engaged in the conversation, feels understood, and the focus is clear. You want to be sure throughout your conversation that he feels understood and not pressured to make a decision or move at all. Most often, though, you will begin the evoking process after some time, when you feel that you understand the situation and he feels understood.

We describe typical strategies on how to evoke in a moment, but it can be really just as easy as being curious about why this person is considering the change. What does she want or hope for? Why might she want to change? Why does she believe that she might be able to do this if she decided to, and what reasons does she have for thinking that this change will benefit her? Again, change language is already present, but leaders often fail to look for it and consequently do not hear it. Leaders like yourself typically hear all the reasons why an employee is not making the change—reasons that they likely label as resistance, excuses, or complaints. However, when you start to understand that your employee is conflicted and that what you are hearing is ambivalence, rather than unwillingness or resistance, you will begin to hear change language and can then selectively focus on the part of the conversation that will help her move forward.

Let's look at this example. Karen served as the supervisor of a social worker named Ken. Ken had many projects on his plate and was falling behind. He had no grasp of how to focus his time or what to prioritize. He would work on everything a little at time, missing deadlines, and ultimately did not deliver on any of his projects with a high level of quality. In Ken and Karen's weekly meetings, Ken brought up the list of the many projects he was working on. To help structure the conversation, Karen asked, "Would it be helpful if we talked a bit about how you are managing and handling these many priorities?" Ken said that it would be helpful. Here is how he described the dilemma. Listen first just for understanding. Then listen again with your ears tuned toward change language.

"I really don't know where to even begin. It seems that everything is an important priority and needs to be accomplished today. I know you are going to ask me what can wait, or what can I scrap, but I really don't think anything can wait or be scrapped. I have already considered that. I know I can't manage all of this and can't focus on everything at once, but I really don't have any other option. I just work on each project a little at a time in the hope of making an impact on them all. It is frustrating, and it feels like I am drowning and not making progress and not delivering the level of work of which I am typically capable."

What did you hear? If you are listening just for meaning, you might hear and reflect:

"You feel you are drowning and are not sure where to even begin. You want things to be better, but you simply don't know how they can be."

Or you might say:

"Things are just piling up, and you can't seem to come out from under the pile. You keep working in a fragmented way, but you are not seeing any improvement and the pile keeps increasing."

You might also think for a moment about what your response might be. How might you reflect understanding and express empathy? Remember to avoid giving advice or trying to solve the problem, and try to resist your righting reflex. Try to simply reflect empathy and understanding.

Now, if you instead turn your attention to listening for and cultivating change talk, you may hear and reflect:

"You want things to be better. You have even considered trying to let go of some work. It is important to you to deliver quality work, and you know that means figuring out a different way than what you are doing now. You are trying to come up with a solution that makes sense and does not devalue any of the important projects you are assigned."

How is this example response different? In this response, the emphasis is on what is important to Ken in the direction of change ("It is important to you to deliver quality work"; "You want things to be better"). The reflection in this response also focuses on Ken's ability or confidence ("You have tried to let go of some work"; "You are trying to come up with a solution"). By strengthening and reflecting change language, this reaction typically will elicit more from Ken. His likely response will be to share with you more about what is important to him and what he has tried or is considering.

You might ask why responding this way is so important. The research is clear, and our experience also tells us, that it is in the understanding, expanding, and mining of change language, that the employee starts to open up to the possibility of changing. By providing a platform in which he can safely listen to himself and explore his own thoughts, and by reflecting back to him what he is indeed articulating, you help him sort out and strengthen his *own* arguments for change.

Of course, everything that has already been discussed has to remain in the picture as well. It's not a matter of simply using the evoking strategies to magically make change happen. MI is not something you do to someone; it is a particular conversation *between* people that is grounded in partnership, acceptance, and trust. Change happens in the context of a compassionate relationship, which is built on understanding, empathy, and collaboration. In essence, the leader helps guide the employee toward what he already has within him.

Often you will find that when exploring change language, you can visually see your employee light up and start looking at ideas he has not yet considered. We typically describe this reaction as the person talking himself into the change. Your job is simply not to miss change talk when it is present and to help mine for more of it when you can.

IMPORTANCE AND CONFIDENCE

It can be helpful to think about listening for and strengthening change language in terms of two areas, importance and confidence. Importance and confidence are at the heart of ambivalence. People are typically ambivalent if they have competing priorities or competing aims that are important to them, or if they fail to see the importance of making the change presented to them. Or they may be stuck because they do not believe they could make the change even if they wanted to; they lack the necessary confidence. Knowing whether the ambivalence is due to a lack of, or competing, imperatives, or a lack of confidence, or both, will help you target which area to explore. For instance, if your employee says, "I absolutely know that I could make this happen if I wanted to, I just don't know if I want to," you will want to spend time getting a grasp of what she does want. Her confidence is very high, and she may even have ideas about what she would do, but for now the conversation is about exploring the importance of making this change. Similarly, if she says, "I have to make this happen, or I will lose my job, and I love my job. I really want to figure this out, I do. I just don't know if I can." In this instance, her sense of importance is very high, but her confidence is low, so you will spend time exploring her abilities, strengths, and level of confidence.

We next present a list of typical strategies for evoking. However, these strategies are simply tools to explore and strengthen importance and/or confidence, and the list is not comprehensive. You may have some strategies that you can think of, too. While exploring, it is critical to maintain the collaborative relationship you have developed by continuing active empathetic listening. Often, change talk is already present and does not require cultivating. If it is already there, you can simply reflect it back and ask the employee to elaborate.

If, however, you cannot hear change talk directly, there are a number of simple strategies that you may use to make it more likely that the employee gives voice to the part of her ambivalence that argues for change. You may consider using the **classic list of strategies** presented by Miller and Rollnick (2013).

ASKING EVOCATIVE QUESTIONS

Evoking for change talk can be as simple as asking for it. You do not have to be clever and come up with perfect questions. You can simply ask open-ended questions based on the DARN areas, as described in Chapter 2.

Desire

If you want to evoke change talk around desire, you might pose questions that include words like *wish* and *want* (in the direction of change). Here are a few examples, and you will likely have your own to add:

- "How would you like things to change?"
- "What do you hope will change?"
- "Tell me what you don't like about how things are now?"
- "What do you wish could happen?"
- "What do you wish was different?"

Ability

If you want to evoke change talk around ability, you wish to help the employee begin to think about what she can do, what she believes she is able to do, and what she believes could happen if she decided to make the change. You may then ask:

- "If you decide to make this change, what could you do?"
- "What do you believe you might be able to do?"
- "How confident are you that you could _____ if you made your mind up to do that?"
- "Which of all your ideas do you consider the most likely to succeed?"

Reasons

If you want to evoke around reasons, you encourage the employee to give voice to the specific why. Why would she make this change? You may use if/then statements when you ask her questions, such as:

- "If you did try that idea, what would be the benefit of it?"
- "What do you imagine would be better if you solved this issue?"
- "What would make it worth your effort and time to make this change?"
- "What are some of the advantages to be gained if you decide to make this change?"

Need

If you want to evoke around need, you want to help the employee think about her level of urgency and the importance of making this change. Possible questions in this area may be:

- "How urgent is it that you make this change now?"
- "What do you see as needing to change?"
- "How significant is it to you that this changes?"
- "What has to change?"

The Wrong Questions

Just as these questions are likely to evoke change language, there are some questions that you should avoid because they can be heard as judgments and/or can reinforce staying the same and not invite more change talk. Some questions should never be used because they can be perceived as solely judgmental. Others might make sense in the context of understanding, but in the process of evoking should be asked only with caution, because they might evoke arguments for the opposite side of the ambivalence, the sustain side. We present a few examples of these questions to give you an idea of what we mean, but we are sure you can think of others that you might want to avoid.

- "Why haven't you changed? Why haven't you already done that?"
- "What keeps you from doing that?"
- "What were you thinking about when you messed up?" Or just "What were you thinking?"
- "Why aren't you trying harder?"
- "Why can't you _____?"

ILLUSTRATING IMPORTANCE
AND CONFIDENCE BY MEANS OF MEASUREMENTS

There are still more strategies that are used in MI to help explore or elaborate on change language.

Rulers

The change ruler, for instance, may help guide the employee into a series of questions in which she evaluates the importance of, her confidence in, or her readiness for making this change.

By asking the employee questions like "On a scale of 0 to 10, how important is it to you to make this change, with 0 being not important at all and 10 being the most important thing in your life? What number would you give yourself?," you invite her to consider how important the change really is. Often, it is completely new to the employee to think about the issue this way, to put it into perspective. When she answers, you listen to understand what that number means to her, and then ask, "Why is it a 5 and not a 2 [always pick a number lower than the number she chose]?" And again, it allows you to listen to understand why the change is important. You may continue by asking, "What would it take for it to be 7 [pick a number higher than the number she chose]?," and you will likely hear what may make the change even more important. The flow of the conversation follows this structure:

- "On a scale of 0 to 10, how important is it to you to increase your focus on detail? 0 being it is not important at all and 10 being it is the most important thing on your mind."
- "You gave yourself a 5. Tell me about your 5." Reflect, reflect, reflect.
- "Why did you choose 5 instead of 3?" Reflect, reflect, reflect.
- "What would it take for your 5 to be a 6?" Reflect, reflect, reflect.
- Summarize.

Let's look at a real example. In this example, an employee, Judith, is considering learning to use trauma-focused cognitive-behavioral therapy (TF-CBT) in her clinical approach. Judith is worried that it will take a lot of time and supervision to learn this model but also believes that it would help her achieve better results with her clients.

MANAGER: On a scale of 0 to 10, how important is it to you to incorporate this new clinical approach [TF-CBT] into your practice, with 0 being not important at all and 10 being the most important thing you can think of?

JUDITH: I guess I would say it is a 6.

MANAGER: It sounds like it is rather important to you. What makes it a 6 and not, say, a 4?

JUDITH: Well, I guess it is important because I do not feel that I am that experienced in helping people with trauma, and TF-CBT will help me feel more confident in helping my clients. I also think it is the best approach for me because I already know CBT and just need to see how it is modified for dealing with trauma.

MANAGER: You are thinking it might be easier for you to learn TF-CBT because of your experience with CBT. You want to feel more confident with clients who have experienced trauma, and you believe this will increase your skills and confidence.

JUDITH: Yes. I don't like feeling like I might be missing something with clients, and I feel that way a lot when someone has a trauma background. More and more of my clients present with trauma, so I feel I have to do something.

MANAGER: The time is now because you see that you need to increase your ability to serve clients with trauma.

JUDITH: Yes. I really want to be able to help my clients in the best possible way.

MANAGER: So, let's go back to your 6 for a minute. What do you think it would take for that 6 to be, let's say, an 8?

JUDITH: Well, I guess if I knew I would have the time to commit to the supervisions and coaching after the training. If I knew how to fit this additional approach into my schedule and not reduce my time in helping clients, it would be higher.

MANAGER: So, let me make sure I got it right. It is really important to you to provide the best therapy to all your clients, and you know you want to improve in your ability to help clients with trauma. You think TF-CBT will do that, and you are just trying to figure out the logistics of incorporating the coaching commitments into your schedule. Did I miss anything?

JUDITH: That sounds about right. I just want to feel better about helping clients with trauma.

MANAGER: So, what do you think you will do?

JUDITH: I guess I will take a look at my schedule over the next 6 months and see if I can find a slot for the 2 hours of coaching.

You can swap out the words *important* with *confident* or *ready* if you want to understand and cultivate the employee's confidence or readiness.

If you use this scaling strategy to put importance, confidence, and readiness into perspective, it is vital not only to know how to ask the initial questions but also how to move on and ask why. When you have heard the number that the employee gives herself, you ask, "Why not lower?" because then you will be asking in the direction of change, and allowing your employee to hear all the reasons why the change is important. Contrariwise, if you ask, "Why not higher?" you will likely only hear all the reasons why it is *not* important. You will end up exploring why change may *not* be an issue. Similarly, when you ask, "What would it take for it to be higher?" you explore what might happen that would make it even more important.

Here is a brief model of how to use confidence rulers in an MI conversation. Remember, you can switch out confidence with importance or readiness as well:

- "On a scale of 0 to 10, how confident are you that your team can improve its performance, with 0 being not confident at all and 10 being so confident you would bet your reputation on it?"
- "You gave yourself a 7, Tell me about your 7." Reflect, reflect, reflect.
- "Why did you choose 7 instead of 5?" Reflect, reflect, reflect.
- "What would it take for your 7 to be an 8?" Reflect, reflect, reflect.
- Summarize.

Querying Extremes

Another strategy you may consider in order to cultivate change is that of exploring the employee's concerns were she to do nothing different:

- "If this problem/issue never changed and continued as is, what are the worst things that could happen?"
- "If you do not change, what will the situation look like in a couple of years, if you look at the worst-case scenario?"
- "What concerns you most about this area?"
- "What do you imagine will happen to others if this continues, even if you do not think it will happen to you?"

You may then continue and explore the other extreme, that is, what might be the best outcome of change.

- "What do you imagine might be the best thing that could happen if you did make a change here?"

- "If you make the change, what might the situation look like in a couple of years at best?"
- "If you were successful in making this change, what would be different?"
- "If this problem was gone, what would it be like?"

Looking Back

It may also be helpful to ask the employee to think back to when this current problem or issue was not a problem. You could ask questions about what work was like before this was a concern.

- "Can you think of a time where you felt successful here or in your job? What has changed?"
- "Before you were struggling with this issue, what was your work life like?"
- "What is the difference between your work life now and 5 years ago, before this was a concern?"

Looking Forward

Helping the employee envision the future is another way to elicit change talk. This may be done by inviting the employee to think about and describe how her work life might look after a change:

- "If you did decide to make this change, what would you hope might be different at work in the future?"
- "Tell me how you hope things at work will look for you in 5 years."
- "Tell me what you hope your next performance review will say about this issue."
- "I can see this is really weighing on you. What do you want to be different in the future?"

Exploring Goals and Values

In order to really support the employee in resolving ambivalence and making the right decision, it may be helpful to explore the employee's goals or values in relation to the concern at hand. Understanding what is most important to the employee and how he sees his values or goals as being better achieved by the potential change can help increase his motivation. Most leaders find it a natural part of their job to try to understand what employees want to accomplish in their careers or during their time with the company. However, leaders often feel that values, or what someone holds dear, may not be appropriate for exploration in the workplace. We disagree. Understanding the key values your employee lives by everyday will help you to appreciate when he might be in a values conflict at work or how a particular value might help him achieve a goal that he has set for himself. You will likely recall the story of Henry, who found himself in a values conflict when he took on a fund-raising role. He felt that asking people for money meant that he had to be insincere. Two of his strongest values were honesty and integrity. Though he could "act the part" with the best of them, intentionally acting insincerely meant that he was an ineffective fund-raiser and a very unhappy one. When his supervisor asked him how he thought about his values in relation to the job, he glimpsed the possibility of changing. He became aware that he needed to find a better way to be both sincere and honest to be able to fund-raise.

Clarifying or exploring someone's values or goals in relation to the issue or target at hand can help evoke reasons to change and can also develop discrepancy. *Discrepancy* is another word for conflict or distance between two areas, as for instance, when goals or values are at odds with a current situation or behavior. When a person realizes that there is a discrepancy between his fundamental values and what he is currently doing and where he is heading, it often leads to ambivalence and to giving serious thought as to how the conflict might be resolved. And remember: experiencing some or even a lot of ambivalence is often the first step on the road to making a decision about change. Keep in mind that the goal is to evoke the employee's own reasons, not to convince him to change or to see the issue through your eyes. The aim is to allow the employee to see his own goals and values in relation to the issue at hand. The leader could ask:

- "What is most important to you in life?"
  - Reflect the answer.
  - "How does that relate to the change you are looking at?"
- "What are your goals here at work?"
  - Reflect the answer.
  - "How do you see this issue in relation to that goal?"
- "What are your professional goals for yourself?"
  - Reflect the answer.
  - "How do you see these goals in relation to this issue?"
- "What do you see as your most important values that you try to live by?"
  - Reflect the answer.
  - "How do you see these values in relation to this issue?"

RESPONDING TO CHANGE TALK: HOW TO MAKE IT GROW

When you begin to hear change talk from employees, even when it may be mixed in with musings about *not* changing, the so-called sustain talk, you want to make the change talk grow. In essence, you wish to create more opportunities for employees to express change language and talk themselves into changing. How do you do that? What do you do, when you hear change talk? How do you respond? How can you cultivate change talk? How can you make it grow?

The good news is that you already know how to respond. You will use the same skills that you have been using all along. You can simply use your OARS (open-ended questions, affirmations, reflections, and summaries) skills. The only slight difference is that now you may be a little more selective in what you focus on and in what you wish to high-light for the employee. In MI, we often use *EARS* skills to emphasize this shift in intention. In the process of evoking, you are selectively asking open-ended questions to encourage the exploration or *elaboration* of change talk (*E*). You are *affirming* strengths or change attempts (*A*). You are *reflecting* the importance and confidence change talk you hear from your employee (*R*). And you are *summarizing* and linking up elements of change talk in your employee's responses (*S*). By using your EARS, you will hear even more change talk and can simply continue to listen, use your EARS skills, and not have to be clever in thinking about other strategies to try.

MOBILIZING CHANGE TALK

The flow of a conversation about change may be viewed through the lenses of an analogy, first presented by William R. Miller and Stephen Rollnick (2013).

The conversation may be compared to climbing up and down a hill, as in Figure 9.1.

The engaging, focusing, and evoking processes are part of the walk uphill. During this climb, you may cultivate and hear DARN language—the *preparatory change talk*. When you arrive at the peak, you start hearing commitment language—the *mobilizing change talk* (CAT). It is downhill from there. The conversation becomes much easier. Uphill, you help your employee prepare to decide by letting him consider change. You have sought to understand his ambivalence, you have elicited from him all the arguments that he has for change, and helped him investigate his thoughts that favor change. All the change talk so far can be seen as preparatory language. If the change turns out to be what he really wants deep down, and if it is aligned with his values and thoughts about

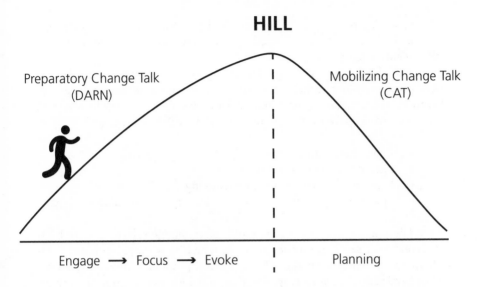

FIGURE 9.1. MI hill metaphor.

his future, you will likely begin hearing mobilizing language, signaling a movement toward resolving the ambivalence and becoming ready to make a decision.

Mobilizing language can be heard in different ways, and may be captured by the acronym CAT, part of the DARN CAT described previously. *Commitment language (C)* itself is the clearest example of mobilizing change talk. Commitment language is a statement of resolve, saying "I will." Commitment language may sound like:

- "I will start tomorrow. . . . "
- "I am really going to do this."
- "I promise to . . . "

("I will start using those reports next week"; "I am really going to set up the team meeting, and it will happen by the end of the month"; "I promise next time this comes up with my team, I will address it immediately and not let it drag out.")

Commitment can also sound like *activation (A)*. This is language that indicates movement.

- "I am willing to . . . "
- "I am ready to . . . "
- "I am prepared to . . . "

("I am willing to meet with the coach"; "I am ready to make this a priority for my team"; "I am prepared to have that conversation and get past this negative team dynamic.")

The third kind of mobilizing change talk is indicated not by the wording itself, but rather by what becomes apparent when listening. Activation language is used when the employee tells you how he has tried or begun to prepare for the change. It is called *taking steps (T)*.

- "I have bought a textbook."
- "I attended a class on this."
- "I set up my calendar to start tracking this."
- "I have set up the meeting with my supervisor to address this."

These are examples of how mobilizing change talk may sound. Of course, there are many other ways in which you might hear preparatory or mobilizing language. The important point is to notice the difference between when your employees are considering changing something and when they are moving toward taking action. It is also important to remember that, just as when cultivating preparatory change language, the easiest way to develop and cultivate mobilizing language is not to hand it to the employee, but to ask for it:

- "What will you do?"
- "What is the next step?"
- "What do you conclude from our conversation?"
- "What might bring you closer to making a decision about this change?"
- "What might you try to do?"

Mobilizing change talk signals that it is time to move to the planning process that we discuss in Part IV. But before we turn to this process, we will spend a little time examining what the evoking process may look like when it's your organization that you wish to guide toward change, and not just a single employee.

SUMMARY

When the focus is established, the process of cultivating change talk becomes more prominent. Cultivating change talk means listening for all aspects of what has been said, directly or indirectly, that lead in the direction of change or a decision. We gently increase the volume of the sound of change by reflecting it and asking for more. We help our employees hear themselves talk about the positive aspects of change, including the feeling of need for the change. We may increase the volume by creating opportunities for individuals to give expression to the importance of change and their belief in their ability to change, while reflecting back to them what they express.

Employee Vignette

Susan has been struggling with a particular part of her job, and wants to get better at enrolling new clients. So far, we have come up with a focus, which is helping her think about how she evaluates her progress and how this affects her ability to enroll new clients. Let's listen and see where the conversation goes, now that we have a focus. Listen also to how Ashley begins to think about evoking change talk (the importance of, confidence in, and readiness for doing something new) from Susan, in the hope of helping her achieve her goal of meeting the job expectations and not getting fired.

ASHLEY: Tell me a little about the new things you are doing to improve on the client enrollment part of your job, and how you are evaluating your progress? (*open-ended question*)

SUSAN: Well, I do a lot of things actually. I practice with my peers and my supervisor in our meetings. Using the skills I have learned, I am able to enroll pretend clients in role plays with my teammates and my supervisor. I am able to listen and not worry about whether someone wants our service when I am practicing, but when I am with a real client it is different.

ASHLEY: So you are practicing a lot with your peers and your supervisor. You actually know you can do it because you are doing it with them. (*reflection*)

SUSAN: That is what is so frustrating. I am great in training with peers and with my supervisor, but on my own with clients, I suck.

ASHLEY: What do you make of that? (*open-ended question*)

SUSAN: I guess that in my training with these groups, I don't worry about the answer because it doesn't actually matter. I really am focused on listening to whoever is playing the part of the client and am able to understand what is important to that person and whether she thinks our service can help. I don't worry if she doesn't want our program, because if what is important to her is not our program, that is fine. But, you know, in training, it's all acting. It's not real. It's fake.

ASHLEY: When you aren't worrying about the outcome, you are able to hear what is most important to your client. (*reflection*)

SUSAN: Yeah. I don't do that on the phone. I worry more about the fact that this person does not want the program, than I care about what is important to them. I worry about me failing more than about what they are saying.

ASHLEY: So, you know that when you listen to the client and care about what she wants, you are more successful. (*reflection*) How does that apply to your clients and not just in training? (*open-ended question*)

SUSAN: Well, like I said, with people who are already in our program, I can do that, and it goes very well. I am just not doing it with new people.

ASHLEY: Because you are focused on their agreeing to the program and not on what they are wanting or saying. (*reflection*)

SUSAN: Right.

ASHLEY: If you could look 6 months down the line, and you knew that you would by then have overcome this initial learning phase, what would you hope might be different? (*open-ended question, evoking*)

SUSAN: Well, I hope I am still working here. I also hope that I am able to interact with clients the same way that I interact in training—calm, open, and not focused on trying to sell our service.

ASHLEY: Being calm, open, and not focused on selling are part of what you hope to change. (*reflection of change talk*)

SUSAN: Yeah, I just wonder why I am not doing that now.

ASHLEY: Yeah, I was wondering the same. Why do you think that is? (*open-ended question*)

SUSAN: I guess I am so worried about getting fired that it just takes over. I know I have about 30 days before I am going to be told that I am fired, and I am nowhere near close to the goal.

ASHLEY: You know that focusing on getting fired is not working for you. It is actually the reason you are not doing well in the first place. You are just not sure how to let it go, because you know the clock is ticking. (*reflection*)

SUSAN: Right. If I could let it go, I would. I know if that I did, it would help.

ASHLEY: What do you think might help with getting you to the place you want to be in, open, calm, and truly listening, and not worrying about getting fired? (*open-ended question, asking for change talk*)

SUSAN: I guess if I knew for sure how much time I had to improve and saw some improvement each day I would be able to stop worrying.

ASHLEY: So knowing the time frame would be important to you. (*reflecting change talk*)

SUSAN: It would.

ASHLEY: What do you already know about the time frame that you have in which to meet this expectation? (*open-ended question*)

SUSAN: Well, I guess it is fuzzy. Some people seem to have a little more time than others. I'm not really sure.

ASHLEY: Would it be helpful if I told you a little bit about the time frame and process for determining when someone is let go? (*asking for permission to give information*)

SUSAN: Yes.

ASHLEY: Typically, if an employee is making progress and is close to the goal, we keep working with that person, and most people end up being successful. There are times where an employee finds he doesn't like the job and chooses to leave, and there are times when an employee does not make progress and we have to let him go. Typically, that is about 6 months from hire. People seem to learn this job at different paces. So as long as they are trying, using supervision well, and making progress, we keep working with them. (*giving information*) What do you make of that? (*open-ended question*)

SUSAN: Well, it's still a little scary, because that sounds like I have 2 months before I will be fired. But I guess also that if I show improvement, you might still work with me.

ASHLEY: Right. I wonder how you think you might make progress. (*asking for change talk*)

SUSAN: Well, if I could find a way to not worry about not enrolling people over the next 2 months, and just practice what I do in training, that might make some progress.

ASHLEY: Focusing on applying what you are practicing in training to real clients might help. And part of that is not focusing on enrolling people or on selling. (*reflecting change talk*)

SUSAN: Yeah. I am just not sure I will do that. My mind keeps going back to "you are going to get fired."

ASHLEY: You know not focusing on getting fired will help. You are just trying to figure out how to do that. (*reflection*)

SUSAN: I am.

ASHLEY: So, what do you think might help? (*asking for more change talk*) If I understand you properly, you know that focusing on failing or getting fired is why you are not open, calm, and able to use your skills with your clients. You also know that you are able to use these skills, because you use them well in training. (*summary of change talk*)

SUSAN: I am not really sure. I just don't want to be blindsided and fired all of a sudden. And if I am going to be fired, I need to start looking for another job now.

ASHLEY: So what would help you with that? Not feeling blindsided? (*asking for change talk*)

SUSAN: Not sure. (*pause*) Is there any way you could tell me for sure that I won't be let go before the 60 days are up? Maybe then I could focus at least for the next 30 days without worrying about getting fired, and then have 30 more days to worry if I don't improve.

ASHLEY: So, knowing for sure you have 60 days to improve would help you. (*reflecting change talk*)

SUSAN: It would.

ASHLEY: Yes, I can tell you that you have at least 60 days to improve. (*giving information*)

SUSAN: Okay. So, I just need to do this now. Try not to focus on the outcome, and just care about the clients.

ASHLEY: Makes sense to me too. Is that something you are going to do? Not focus on the answer while listening to new clients? (*asking for commitment*)

SUSAN: Yes. I am going to try.

SELF-REFLECTIVE EXERCISE. EVOKE WITH YOUR EMPLOYEE

You now have an understanding of your employee's ambivalence and a focus. You will continue the process with both of them in mind. You will move on to the engaging process of reflecting understanding and will gently guide the conversation to this focus as you continue the evoking process.

Continue the conversation with this person about the change. The conversation can be free flowing, and our evoking questions can be used as guides. Always remember to continue the engaging process too by reflecting understanding when the person shares her thoughts.

The *goal* of this process is to help the employee build the sense of the importance and confidence needed to make the change in this target focus upon which you have just agreed. Remember, the goal is not to fix or solve the problem or give advice. It can get hard at this stage to avoid doing so because the employee might start sharing ideas or solutions. You want to reflect your understanding when the employee does that, but not yet move to planning action until you hear readiness.

Remember, the change language the employee shares with you cues you as to whether she is just thinking about change (desire, ability, reason, or need to change) or is committing to change (commitment, activation, or taking steps). You may stay in evoking for a little while and, if you hear commitment, you can always check it out with the employee and move to the next exercise to begin planning.

You can use the following questions to help guide the evoking process. You may find, depending on how the employee feels about the importance of this change or her confidence in making it, that you use some questions more than others. That is fine. Just keep in mind that the goal is to build importance and confidence so the person feels ready to make the change. Both are needed and necessary.

Questions to Guide Evoking

Remember to reflect understanding before asking more questions.

Importance (Questions to Explore and/or Increase Importance [Reasons/Need/Desire])

- "What makes this important to you?"
  - Reflect what you understand. "Tell me more about that. . . . What else?"
- "What reasons do you have for making this change? What reasons do you have for not staying as you are now?"
  - Reflect what you understand. "Tell me more about that. . . . What else?"
- "When do you think this change needs to happen? How urgent do you feel this change is?"
  - Reflect what you understand.

Confidence (Questions to Explore and/or Increase Confidence [Ability])

- "If you decided to make this change (the focus), how confident do you feel about carrying out the change?"
  - Reflect what you understand. "Tell me more about that. . . . What else?"

▨ "If you did decide to make this change, what ideas do you have already about how you would do that? Tell me more about that."
   ◆ Reflect what you understand. "Tell me more about that. . . . What else?"

▨ "How do you envision making this happen?"
   ◆ Reflect what you understand. "Tell me more about that. . . . What else?"

▨ "What kinds of things will need to be in place for this to come about?"

▨ "What might make it easier for you to make this change?"

▨ "What other resources might be helpful to you at this point?"

Later, after you have had the conversation, reflect on the process.

▨ What did you notice?

▨ What did you notice in what the employee shared relating to the importance of the change and her confidence in making the change?

▨ Were there times that you found it hard not to give advice or solutions? If so, what are your thoughts about why it was harder at those moments?

▨ Were there times it was easier to listen and guide? What did you notice about those times?

CHAPTER 10

Evoking with Your Organization

MI in organizations builds on the assumption that the solutions, the ideas, and the reasons for change are already within the organization, and that they flourish in a collaboration between you, the staff, and maybe your customers. Leaders can use the process of evoking to gently steer the organization in the direction of change by listening for and expanding the staff's reasons for and ideas about how change will happen.

Just as was discussed in the context of evoking with employees, you may think it quicker to simply jump to a decision or solution, providing it yourself. You may also wonder whether delivering solutions is not, in fact, what is expected of you. The problem with your providing the solutions to organizational dilemmas is that they are your answers only, and not the organization's. Even if the organization accepts the solutions you provide, the underlying message is that the employees are not able or expected to develop them. You are saying, indirectly, that answers or solutions can only come from you and/or your company's leaders. The message that all ideas must flow from the top kills organizational innovation, creativity, and effectiveness. When the solutions emerge from the whole organization, implementing them is far more likely to succeed. If the staff are involved in creating the solution, they are more likely to follow through on the proposed ideas and to embrace the change wholeheartedly, compared to keeping the change at arm's length. Additionally, when you understand that there are answers latent in all areas of your organization and you involve your staff in developing solutions, you have access to a greater number of ideas and a higher chance of finding a successful outcome. Also a leader's main priority is to support the organization's growth by increasing staff skills, abilities, and confidence, and evoking can help you do just that.

LISTENING TO AND EVOKING CHANGE LANGUAGE IN ORGANIZATIONS

How do you listen to and grow change language in an organization? You may remind yourself again that the organization is a group of people, and it is all about listening to them. So, in that respect, you may turn to the previous chapter on evoking ideas from your employee. Some of those same approaches and strategies also work with organizations. However, when listening to large groups of people and to what may lead the collective in the direction of change, you need to tune your ears to pick up patterns and learn a bit about groups and how group processes work.

Your staff consists of groups of people. It may be teams working in specific areas (i.e., intake of patients, aftercare, or outreach), and it could be groups of professionals working with specific remits (i.e., nurses, social workers, secretaries, doctors). Often, a team or group has members with different formal or informal roles. It may be that one is the spokesperson, another is the voice of concern, and another gets easily bored with discussions and just wants to "get on with it." One group may take the view of the customer, another easily gets excited about any new idea, and yet another tends to be the devil's advocate, always predicting what will go wrong. The same pattern can be seen among different kinds of teams: One group may be willing to try out almost every new idea, while another group almost always has second thoughts about any proposed suggestion. Everett Rogers describes these group dynamics according to what he calls five adopter categories. He explains how each of these categories of individuals or groups illustrate their readiness to implement new innovations or changes: the *innovators*, the *early adopters* (the opinion leaders), the *early majority* (the deliberators), the *late majority* (the skeptical), and the *laggards* (the traditional) (Rogers, 1995 p. 263ff). The *innovators* are immediately willing and ready, are often aware of new ideas before the others, and see the benefits right away. The *early adopters* are more integrated into the social system than the innovators and have the greatest number of team opinion leaders. The staff considering the new idea may look to early adopters for advice and information. The early majority, however, adopt new ideas and change deliberately, and typically before the average member of a system, but seldom hold positions of team opinion leaders. This group typically consists of one third of the members of the system. The *late majority* are more skeptical and adopt new ideas just after the average member of the system. The late majority are also deemed to make up one third of the members of the system. In the fifth category are the *laggards* or late adopters, who are the last in a system to adopt an innovation. Their point of reference is the past, and they tend to be more suspicious about change (Rogers, 1995).

Taken together, the individuals from all the groups and categories may represent organizational ambivalence, with some expressing interest in changing by sharing importance language (desire, reasons, needs) and confidence language (ability to change). Whereas others are sharing status quo or sustain talk. Understanding what is happening will help you think about how best to use and/or adopt MI with each group. For instance, if you are talking with an innovator, you might spend most of your time on building her confidence and belief about her own, her team's, or the organization's ability to implement this new idea, because she already recognizes the importance and/or value of the innovation. However, if you are talking with a laggard, you might spend your time on instilling importance, on how he sees this idea as important to the overall mission and goals of the organization, while also eliciting his ideas about his own and his team's ability or confidence to put it into practice if the organization decided to implement the change. In Figure 10.1, you can see examples of how leaders (the individuals with a bag in their hands) may respond to the employees (the individuals without a bag), depending on the employee's readiness and willingness to change.

NOTICE THE LANGUAGE OF CHANGE IN THE ORGANIZATION

Knowing how the group or employee approaches innovation is important, and it is also important to know how to resolve group ambivalence as well. How do you help change language to grow without deepening the organizational ambivalence? How do you evoke change language from the staff or groups? If you simply join the choir of those supporting the change—the innovators and early adopters—you may, in fact, exacerbate organizational ambivalence because the reluctant groups and individuals may feel that they need to become even more vocal, stepping up their concerns and reluctance about change in order to feel heard. In fact, they may feel so overwhelmed, scared, or anxious about the change that they argue against it ever more forcefully, with the result that they win more support and convince themselves and the rest of the organization that change is a bad idea, not necessary, and not possible. Leaders want to avoid this outcome because it may lead to organizational conflict and stagnation.

Instead of just aligning with the groups that are positive about innovation, you might instead consider treading more carefully. You could

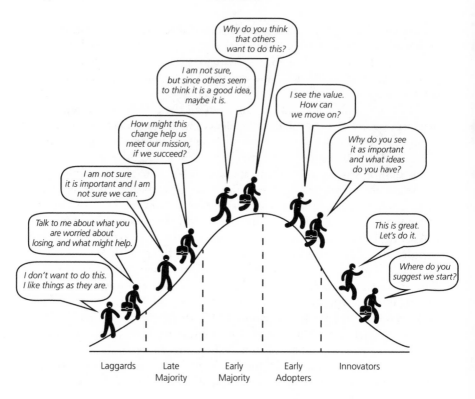

FIGURE 10.1. Examples of how leaders (the individuals with a bag in their hands) may respond to the employees (the individuals without a bag), depending on the employees' readiness and willingness to change.

focus on softening the sustain talk and evoking change language from the groups that are reluctant, while continuing to pay sufficient attention to the groups already ready to change. How do you do that?

The first step is to recognize what change language sounds like in organizations. Just as with individuals, you listen for desire (D). Desire comprises what your staff wants, hopes for, wishes, or would like in relation to the organization. It might sound like "We want our company to be the best," or "We wish we served our clients better." You also listen for language around ability (A). Ability comprises what your staff believe they can do. It might sound like "I know we can do this if we just give it our attention," or "We have done something like that in the past." You also listen for reasons to change (R). Reasons are the "why" your staff might make this change. They might sound like "If we did make this happen, we would better serve our clients"; "We would increase our customer base and be able to hire more counselors to add to our team";

"If we make this happen, we might increase our revenue enough for us to get raises." And you listen for why the staff feel the need for change (N). This is the language around the urgency of the change. It might sound like, "If we don't do this, our department will be downsized"; "If we don't make this happen now, our competitor will beat us to it"; "I am afraid that if we don't do this now, our staff will quit."

However, to be able to soften sustain talk, you also need to be able to recognize sustain language when it is there. You do not listen for sustain language in order to deepen it and make it blossom, but because you wish to acknowledge and learn from it when relevant, and soften it to a level that allows for decisions to be made. To do that you need to be able to recognize the organization's desire (D) for staying the same. It might sound like "We want to keep things like they are," or "We wish we could just keep on doing what we are doing now." You want to recognize language indicating ability (A) to stay the same or expressing an inability to make the change. It might sound like "We have in the past resisted things like this and it worked out; we can do that now," or "Even if we thought we needed to do this, there is no way our team can pull it off." You may also hear reasons expressed for not changing (R). They might sound like "If we change, staff will quit," or "If we don't do this, we will have more time to focus on the work we already have." Or you may hear reasons why the staff do not feel the need for change (N). It might sound like "I just don't think we need to do this with everything else already on our plate," or "No other hospital is doing this. I don't think it is something we have to do." You need to be able to recognize sustain language, empathize with it, and put it to rest. If you ignore it, it will just get louder and stronger. As in the case of MI with individuals, the acronym DARN can help you focus on the language it is most important to pay attention to in a conversation. Understanding what language is pointing toward staying the same or toward changing will help you decide whether you should acknowledge and soften it or elicit and expand on what has been shared. Expanding or eliciting more sustain language will simply keep you and your organization stuck. Table 10.1 provides examples of change language you would want to deepen and sustain language you would want to soften.

RESOLVING AMBIVALENCE IN ORGANIZATIONS

Evoking is the strategy to use when you are trying to grow change language and resolve ambivalence. When you start being selective in what you reflect or ask groups or individuals to elaborate on or explore more, you make an attempt to take a step forward toward change and help the organization focus on the motivation to change that already lies within it.

TABLE 10.1. Change versus Sustain Talk

DARN	Change talk (grow and cultivate)	Sustain talk (understand and soften)
Desire	"We want our company to be the best." "We wish we served our clients better."	"We want to keep things like they are." "We wish we could just keep on doing what we are doing now."
Ability	"I know we can do this if we just give our attention to it." "We have done something like this in the past."	"In the past we have resisted things like this and it worked out, and we can do that now." "Even if we thought we needed to do this, there is no way our team could pull it off."
Reasons	"If we did make this happen, we would better serve our clients." "We would increase our customer base and be able to hire more counselors to add to our team." "If we make this happen, we might increase our revenue enough that we can get raises."	"If we change, staff will quit." "If we don't do this, we will have more time to focus on the work we already have."
Need	"If we don't do this, our department will be downsized." "If we don't make this happen now, our competitor will beat us to it." "I am afraid that if we don't do this now, our staff will quit."	"I just don't think we need to do this with everything else already on our plate." "No other hospital is doing this. I don't think it is something we have to do."

However, all too often leaders miss the change talk that is already there or just below the surface. Leaders tend to only hear all the reasons why a team or a group does not wish to change: reasons that you likely label as resistance or complaining. When you start listening for change talk, you may find that it is easier than you thought to move your organization in the direction of change. You may even find that it is like traveling within your organization, looking for and finding hidden treasures and beautiful spots. Cultivating change talk and creating opportunities for the organization itself to fuel the change process is often easier, quicker, and more enjoyable than trying to persuade the organization to change.

When you start to understand that what you are hearing from some corners of the organization is a sign that the organization is ambivalent, and that the reason the new ideas are not being implemented is because the organization feels stuck, you can train your ear to hear the change language that is mixed in with the expressions of worry. You can choose to focus on and expand that part of the conversation to help move the organization forward. You should not ignore the concerns that you hear. You can gently recognize that both arguments for and against change are there and allow the group to consider both sides. Strategically, when you recognize organizational ambivalence, you can avoid bringing groups or employees into situations in which they feel a need to express their worries more and more strongly, and instead ask them to reflect on why they might want to change and how they think they might if the company decided to go ahead with the new way of doing things. That is not to say that if people share their worries, you should shut them down and not listen. Not at all. Instead, when staffers voice concern, you listen in order to learn, and you reflect your understanding so that they feel understood. At the same time, you constantly focus the conversation on what the employees and teams add to the urgency of or confidence in the organization's ability to implement the new idea. You continually focus on, reflect on, and acknowledge that ability to help it grow.

One practical strategy for evoking change talk and resolving ambivalence in organizations is the use of staff group conversations. For example, you might establish a conversation about a specific area of the organization needing improvement—intake of patients, say—and invite your entire organization or a cross-functional team to discuss the issue. In the setup, you ask the entire staff to briefly describe what is working well already, and what you all should be careful not to lose in a future process. You can guide the group discussion by first asking each member, one by one, to spend about 2 minutes describing everything that he feels works well in the intake of patients. While one group member is speaking, the rest are asked to listen quietly, while the leader writes all the ideas that are offered on a whiteboard, asking for clarification if needed. When all group members have spent their time describing what is already working well, you ask the group to spend a few minutes looking at the whiteboard, while the leader summarizes its contents. After a break, the procedure is repeated, but this time, all members are asked, one by one, to describe improvements and what they might want to see change. Again, the group is asked to listen quietly while each member is speaking, and the leader is writing the suggestions on the whiteboard and reflecting understanding back to the speaker as needed. When all members have offered their suggestions and ideas, the leader summarizes and reflects what has been shared. This process creates a platform for recognizing concerns that need to be taken into consideration (softening sustain language), while inviting support for implementing the change (cultivating change language). Again, note that change language is often there already. Instead of battling with the members of the group that are against change, you listen to them, while also allowing and cultivating the change talk in the organization expressed by other members—or even change talk intertwined with sustain talk—and you display change talk and sustain talk side by side, gently and respectfully placed in the context of the company's goals and mission.

For example, Carol, the leader of a drug and alcohol agency, was working with her team, who was responsible for initiating acute treatment in clients with alcohol problems. Due to a new structure in the organization, the team had many new tasks assigned to it and felt that it lacked resources. Several members of the group felt stressed and thought that the workload was too high. Conflicts began to emerge. In a meeting, they all argued that the new structure was not feasible. Carol asked, "Would it be helpful if we talked a bit about how the team is managing and handling all the tasks?" The team agreed that it would be helpful. Carol used the format we just outlined for the group conversation. Here is how the team described the dilemma. Listen first just for understanding. Then listen again with your ears tuned toward change language.

This is what the team said: "The not-so-good things (and things that we should consider improving) are as follows: It is difficult to get enough time for documentation. The waiting time for clients has increased, and we are not sure that we are doing everything right. It is difficult to remember all the new steps in the new routines. We worry about our colleagues and their being exhausted. Occasionally we need to get in contact with a doctor, but cannot reach him. It is frustrating, and we feel like we should be better at what we are doing, and that we are not delivering the level of work that we used to be able to."

"The good things about the new situation: We like working together. The new working routines are safer for the clients, and clients now receive better information before treatment starts. We have improved our efforts on informing clients about the potential side effects from medication. The documentation of our work is good, too. We are better at involving significant others in the early phases of treatment. Our clients are happy and satisfied with our service."

What do you hear and wish to summarize or reflect back to the team? If you are listening just for meaning, you might reflect: "The team feels overwhelmed by the work overload. You want to serve your clients well, but you just don't think this is the answer. The team needs more staff members and better access to doctors." (The underlying message is that management should provide a solution and add more resources to the team.)

If you instead focus on change language in your summary, you might reflect: "The team worries because so far it seems that the procedures take longer, and you are not always sure if you can remember it all. It is important to you to deliver satisfactory service to your clients and you try hard. The team really wants to provide quality treatment, and you also care about each other. You are all engaged in the work, and are happy that clients are more satisfied, and the documentation of your work has improved, too. You want to make sure that clients do not have to wait. You collectively are trying to come up with a solution that makes sense." (The underlying message is that the team is able to produce a solution—perhaps guided by management.)

In this example, you are reflecting back and also emphasizing what is important to the team in the direction of change ("It is important to you to deliver quality work. The team wants things to be better"). You are also focusing on the team's ability or confidence ("You are trying to come up with a solution"). By strengthening and reflecting the change language present, you are typically met with more change language. Your team's likely response is to share more with you about what the team believes is important and what it is considering.

Understanding, cultivating, and mining change language among employees, teams, and groups help leaders guide the organization toward opening up to the possibility of change. But remember, as in the case of individuals, simply using the evoking strategies will not make magic happen, with the organization suddenly willing to change. Just as MI is not something you do to someone, nor is it something you just *do* to the organization. Change happens in the context of a relationship between a leader and employees that is built on trust, understanding, empathy, and collaboration. Successfully implementing change is grounded in the mutual understanding that leaders are there to help guide staff to collaborative design solutions because they are the experts in their roles. Implementation of change in an organization by means of MI does not equate to leaders pushing change processes through and forcing the staff to behave differently. Rather, it is a way for leaders to create opportunities to instill motivation to implement change by exploring the employees' preferences, knowledge, and expertise.

When you explore and cultivate change language in the organization, you need to be aware of not only the spoken language, but also the written and unspoken language. Weekly or monthly company newsletters may be a means for cultivating change talk. You can share change stories, describe instances of customer satisfaction, or give feedback on implementation status, using them as opportunities to reflect what you are seeing and hearing from the organization in the direction of the desired change. Similarly, minutes from meetings may also be a means for cultivating change language, just as small talk over lunch with staff can create an opening to not only understand, but also to encourage motivation. Recognizing the desire, ability, reason, and need for change in the organization, and reflecting it back to the staff on all platforms, and in all forums and situations, is a way of being with your organization, recognizing potential ideas, and cultivating positive change.

WHAT IF PARTS OF THE ORGANIZATION ARE RELUCTANT TO CHANGE AND OTHER PARTS ARE NOT?

Typically, when faced with new ideas, some parts of an organization are quick to accept change, while other parts are more reluctant. This is an expression of organizational ambivalence, and it is a high-risk situation that can evolve into real conflicts if not handled carefully. What should you be aware of in these situations? First, it is important to be aware that when staff and teams show resistance to change, they do so with the best of intentions. It can be due to a lack of knowledge about how to change or because they feel uncertain about what to do or how to do it. They rarely resist change just because they reject it per se. Second, it is important to be aware that if you ignore the parts of the organization that is against change, you are running the risk of creating and cultivating further resistance to change. If you continue to focus on pushing through the change, you are, inadvertently, inviting the parts of the organization that feel reluctant, scared, or insecure to raise their voices even louder in order to be heard.

When resolving organizational ambivalence, it is crucial to make all parts of the company feel safe in the process. One way of creating a safe space is by affirming staff efforts to take ownership, and caring enough to be concerned. You may also explicitly communicate that you will not allow the coming change to destroy valuable assets in the organization during the process of implementation. Instead of arguing and trying to persuade the groups that are reluctant or critical about a proposed change, you may thank them for sharing their worries, and maybe invite them to be your special advisors and even to play devil's advocate (whose job it is to think through all the ways the change might not work or be a good idea) to make sure that you do not miss anything in the process ahead. You may even offer to collect data to monitor the outcome and promise to evaluate the change at a specified time. You may invite the reluctant parts of the organization to give their perspectives, at a specified time, on what has been gained or lost during the process. It is our experience that all such options (encouraging the reluctant segment to share their concerns with you, inviting the groups or their representatives reluctant to change to be your advisors, and—in particular—collecting data and evaluating the outcome of the change together with both the reluctant and the willing parts of the organization) are feasible approaches that put the worry to rest, rather than producing resistance and conflicts. Again, the point is not to launch into trying to persuade these groups not to worry, but rather to recognize their reluctance and to engage them in a process that evaluates the outcome of the change. You might even consider separating the evaluation into small parts (make interim evaluations, perform quick surveys) to demonstrate your willingness to listen to them and make relevant adjustments when needed.

Another important consideration when you are working with an organization that is partly ambivalent is to listen for anxiousness about change. Staff may be reluctant to change due to fear of making mistakes or of moving into unknown territory. Recognizing this fear and making sure that staff feel safe in relation to the change can also help resolve organizational ambivalence. Let's revisit the example of Marie, the leader of a drug and alcohol agency, mentioned in a previous chapter. You will recall that she developed a quality-assurance group within her organization and used an audit team as one of many platforms for listening to the organization. The audit team consisted of management as well as representatives from all staff groups (nurses, social workers, doctors, etc.) and was given the authority to regularly review the quality of the services that the organization delivered. In order to ensure that the discussions were fruitful and that everyone felt safe, the audit team decided its motto would be: Mistakes and errors belong to the organization and not to individuals. The team wanted to be clear that individuals were not to blame when quality was low or mistakes were made. The team knew that all members needed to feel safe when they shared team, individual, or leadership errors, so that it could really understand what was happening and focus on the right areas to improve outcomes. In other words, the task of evoking change talk also meant recognizing fear and anxiety and putting them to rest. Leaders need to listen for staff anxiety in order to able to understand, express empathy, overcome any worries, and cultivate change talk in the direction of change.

THE IMPORTANCE OF TRUST

To create an environment where employees can let go of their worries, they must be able to trust that there is no risk involved in trying something new. Leaders need to model consistently that an organization learns through making mistakes and through trial and error. These lessons are important for a company and are the only way it will know what to focus on and what to improve. True leadership is also about consistently telling employees of the organization that it is safe to talk about what they are currently doing wrong—in terms of errors, mistakes, and systems that are not currently working. Cultivating change talk and evoking resources for change are not just about sounding excited or cheering efforts to make change happen. They are also about creating and securing a safe atmosphere in which to try something new.

IMPORTANCE AND CONFIDENCE

Even if your employees feel safe in modifying what they are currently doing, they still might be ambivalent. You will likely recall that we have talked about importance and confidence being at the heart of ambivalence. Groups are also often ambivalent if they have competing priorities that are important to them. Or groups may be stuck because they do not believe they could make a change even if they so wanted. Knowing whether ambivalence exists because the group does not consider it important or because it lacks confidence, or both, will help you know where to focus your exploration. For instance, if a group does not consider a specific change necessary because it believes that other aspects of the organization's services are more critical, you would want to spend your time understanding what the group finds more important and how it views these new ideas in relation to those areas. The staff may indeed be confident that they can perform the change, and they may even have ideas on how it should be done, but for now, in the conversation, you want to explore to what degree the staff find it important to make this change. Similarly, if a group of employees recognize that a particular change is very important, are really excited about supporting the change, and look forward to doing so, but do not know how to start or how to make the change happen, then the sense of importance is very high, but organizational confidence is low. You would then explore the staff's strengths, confidence, and past successes and discuss how competencies could be developed.

You want to remember to build on the foundation you have already established. You also want to remember that often the organization already has the motivation and that change talk is intertwined in the conversation. You can simply reflect it back and ask the staff to elaborate more. Evoking change talk can be as simple as asking for it. You do not have to be clever and come up with the perfect questions. You can simply ask your team or staff open questions. If you want to evoke around desire, you might pose the following questions about desire to them, thinking of words like *wish* and *want* (regarding change).

- "What would you like to happen to improve the quality of the services we deliver?"
- "What does your team wish to improve?"
- "What do you as a team wish could happen?"
- "What difference would you as a team like to make when at work?"

If you want to evoke around ability, you need to think about what the organization as a whole can do, what the staff believe that they are capable of doing, and what the staff believe could happen if the organization decided to make this change. You might ask questions, such as the following:

- "What can your team offer?"
- "What skills and competencies would your team like to leverage more?"
- "What ideas do you have to make the competencies in the team grow?"
- "What do you think is possible with the team and resources you have?"

If you want to evoke around reasons, you need to get to the specific "why." You may ask if/then questions, such as:

- "If we let the overall goal of the organization be a guiding point, how can the team better support the goal?"
- "If the team did try out that idea, what would be the benefit of it?"
- "What are the advantages if the organization should decide to make this change? Or what would be the disadvantages if we decided to not make this change?"

If you want to evoke around need, you want to think about your organization's level of urgency in making a change. You may ask questions, such as the following:

- "What do you see as needing to change to accomplish the mission of the organization?"
- "What has to change?"
- "How soon do you think this change needs to happen?"

Helping your staff envision a changed future is another way to elicit change talk. In asking questions such as the following, you want your staff to think about, and tell you, how the work they do might be different after a change.

- "If our organization succeeds in making this change, what do you hope might be different in relation to the quality of the services delivered?"
- "What should our services be like in 5 years?"
- "What does your team wish to be different in the future?"

EXPLORING GOALS AND VALUES

You could also explore the change in relation to your organization's goals or values. Understanding what is most important to your company and how the staff see these values or goals being better achieved by this change is an important way to increase motivation. Showing that the organizational goals and values are at odds with the current status of the delivery of services is one of the most effective ways to resolve ambivalence. People may have originally join your organization because they need the job or the salary or because the job fits in with their daily life. But most often the reason employees stay in your company is because they find it a meaningful way to spend their professional time. In other words, they feel proud of their work and a part of something greater than themselves because they believe in the mission and values of the organization. Daniel Pink (2009) explains that the key to employee motivation involves creating a workplace culture in which employees can devote their efforts to becoming better and better at something that matters, a trajectory of improvement that connects their quest for excellence to a larger purpose.

When deciding about shifting tasks, procedures, or structures in the organization, it is important that the change is guided by the company's mission and its larger purpose, and is performed in accordance with company values. Your goal is to steer the conversation in a direction where both staff and management view the change through the prism of the organization's mission. You could ask:

- "What is most important to the organization? How does that issue relate to the change we are looking at?"
- "What are our goals here in the workplace? How do you see this issue in relation to these goals?"
- "What do you consider to be the most important values in our organization? How do you view these values in relation to this issue?"
- "With this change in mind, how might it help us live our organizational values more fully?"

RESPONDING TO CHANGE TALK

What do you do when you hear change talk in your organization? How do you respond? Again, just as in the case of MI with individuals, you already know how: You show the organization what you hear. You reflect and acknowledge what has been shared. You affirm the efforts and enthusiasm presented to you, and you keep exploring in the direction of change. In other words, you use the same skills that you have been using all along. You keep offering open-ended questions, affirmations, reflections, and summaries, only now you are selectively focused. You use your EARS skills, just like you would with individuals. You selectively ask for exploration or elaboration of change talk (E). Affirm strengths, positive intentions, or change attempts (A). Reflect the sense of importance, confidence, and the change talk you hear that supports the mission and values of the organization (R). And you summarize and connect up the elements of change talk that appear in responses from all areas of the organization—individual staff members, teams, management groups, and customers (S). Many of the strategies previously mentioned are open-ended questions that focus on—or even ask for—change talk. You do not need to persuade and struggle with your staff. It may even become fun to steer change processes, and it is a great feeling when you can say that you and your organization implemented the change together, instead of the change being something that you feel you forced upon it.

MOBILIZING CHANGE TALK

Remember the analogy used by Miller and Rollnick (2013), describing the movement toward change as climbing over a hill (see Figure 9.1 in Chapter 9)? Once you hit the peak and start hearing commitment language, or mobilizing change talk, it is all downhill. It becomes much easier, and you can focus on planning and initiating the course of action. Our way uphill takes more effort because you are helping the organization prepare by talking about change, by understanding the ambivalence, and by gently steering it in the direction of the most relevant change or place to start. In the process, you have also continuously kept an eye on sustain talk and either put it to rest or learned from it, without letting it overwhelm or stop the process, while at the same time evoking change talk. When you start hearing commitment to change, you move downhill. Uphill, most of what you did was to help the organization resolve its ambivalence about desiring change or believing itself capable of it. When you begin to hear commitment language, the ambivalence in the organization is likely about to be resolved. Commitment language indicates the imminent likelihood of action, and that it is time to assess readiness to move to planning.

How does commitment language in organizations sound? Just as with individuals, commitment language expresses a commitment to change, a willingness to plan or, indeed, even the start of planning, hinting at steps aimed at trying the new ideas. You can hear both preparatory talk (DARN) and activation, or mobilizing, talk (CAT) in organizations, too, just as you can when you talk about change with an individual. CAT in organizations could be a team that reports back to you about its discussions on how to start implementation. It may be the staff discussing how the thinking informing the change is being received by clients or customers. Or it could be the staff describing to you how they have started preparing for the upcoming change. The important point is to notice the difference between when the organization (or a part of it) is just considering a change and when the organization (or a part of it) is gearing up to take action. The latter development signals that you can move to the planning process that we discuss in the next chapters.

SUMMARY

Cultivating change talk is tricky in organizations. Understanding how groups and people may respond differently to the same change can help guide your path to evoking change. Evoking and cultivating change language in and from the organization involves several strategies. Having an infrastructure for conversations, platforms for collective communication, and companywide conversations are central. The use of strategic reflecting back to the entire organization what is said that points in the direction of change is important. The leader should, however, always also pay attention to sustain talk and to the fear and anxiety in any part of the organization in order to put them gently to rest without creating resistance.

Organization Vignette

The large outpatient alcohol treatment facility in which Marie had a leadership role was focusing on improving the quality of its treatment. Marie was engaging her staff in improving overall client outcome performance. Now that the team has a clear focus and a shared understanding, let's see how she led the evoking process.

In order to enhance compliance with treatment, prevent premature client dropout, and improve treatment outcomes (the number of clients not drinking at 3 months following treatment start), the audit team narrowed the series of improvement areas to the following: acute treatment (detoxification and treatment of withdrawal symptoms), involvement of the client's significant others in treatment, information material provided to clients, and training of the staff in evidence-based treatment methods.

> MARIE: (*to the audit team*) Tell me, what are the most important reasons for improving our delivery of acute treatment?
>
> NURSE: If we do not manage detoxification well, unmanaged withdrawal symptoms increase the likelihood that clients will start drinking again.
>
> SOCIAL WORKER: If the client and his family do not know what is going to happen during the acute phase, he is likely to drop out. We should make sure that both he and his family are well informed.

The members of the audit team offered multiple reasons for improving acute treatment, and Marie noted them all in the meeting minutes. While writing, she projected the text onto the large screen, allowing all members of the team to read along and asking them to correct her if she had misunderstood something or written it down incorrectly.

> MARIE: Okay, if we decided to improve acute treatment, do we feel capable of doing that? (*evoking confidence*)

The audit team members claimed that it was possible. The organization had the doctors, the nurses, and the resources that were needed. Marie noted this in the minutes.

> MARIE: Okay, if we are going to focus on improving acute treatment, are there specific parts of that treatment that we need to consider because changes there could create problems for other areas of our services? (*open-ended question, asking for change talk*)
>
> NURSE: Yes, there are. I'm glad you've mentioned this. If acute treatment is finalized too quickly, clients may start the planned treatment phase before they are, in fact, really ready for it. We need to make sure that we plan the transition from acute treatment to planned treatment properly.

Marie thanked the nurse and put her comments in the minutes. She then read aloud all the arguments for improvement (reflecting change talk) and mentioned that a change in how the acute treatment phase was performed should include considerations about how to integrate the acute phase and the phase of planned treatment.

SELF-REFLECTIVE EXERCISE. EVOKE WITH YOUR ORGANIZATION

You know that you have an understanding of your organizational ambivalence and a focus. If you identified more than one focus in the last exercise, choose just one for now to use in this process exercise (and in the related planning exercise in Chapter 12). You can practice the evoking and planning processes with more areas of focus later. You will continue to the engaging process of reflecting understanding and will gently guide the conversation to this focus as you continue the evoking process.

With your team assembled, and the clearly defined focus now on the whiteboard, ask your team members to share their thoughts on why this change is important and their confidence in the collective organization's ability to make it happen. Your conversation can be free flowing, and these evoking questions can be used as guides. Always remember to continue the engaging process too by reflecting your understanding through sharing with your team the themes you are hearing or writing them on the whiteboard.

The *goal* of this process is to build a sense of the importance and confidence needed to make the change in the target area (focus) upon which you have just agreed. Remember the goal is not to fix or solve the problem or to give advice. It can get hard at this stage to avoid doing so because your team might start sharing ideas or solutions. You want to reflect your understanding when this happens, but not yet move to planning action until you hear readiness.

Remember, the change language the team members share with you cues you as to whether they are just thinking about change (desire, ability, reasons, or need to change) or are committed to change (commitment, activation, or taking steps). You may continue evoking for a little while and, if you hear commitment, you can always check it out and if appropriate move to the next exercise to begin planning.

First post your mission and values. Before you turn to the evoking questions, ask the group to say out loud what your organization's mission is and what values it holds. It is a good idea to post these comments on the whiteboard also, so you can keep them in mind, next to your focus, as you continue evoking.

You can use the following questions to help guide the evoking process. Depending on how your team members judge the importance of this change or their confidence in making it happen, you may find that you use some questions more than others. That is fine. Just keep in mind that the goal is to build a sense of importance and confidence so your team feels ready to make the change. Both are needed and necessary.

Questions to Guide Evoking

Remember to reflect understanding before asking more questions.

Importance (Questions to Explore and/or Increase Importance [Reasons/Need/Desire])

- "What makes this change important to you and/or our organization?"
  - Reflect what you understand. "Tell me more about that. . . . What else?"
- "What reasons do we have for making this change? What reasons do we have for not staying as we are now?"
  - Reflect what you understand. "Tell me more about that. . . . What else?"
- "When do you or your team think this change needs to happen? How urgent do you feel this change is?"
  - Reflect what you understand.
- "In what ways do you see this change improving upon our mission or demonstrating our values?"
  - Reflect what you understand. "Tell me more about that. . . . What else?"

Confidence (Questions to Explore and/or Increase Confidence [Ability])

- "If we did decide to make this change [the focus], how confident would you feel about our organization's, your team's, and your own ability to carry out the change?"
  - Reflect what you understand. "Tell me more about that. . . . What else?"
- "If we did decide to make this change, what ideas do you have already about how we could do that? Tell me more about that."
  - Reflect what you understand. "Tell me more about that. . . . What else?"
- "How do you envision we could make this happen?"
  - Reflect what you understand. "Tell me more about that. . . . What else?"

- ▨ "What ideas have you already thought of that you or your team could do to make this happen?"
- ▨ "What kinds of things will need to be in place for this to come about?"
- ▨ "What might make it easier for you to make this change?"
- ▨ "What other resources might be helpful to the team and our organization to make this happen at this point?"

Later, after you have had this conversation, reflect on the process.

- ▨ What did you notice?
- ▨ What did you notice in what your team members shared relating to the importance of the change and their confidence in making the change?
- ▨ Were there times when you found it hard not to give advice or solutions? If so, what are your thoughts about why it was harder at those moments?
- ▨ Were there times it was easier to listen and guide? What did you notice about those times?

PART V

PLANNING

CHAPTER 11

Planning with Your Employee

The last process in an MI conversation is planning, a process with which leaders are typically well acquainted. Leaders are trained on how to develop measurable and effective plans, to execute goals, and to hold employees accountable. There are definitely skills and specifics you likely have learned that will help you in the planning part of an MI conversation.

The most important intention to keep in mind in the MI planning process is that planning is done by the employee. Helping employees through the planning process means helping them come up with a plan that they are willing to follow now that they have decided to make this particular change. It means that the leader helps employees think about what they might need to consider, put into action, or modify as they take steps to make this change. The development of a plan is not intended as a means of "holding them accountable." Rather, the plan is a tool for employees to use to help them succeed. Employees may not even need you to help them plan. They may want to work on their plan on their own. It is not uncommon for people to make a decision to change and simply move forward without the planning process. Sometimes just working through and resolving their ambivalence is enough for employees to become ready and able to make the change.

ARE THEY READY TO PLAN?

Before addressing the questions of whether the employee wants to plan and whether she wants to plan with you, it is important to first evaluate what the employee has shared thus far. Leaders typically like to solve problems, and, as discussed previously, often consider this responsibility to be the most fundamental part of their role. They are often tempted to jump to the planning process before their staff are ready. They tend to want to speed things along in order to actually see something change. However, if leaders push when employees are still ambivalent, the result is often resistance. Deep in all of us lies the belief that we only embark on something new when we feel pretty sure that it is something we can do and that it is what we want. If an individual is in doubt, she pauses. And if she feels pushed, she resists. At this stage of the conversation, the leader should avoid pushing the employee and trying to persuade her to launch into making the change. Instead, it is much more helpful to focus on the employee's language. What is the employee telling you? What are you hearing? If you hear mobilizing change language (commitment: "*I will . . . *"; activation: "*I plan to . . . *" ; or taking steps: "*I have already . . . *"), you can explore whether the employee has made the shift from thinking about and considering the change to indicating that she is ready, willing, and able to move forward. There are many ways you can assess whether the employee has shifted her thinking, but it may be as simple as checking out a hunch. You might reflect, "You are really ready to do this"; "You have decided you are going to make this change." If the employee answers in the affirmative, you can ask if she would like to talk more specifically about how to make the change. Again, in a collaborative process, it is the employee who should decide whether she is ready to move to the planning process. The leader should not push her further than she wants to go. You could ask, "Would it be helpful if we thought about this change you have decided to make and how you might best set yourself up to be successful?" or "Would you like to spend a few minutes thinking through your plan to make this change happen?"

It is important to be aware that often employees will move back and forth between readiness and reluctance to change if they are even the slightest ambivalent. They may become more ready to change during the MI conversation, but when they get closer to actually carrying out the change, they might feel ambivalent again. This is a sign to the leader to slow down a bit and backtrack a process or two. The transition through the four processes is both linear and recursive, and you move through them in order, building on the preceding one. But you also return to any previous process according to what you hear from the employee. We typically draw an analogy between this process and two dancers dancing up and down a staircase. Ginger Rogers and Fred Astaire spring to mind. When you hear commitment language or signs of readiness, you can move toward planning. If you hear ambivalence, however, you might want to move back to engaging or evoking. And if you are not sure, you can ask key questions to assess the employee's readiness. Such questions might include:

- "Where does that leave you?"
- "What are you thinking about at this point?"
- "I wonder what you might decide to do."

WHAT IF THE EMPLOYEE IS ALREADY COMMITTED?

There are certainly also times when your employee might come to you in order just to plan. He may already have resolved how to make this change, be committed, and may just need help with the planning part. You need not necessarily spend a lot of time on evoking or focusing. You may simply want to understand why the employee has decided to make the change, why it is important to him, and why he believes he can. It is important to keep these beliefs center stage during the planning process. Having the employee hold on to his own reasons for making the change and to his own ideas about how he can change is the fuel needed to move through the planning part of the change process, especially when the going get hard, or if he does not succeed at first. When we described this process once in a training, one of the attendees said, "I get it." This person was pregnant at the time, and she observed, "It is like when I am exercising. I hate exercising. But when I am exercising, and I want to stop or don't even want to start, I chant, 'It's for the baby, it's for the baby,' and I keep going." Exactly. The leader wants to help the employee say out loud what his "for the baby" is—not so that the leader may know, but so that the employee will have his beliefs about the change at the heart of his thinking.

Imagine the situation for yourself. If you decided to do something new that is important to you for the first time, how would you feel? You might feel excited, scared, nervous, or exposed. You hope it will go well, but you cannot be sure. Brené Brown (2012) describes these emotions as signs of vulnerability. That when you try something new, you put your-self out there, and you're all in, even though you cannot be sure of the outcome (Brown, 2017). Have the employee say out loud why she would want to do this. Why would she put herself in a position of vulnerability, risk, emotional exposure, and uncertainty? Why is this change so impor-tant to her, and why does she believe that she can pull it off? This change language helps her stay focused and able to carry on even when she feels uncertain and unsure.

Let's look at an example. Carl worked on a hospital unit, and was leading a team that was experiencing a lot of conflict. The team was made up of very talented and passionate people, each of them very keen for the team to be successful. But it was also their passion that led to conflict in their day-to-day work. Carl knew that he had to address the team's relationship dynamics. He knew that the team needed to set aside a day to work through the conflicts and struggles that were getting in the way of the team accomplishing its goals, and he was resolved to make it happen. He also knew that the team would have to have tough conversations, and that the team members, including himself, had to look at how each of them contributed to the team's problems, apologize, take responsibility, and commit to a new way of interacting for the greater good. Carl also knew, as the leader, that this meant that he had to go first and model that it was okay to be vulnerable and hear what others needed to say about his own performance. He had to be willing to hear how he was not supporting the team and how he might need to change. He was committed to having this conversation. He was committed to doing whatever it took to get the team back to a place of success. Yet, he was also scared. He worried that the conversation might make things worse. He worried that he might not be able to handle all the strong emotions that would surface. But he also knew that the only way to move forward was to hold this off-site meeting and try. When the morning of the meeting came, and he walked into the room, he paused for a moment. "Why am I even doing this?" he asked himself. He reflected, "I do not want my team to suffer any more. I don't want to suffer either. We are all tired of coming to work every day unhappy because of all the stress this team dynamic creates. I really want my team to know that I care about them. I want them to know that they matter and their work matters. I also want to show them that being open, vulnerable, and willing to take responsibility and make a change is hard but also doable." These "whys," along with his confidence that he could pull it off, enabled him to walk into the room and start the meeting. It is also what he reflected on when the conversations were emotional and difficult, and he just wanted to give up.

It is both the "whys" and the confidence to move forward that helps individuals to make changes that are hard and not always enjoyable. If you have ever tried to lose weight, quit smoking, or start exercising, we guess that you can recognize this process too. Understanding it before moving to planning is critical.

HOW TO HANDLE "FAILURE"

Before we discuss the process of planning and the steps involved, let's consider for a moment how to look at "failure." It is well known that "failure" is part of the change process. In most engineering programs, students are taught how to fail, fail fast, fail again, and fail better. This approach is taught as a way of communicating that the only way to do something new is to fail and to keep going. Achieving complete success the first time around is highly unlikely. You may see improvement, in the form of steps taken toward the goal, and yet the issue at the center of the change might still be there. When you work through planning with your employee, you can address this roadblock directly and discuss with her how she might evaluate progress toward her goal and how she will measure success. But first, it is important for leaders to consider how they and the organization really think about failure.

Donna was working with an employee, Kathy, who was very passionate about her work. Kathy often let her emotions drive her behavior and her decisions. Her strong feelings made it hard for others to have discussions with her, because they felt that she was uninterested in their thoughts and too overzealous to debate an idea. Donna and Kathy talked about her emotions and how they were impeding her goal of working collaboratively with other team members. Kathy was actively working to improve. She wanted very much to work with others, consider their ideas, share her own, and come up with collaborative goals. Kathy acknowledged that her passions often got the better of her, but averred that she wanted to improve and actively worked to make that happen. As her supervisor, Donna saw tremendous improvement when she watched Kathy in team meetings. Donna observed times when Kathy stopped defending her own line of thinking, concentrated on her breathing, became curious, and asked others to share their views and help her understand. Donna could tell that the situation was not a comfortable one for Kathy. She could also see how much effort Kathy was putting into making this shift and how much her overall team interactions had changed for the better. What was disappointing, though, was that when Kathy had moments of slipping back into her old habit of shutting down a conversation or overpowering her conversation partners, the team or other staff discounted all the progress she had made. It was as though the team did not even see Kathy's improvements. Kathy kept working at getting better but it was hard for her. Donna and Kathy often talked in their meetings about how demanding it was and together modified her plan to help her keep improving. However, because of the team response and the lack of acknowledgment of her improvements, Kathy ended up leaving the organization. Donna considered her departure a huge loss, not only for the team and the organization, but also for all those left behind. It signaled very clearly that if you did not improve the first time, or if you failed, you were on your own and the team was not going to help or support you. What message did this send to the next person who might want to try and make a change or improve in some way? How were the rest of Donna's staff going to be able to make needed improvements?

The leader, in our view, is responsible for setting the tone and for creating an environment where change is truly possible. A big part of this is about establishing expectations around change and how the organization responds or reacts when people are on the path to change. In trying to create an environment for growth, a leader also needs to create an environment where the employees are safe to fail along the way. Employees need to feel that they can allow themselves to be vulnerable, knowing that the team and the company will support them. It also means the leader must take the initiative. The leader needs to model his or her own vulnerability and professional growth. Workplace culture starts and ends with the leader. If the leader believes that the staff are expected to change, she also has to be open to changing herself.

DEMONSTRATING THAT IT IS SAFE TO SHOW VULNERABILITY

How does your organization respond to "failure"? How would you respond? How do you establish an environment that accepts trial and error? How do you talk about or model the fact that change includes unsuccessful attempts? We all know that slipping back into old habits is part of the process. How many of us have been on a diet and yet had a "cheat day," or moments of not sticking to the diet 100%? Yet we still lose weight and keep moving forward as we continue to lose more. Perfection is not required to be able to make long-term successful changes. It is the same with growth in the workplace. If the employee is trying something new, she will make mistakes and slip back into old patterns every now and then. This backsliding does not mean that she is not improving, or not changing, or won't someday be past this issue altogether and onto her next change.

Recognizing employees when they backslide and supporting them in getting back on track is an important part of the process. There are several ways to communicate to your employee and organization that this is an expected part of implementing new behaviors. It may, for instance, be helpful to talk about "relapsing into old habits" openly with your staff, using personal examples. The talks could include telling stories about some of your own relapses and chuckling about how long it takes to fully become comfortable with new routines. You might openly ask your staff to point out to you when you fall back into a work behavior that you had decided to improve.

WHAT IF FAILURE IS NOT AN OPTION?

This important question typically arises around performance issues or when a problem has gone on for so long that time has run out and the change has to be implemented right away. This is likely a situation in which MI is not the communication style to use. You might instead have to set up a progressive discipline conversation around expectations, explaining why and by when this change has to occur, and what will happen if it does not. You might also ask how you can help the employee succeed. It is important to remember, though, that the employee still has her autonomy to choose to make this change. She can decide to change, or she can decide to accept the consequences. Either way, she remains in the position to decide. You cannot decide for her. Your role is to be empathic, compassionate, understanding, and clear. It is not helpful to pretend that the issue does not exist or that this is not the reality of the situation.

WHAT IS GOOD PLANNING?

The planning process helps the employee work through what might happen in the change process and prepare ahead of time. People do not tend to achieve the change they want by jumping into action without planning. The first time they fail, they give up and say, "See, I can't do it." If the leader helps the employee to think in advance about all that goes into making a change, she is more likely to overcome the obstacles when they arise. There are many ways to formulate a plan, but there are some specific guidelines that can help steer the employee in developing strategies and thinking through the many contingencies that might arise when executing a plan.

Specific, Observable, and Measurable

A helpful plan is specific, rewarding, and open to revision. By *specific,* we mean that it is observable and measurable. How might your employee know that she has actually achieved her goal? If a goal is not specific but general, it will be hard for the employee to know whether she is making progress. For instance, if the employee says, "I want to improve my management approach," what does that mean? How will she know if she is getting better or getting worse?

When you help your employee create a plan that is specific, you might, for instance, ask the employee, "How will you know when you have reached this goal? What will be different?"

The employee may reply, "I will know that my management approach has improved if I am able avoid reacting emotionally to my staff, seeking instead to understand their views so that we can solve problems together," or "I will know that I have improved when my team survey results show an increase in the percentage of my staff who say they feel cared about and supported by me, and when jointly we are achieving almost all of our deliverables on time." The goal is to help the employee have a clear view of what she is working toward and whether she is making progress or might need to revisit and revise the plan.

The likelihood of success also increases if the employee's plan is *rewarding*. This means that the progress the employee makes, and/or the improvement itself, is rewarding, or that she specifically develops ways to reward her efforts along the way, such as celebrating small milestones. For instance, in the example of Kathy discussed earlier, every time she stopped talking in a conversation where she felt she was overpowering her peers and listened to them instead, she felt rewarded by the reaction from the team. However, sometimes the emotional energy it took to keep trying was draining, so she would journal how many times a day she was making the choice to shift; when she'd done so at least once a day every day, she brought in her favorite doughnuts for herself and the team.

Feeling rewarded is unique to each person, so it is important to think about what works for the person in question. Sometimes the improvement itself is rewarding, whereas at other times, finding ways to measure and reward the milestones can help the employee persevere. You might ask, "In your plan, how might you build in rewards along the way? What feels rewarding to you? And is the reward sustainable and doable?" Again, it does not matter what the reward is—only that it is experienced as such by the employee.

A well-functioning plan is also *open to revisions*. Leaders know this well. Often leaders start out with a very specific company plan and when they start to implement it something changes or does not work, so they modify the plan and create a new one. Rarely does the first plan address all the challenges that may arise. The same is true with an employee's plan for change. Rarely is the first plan complete. Sometimes the steps that the employee develops at first end up not being helpful at all. So, you could discuss with your employee how she will know if it is time to revise or rework her plan. And how might she incorporate these revisions into the evaluation of her progress? How will she evaluate the plan itself, and not just whether she is making progress?

In order to help your employee think about how to make the plan open for revisions, you may ask:

- "How will you evaluate whether your plan is working for you, as distinct from whether you are achieving your goal?"
- "If you feel the plan needs to be reworked, how do you imagine doing that?"

If we are writing down the plan, we might even include the answers to these questions.

Clear, Concrete, and Achievable Goals

Any good plan includes specific goals that are *clear, concrete,* and *achievable*. Just as the plan needs to be specific, so do the goals. If the employee says she wants to improve her interactions with her team members, how might she make that goal clear and concrete? You might ask, "How will you know that your interactions with your team have improved?" The employee might say, "I will know because I will spend more time listening to their ideas rather than arguing for my own." Then you might ask, "How will you know that you are doing that?" The employee might say, "Every time a colleague shares an idea, I will reflect what I take their idea to be until they agree with my understanding. Only then will I share my own idea. I will do this consistently over the next 2 months." This turns the idea of improving relationships into a *clear* and *concrete* goal. She can now measure the change, and can determine whether it happened or not.

The plan should also be *achievable*. When it is clear and concrete, you can help the employee to decide if it is achievable. How confident is the employee that she can do this? For instance, in our example, how confident is she that she can reflect *every* time a colleague shares an idea? It may be that she feels this is definitely achievable, or she may say that reflecting three out of four times would improve the relationship. Remember, plans can always be revisited and revised. So, if it feels achievable to aim for a 50% improvement, she could certainly start there, and if it turns out to be even easier than she thought, she can increase the frequency.

When planning, it is important to give the employee an opportunity to reflect on what feels achievable. For instance, when a person wants to lose weight, he may tell himself that he would like to lose 30 pounds in 30 days. This goal is not likely to be realized and was often the reason why he previously stopped trying and reverted back to old habits. However, when he thinks about whether his plan is realistic and opts instead to try and lose 1 to 2 pounds a week, he might feel that this goal is actually possible. It falls short of what he wants, but it is achievable, and it will get him to his actual goal of losing 30 pounds, just a bit slower than he might wish. You can also revisit the topic of revising the plan if the goal is too aggressive. You can ask how the employee will know that he might want to revisit the plan to check if his time frame for achieving the goal needs to be revised. He does not need to revise the overall goal, but might find that the time frame for achieving it is hurting his motivation to continue and it might need to be reworked.

The Employee's Reasons for the Change

So far, the planning process we've discussed is probably similar to other types of planning strategies you have seen or used before. The only possible difference is that the focus of the planning process must be a plan that the employee herself has created. In the MI planning process, in addition to ensuring that the employee has authored the plan, you also want to be sure to specifically ask about and clarify the *reasons for change*. You may suggest that the employee articulate, write down, or clarify her reasons—her unique specific motivation—for committing to this goal. You could also take a minute to connect her reasons to her life goals and values. Remember that the employee's reasons for change are the fuel that will keep her moving forward, even when things get hard or she does not see immediate success.

Steps/Strategies

It is also helpful for the employee to incorporate *steps* and *strategies* into her plan. Depending on the level of complexity of the goal, there are times when a plan does not have to be very detailed. Sometimes it is simply enough to have a clear goal, the reason the employee wants to do something and believes she can, and then just get on with it. However, more often than not the goals are complex and are not reached quickly. By having a plan with specific steps, within a time frame that the employee sees as doable, she can see that she is making progress toward a larger goal.

For instance, let's say your employee, Peter, has decided that he wants to improve his overall ability to manage his projects in a more strategic and detailed way. The goal is not likely to be achieved just by making this decision. Peter might need to take a class on project management. He might need to seek coaching or training from a colleague who is experienced at managing complex and detailed projects. He might try different approaches to using his new skills or knowledge in the context of his projects and get feedback on how he is performing, and whether the approaches are working.

- *Goal.* The goal is to improve his project management abilities.
- *Clear, concrete, and achievable.* Peter will know that he has achieved this goal if his projects are meeting deadlines 90% of the time, all the details are addressed, and strategies are developed around all details.
- *Reasons.* He wants to make this change because he wants to advance to a director position and knows this skill set is necessary to get the promotion. He also wants to do a better job now with his projects because he dislikes being told that they are not acceptable. He does not like the feeling he has when a project fails and he sees the negative impact it has on his team.
- *Steps/strategies.* His first step is to find and take a class recommended by others. He will do some research and have a list of classes within 14 days. He will seek recommendations from his peers as soon as he has this list, and he will have their recommendations within 30 days. He will register for the class and will take the class within 60 days.

If Peter is helped to develop these specific steps and strategies, he can evaluate whether he is making progress, even though he has not yet implemented the new project management skills. He also now has a specific plan that he can reflect on and modify as needed. What if no class is available in the next 60 days? Or the best class to take will be offered at a time beyond the next 60 days? He can easily come back to modify the time frame and still move forward.

Support

Another important part of being successful with a plan is looking for and securing *support*. When you are developing a plan with the employee, it is a great time to talk about how others can help, and to see what the employee believes would be helpful. You might say, "When you think about your goal, who might be able to be genuinely helpful to you in this effort?" or "Who could offer you help in achieving this goal?"

If the employee can identify someone or something that might be of help, you might assist her in clarifying what specific help she wants, how she might solicit it, and how she will know if the support is actually beneficial. A manager shared with us that when she was on a diet, her partner would often comment on what she was eating in an attempt to help. Her partner thought that reminding her that she was on a diet would help her make better food choices. He would say, "Are you sure you want the nachos? I know you want to lose weight and that you want me to support you." For her, this comment was not helpful at all. On the contrary, it only made her crave more nachos, and why not also a margarita. Her partner thought he was being supportive, as she'd requested. However, what would have really supported her would have been not to have the nachos in the house to begin with. So when her partner shopped for groceries, it would have been better if he refrained from buying nachos, which are harder for her to resist. Not buying and bringing home these snacks was a way he could support her. What is helpful and supportive is personal and unique to each person, and other people do not always know what will work. You want to help your employee identify what is helpful and communicate that to others who are willing to be supportive.

Removing Barriers

Plans encounter hurdles and barriers. Since your employee is now sharing that she is ready and willing to move forward, you can look at these hurdles, barriers, and strategies for coping with them with her. Had you brought up this problem at an earlier stage, it might have created more anxiety and resistance to change. It could have made her reflect on how hard the change is, and it could have resulted in her feeling less ready to change and in focusing more on sustain language. But because you are now in a process in which she has talked herself into the change she wants, it is time to talk through and anticipate what she might do when she experiences the hurdles as well as other unforeseeable barriers that are likely to present themselves. You can work with the employee to think about what might get in her way and what she will do when problems arise. You might say things like:

- "What do you imagine might get in your way? How might you handle that if it happens?"
- "What do you already know will be challenging? How might you plan to handle that if it happens?"
- "Who do you imagine might push back on this change? How might you handle that pushback?"

Let's revisit Peter's goal of improving his project management, described earlier. Peter shares that he thinks making time for working toward this goal is going to be hard, because he has so many other daily tasks that need attention. He fears he will get lost in his daily duties and miss deadlines. He also says that he knows that when he makes this change, which involves including more details in projects that he manages, his team will not want to do the work of looking at more detailed plans. He thinks they're inclined to just jump in and get going, and so asking them to focus in the early part of the plan will be hard. So, knowing about these two areas, you could ask Peter how he might handle this problem when it happens. He might reply:

"I can schedule an hour on my calendar each week to dedicate to this. Usually, if I schedule something, it happens. I just need to put it on the calendar and tell myself that that appointment is as important as all my other appointments. For my team, I think if I lead a conversation about my own goal and our team goals and talk about why project management needs to improve, and my own plan to improve it, it would help. Then I could ask them how they might plan around this issue, because we are clear that this is our new way of operating, and then get their ideas on how to move forward. I could do that before I go to the training and again when I return with the details of what we have to do."

Your Role in Support

It is also important to clarify whether the employee wants help with his plan. The leader should not assume that following up on or asking about how the plan is going will always be helpful. The employee might name you as someone who could help, and he has some ideas about how you might contribute. You might then consider taking on this role and committing to do what he asks. He might also ask for something you do not think you can do. In that case, you might say, "My being part of your support is important to you, and you have ideas on what that might look like. I wonder if we could talk about what I think I am able to do now, or should we come back to how I can help after we have finished with the rest of the plan?"

If your employee does not mention you as part of the plan, you might simply say, "How would you like me to support you, and please know that I have no perceived expectation of what my role should be?" or "I am wondering how you would like me to support you in this. I know that we are likely to meet weekly and talk specifically about things related to this goal, so I would like to know what you would consider helpful from me."

You just want to be sure that you have considered what your role with the employee will entail and how you might help or prevent hurting his progress. Brenda asked this question of an employee who told her that if she asked about his progress on a regular basis, it would cause him a lot of stress, so he'd prefer that they set a specific schedule (every 30 days) to check in on his goal. He felt that this schedule gave him enough time to make progress without worrying that Brenda was thinking about his goal and assessing him every time they met. Setting his own schedule would allow him to come to the meeting prepared with his own evaluation of his progress. It also became part of the milestones and signs of success he set for himself. If they had not had this conversation, Brenda would not have known that asking weekly about his progress would make it worse for him. Brenda would have considered her asking how he is doing as support. The conversation also gave Brenda the opportunity to explain how she looked at and evaluated his and others' progress, explaining that she was not measuring improvement on every interaction but was rather looking at the overall gestalt of performance.

Your employees know that part of your job is to evaluate their performance. They are going to be naturally curious about how you go about the evaluation process and what your thoughts are. You are likely the one who makes decisions about promotions, hiring, firing, and pay raises. If that is the case, it is important at some point in your relationship to talk about this issue openly. Let your employees know how you evaluate performance, what you are looking for, and what you see as success. It is also important to establish a process of giving feedback on a regular basis. We have known many organizations in which feedback is only given once a year at annual review time, which is not helpful if feedback is not also given periodically. Your employees want to grow and want feedback to know where they need to focus. If you set up your relationship from the beginning by explaining that you see your role as being there to help them grow and to provide compassionate, honest, and clear leadership, you create the setting in which your employees actually improve. Discussing how you review performance, how best your employees can receive feedback, and how you view their current status enables them to know where to focus their growth efforts. I (C. M.) had an employee pay me a great compliment once when she said, "I always knew where I stood with you. I knew you valued me. I knew you thought I had a lot to offer. I also knew at any time how you viewed my performance. I never had to guess. I knew where you thought I was doing very well and where I needed to grow. I always knew you would do what you could to help me in any way you could. I have grown more under your supervision than with anyone I have ever worked with before." This level of buy-in and engagement is what we are hoping to achieve for all employees.

Elicit–Provide–Elicit

When you are thinking about steps and strategies, you might find that the employee hits a wall because she simply does not know what to do or how to move on. There might also be other times in the process that you have a creative idea that you think might help the employee. We previously discussed the importance of holding back your own ideas and of not trying to fix the employee's problem for her. This means not offering solutions and suggestions up front but evoking, trusting that the employee has her own solutions and ideas. However, this does not mean that you can never share your ideas. Actually, the planning process is a great time to share them, as long as you are sure that you do not overrule the employees' own ideas. One way of sharing ideas is by combining ideas with questions, a strategy sometimes referred to as *E-P-E,* or *elicit–provide–elicit.* To use the strategy, you start by first eliciting the employee's own ideas or experience. Then you can ask permission to provide further information, suggestions, or even advice. Finally, you end by again eliciting from the employee her response to the information or advice. Using the example with Peter and his project management goal, the conversation might sound like this:

Step 1: Elicit

- "What do you already know about learning project management skills? What things might you want to do to improve your project management?"
- "What ideas do you have on how to move forward in improving these skills? How likely is that to work?"

- "What have you tried in the past? How did that go?"
- "What have others suggested to help with this? What did you think about their suggestions?"

Step 2: Provide Information or Advice

- "Would it be okay if I shared an idea with you that you might or might not find helpful?"
  - Wait for permission.
- Then provide the idea.
  - "People I know that are great at project management have shared that attending training . . . "

or

  - "One option might be to work with someone on our team who is already good at this, and ask them to coach you."
- If possible, try to offer a menu of options and not just one option. This might sound like:
  - "I have heard of people taking an online training, attending a specific workshop that leads to a certification, working with a coach, or reading books on project management."

Step 3: Elicit the Employee's Response

- "What do you make of that? How does that sound?"
- "Which, if any, of these ideas makes sense to you?"

It may be that your advice or information is not helpful, or that the employee does not connect with it. That is okay. You do not want to push and try to convince the employee that your ideas are better than his own. Rather, you want just to introduce them into the employee's thinking and let him decide whether they are helpful or not. If they are not, fine, you simply continue to think together about what might be helpful instead. If they are helpful, you might ask what makes them helpful, and how the employee imagines he can add the idea to his plan or to his strategy. It is important to remember that this is still the employee's plan, his life, his change, and his decision. You are just helping him through the process.

Signs of Success

You may also help the employee identify *signs of success* along the way. It is unlikely that he will achieve his goal overnight, but he is likely to achieve specific parts of his plan on the way to the bigger goals. So, helping him set milestones sustains his commitment to the plan. Regarding Peter's better project management goal, maybe the milestones contribute to completing the training or to introducing the new way of managing projects to the team. These accomplishments could be two signs of success on the way to Peter being better at project management. He can see that if he has accomplished these two things he is on his way to the bigger goal. You want to build into the plan the specific milestones he will look to as a measure that he is making progress and is successful as he continues toward the ultimate goal.

Commitment to the Plan

Finally, you will want to *elicit commitment* to this plan. Often, this part of planning is missed because leaders think that because someone has committed to a change, it means that they are committed to the plan. These can, however, be two very different kinds of commitment. It is helpful to conclude the conversation by asking the employee to describe his plan, and then ask for commitment—not in order to hold him accountable, but in order to support his decision and increase his commitment to change. You might ask:

- "Is this what you are going to do?"
- "How confident are you that you can carry out this plan?"
- "What is your next step?"
- "What will you do now?"

If you do not hear the commitment to the plan that you expected, it may indicate there is more work to be done. What is making the employee hesitant? It could be part of the plan that needs to be revised. You can either go back to the evoking process or look at the plan and talk through what makes him hesitant.

In summary, depending on the complexity and details associated with the change, you may or may not need all the elements of good planning. If the change is simple, then it might be enough that the employee just says, "I will." For instance, your manager wants to have a difficult conversation with an employee she has resisted having one with until now. She is actually fairly good at having difficult conversations when she decides to do so. Since your conversation resolved her ambivalence about having the conversation, she might say she will do it right away. The only detail you might need to pursue is when does she imagine having this conversation, and what will she do if she cannot have it then? However, if the goal is more complex or more difficult, then you are likely to want to consider the elements we just discussed:

- Plans that are specific, rewarding, and open to revision.
- Goals that are clear, concrete, and achievable.
- Employee's reasons to make this change.
- Steps/strategies to make this change.
- Support from others.
- Signs of success/milestones.
- Commitment to the plan.

WHAT IF YOU NEED A DIFFERENT PLAN?

What if you feel fine with supporting your employee in coming up with his own goals and plan, but all of a sudden you realize that his plan is not going to work for your organization's goals or for your own goals? Maybe you had not picked up on this conflict before, because you thought that if this person made changes in this particular area, it would be good for him and the organization. But when it turned into a specific plan, it became clear to you that his plan, time frame, or strategies simply will not work for you or the team. Maybe he wants to attend a training he cannot personally afford, and you also know that your department does not have training funds. Or maybe he thinks that he has a year to improve, and you know that if he does not improve sooner, you will need to start talking about the quality of his performance or suitability for the job. If, for whatever reason, you feel that his plan will not meet the organization's expectations, you could talk about it in an E-P-E format:

Elicit

You might say, "This goal makes a lot of sense, but before we work through the plan, I wonder if we could discuss a bit about what your understanding is of the organization's expectation around this goal?" The employee agrees. Then you ask, "What do you know about what the organization [or you, his supervisor] expects regarding this goal and the time frame needed to accomplish it?" The employee might reveal what you know or might reveal what he does not know.

Provide

You can then follow up with "Would it be okay if I shared what my understanding is about this expectation?" and then share the details of what you know.

Elicit

You end the E-P-E process by asking, "What do you make of that in terms of your goal and plan?"

It is important to engage your employee in this strategy because you want to make sure that he has all the information he needs to make informed plans and decisions. You can also use the E-P-E process if you find that your employee might need additional information or might present misinformation. The neat thing about this format is that just by asking "What do you already know about X?" you can hear whether the employee needs the information or not. Often when such questions are asked, the employee will share everything that the leader thought he needed to tell him. So, the leader's information was not needed. He already had it.

If *you* and the organization need a specific plan, and the employee does not have the freedom to make his own plan, then this point is also important to clarify and spell out. It also might mean that MI is not the appropriate tool in this situation. There are certainly times when your other leadership strategies will be more helpful.

SUMMARY

The planning process is the last process in the MI conversation with the employee. The plan should be the employee's own plan, and the leader may not always be an active part of the plan. The leader, however, can be helpful to the employee when guiding the planning process. The leader may also ask the employee how she can be helpful along the way, when the plan is being put into practice. Planning processes can vary, based on the complexity of the change, but in general should include (1) plans that are specific, rewarding, and open to revision; (2) goals that are clear, concrete, and achievable; (3) the employee's reasons to make this change; (4) the steps/strategies to make this change; (5) support from others; (6) the signs of success/milestones; and (7) commitment to the plan.

Employee Vignette

As you may recall, Susan was worried about being fired, and her worrying was getting in the way of her listening to new clients. She decided that over the next 30 days she was going to try to not focus on the clients' answers to whether they were interested in the program and instead just listen openly and calmly to really understand what the clients find helpful.

ASHLEY: Let me make sure I understand. You have decided that for the next 30 days that you are going to use the skills you have learned in training when interacting with your real clients. You are doing this, because it is really important to you to keep this job because you like your team and find what you are doing meaningful. You have also decided that you are not going to focus on whether you are improving while on the call. You are simply going to act as you do in training and not worry about whether the client wants the program. (*summary*) Is that right? Did I miss anything? (*open-ended question*)

SUSAN: That is right.

ASHLEY: Could we spend a few minutes talking about how you are going to do that, and what you might do if problems come up? (*asking for permission*)

SUSAN: Sure, that would be helpful.

ASHLEY: Imagine you are with a client tomorrow and are explaining the program to her. What do you imagine you will do? (*open-ended question, asking for change talk*)

SUSAN: Well, I guess I will just try to understand why she came here. What she was hoping to find. And explain how we help people, and then see what she thinks.

ASHLEY: What do you imagine you will do if you start worrying that she is going to not enroll in your program? (*open-ended question*)

SUSAN: Hmm. I guess, I will just refocus on what she is saying and reflect what I hear. Like I do in training. I will just redirect my attention to practicing reflective listening.

ASHLEY: Anything else? (*open-ended question*)

SUSAN: Hmm. I guess I can also get curious, and try to understand what she wants and is hoping for and let that guide me, even if it means she wants a different referral.

ASHLEY: So, if you feel that you are worried, you will reflect, get curious, and try to see how you can help the client find what she is looking for, regardless of whether that is our program. (*reflection*)

SUSAN: Yeah, that feels good. I can do that.

ASHLEY: How might you evaluate your progress toward doing that? Typically, people do not change overnight, so there might be times when you do worry a little while trying this new approach. So how might you evaluate your improvement? (*open-ended question*)

SUSAN: Well, if I enroll people, it's success.

ASHLEY: It is, but if I understand, you are worried that if you focus on whether people enroll as success, that gets in your way. (*reflection*)

SUSAN: That's true. Maybe instead I could evaluate after each session whether I did reflect and get curious, or whether I focused on them enrolling.

ASHLEY: How might you do that? (*open-ended question, asking for change talk*)

SUSAN: I guess I could keep track of each session and give myself a score, like 80% of the time I did reflect and 20% of the time I worried. Or something like that.

ASHLEY: So, after each session, trying to focus on whether you are using this new skill or approach will help you measure progress. (*reflection of commitment language*)

SUSAN: Yeah. I think that would help.

ASHLEY: What else? (*open-ended question*)

SUSAN: I guess in supervision, which is weekly, I could look at how often I am doing that, and how it is affecting meeting the overall expectations. So not focus on people enrolling daily anymore, but rather just in supervision.

ASHLEY: So, you will measure progress on your own based on whether you stay in this reflective space with clients, while measuring overall progress weekly with your supervisor. (*reflection of commitment language*)

SUSAN: Yeah. That would work.

ASHLEY: I wonder who might help you as you try to do this? And what that help looks like? (*open-ended question*)

SUSAN: Well, Jim, my supervisor, is very helpful. He always points out what I am doing well, and then has me practice where I get stuck. That helps a lot. One peer in particular is helpful, because she had a hard time at first but was able to get through it. She shares with me approaches she tried, and that is helpful. Some of my peers are not helpful, because they keep asking me about how many people I have enrolled and that just makes me anxious.

ASHLEY: So, you know who is not helpful and what help looks like. I wonder how you might talk with your peers about their role in helping you? (*open-ended question*)

SUSAN: Yeah, I could do that. I do know that they want me to be successful, so if I tell them to not ask me about my new clients or share how many new clients they have, they would agree. I also know that both my supervisor and that one particular peer would be happy to keep helping.

ASHLEY: So, you will let some of your peers know that you would like to avoid "new client" conversations, and your supervisor and your other peer will let them know how they are helping. *(reflection of commitment language)*

SUSAN: Yes.

ASHLEY: Sometimes what helps the planning is remembering why you are doing this at all. *(information)* I wonder how you think about that? Why is it important to you to get through this struggle and be able to do this job? *(open-ended question, asking for change talk based on values)*

SUSAN: It is for the clients. I know I can help them if I can just enroll them. I know they want help and are looking for help—they are just scared. I want to make this work because I want to help them.

ASHLEY: Great. So, let me make sure I got it all. You will focus on being open, calm, and curious with new clients. You will specifically focus on reflecting and being curious about what they want and letting that guide you in your first meetings. You will measure whether you are improving in this way by giving yourself a score for the percentage of time in which you are doing that in each session, while also reviewing weekly your overall goal with your supervisor. You will meet with your peers and supervisor to let them know how they can help. You are doing all this because it is very important to you to help your clients, and you know that you can and that they want the help. *(summary, including all the change and commitment talk that has been brought forward)* Did I miss anything? *(open-ended question)*

SUSAN: Nope, that sounds right.

ASHLEY: Great. How would you like my help, if at all, with this? *(open-ended question)*

SUSAN: I guess, if you wanted, you could check in with me and Jim in about 2 weeks and find out how it is going.

ASHLEY: That sounds great. I will do that.

SELF-REFLECTIVE EXERCISE. PLAN WITH YOUR EMPLOYEE

You now have an understanding of your employee's ambivalence and a focus, and you understand why this change is important to her and that she believes in her ability to carry it out. You will continue the process, bearing all this in mind. You will continue to engage by reflecting under-standing, gently guiding the conversation to the focus, and evoking as you move to planning.

If you are considering moving to the planning process, it should be based on the fact that you are hearing readiness (commitment language, taking steps, or activation) from the employee. Keep in mind that at this point in the process it is not uncommon for people to revert back to an earlier process because they might be anxious now that they are getting closer to the change. That is fine. Just go back to the earlier process and continue. However, if you think the employee is ready, you want to start by confirming her readiness.

Continue the conversation with this person about the change. The conversation can be free flowing, and the planning questions can be used as guides. Always remember to continue the engaging process too by reflecting understanding when the person shares her thoughts.

Confirm readiness. You can check out your guess that the employee is ready by asking:

- "So, what do you think you will do?"
- "What do you think your next steps are?"
- "It sounds like you really are ready to do this. Would it be helpful if we talked about how you plan to make this happen?"

Guide through the plan. Once you are sure she is ready, you can use the following to guide the details of the plan. Remember that if the change is very simple, you might not need all these details, but the more complex the change, the more you and your employee might want to think about each part of the planning process together.

Remember that the goal is to have plans that are specific, rewarding, and open to revision.

- Now that you have decided to make this change, what specifically are you wanting to change? How will you know that you have achieved it? How will others know if you have achieved it?
- Does that goal seem achievable for you, or does it feel like a real stretch? (If it feels like a real stretch, how might you modify the goal so that you still achieve what you want but in a way that's within your grasp?)
- You can summarize for the employee all the reasons you have heard about why she wants to make this change. You can remind the employee that it is important to keep these reasons in mind as she continues with the plan. You might ask her in what ways can

she keep her "why" making this change her focus as she continues toward her goal.

■ What specifically will you do, by when, and with whom?

■ Who might support you as you make this change?

■ What does your support look like, and how might you let that person or persons know what you would like them to do to support you, and what you would prefer them not to do?

■ You can remind your employee that sometimes change takes time, and ask her how will she know she is making progress as she continues with the plan. What would be signs of success or milestones?

■ When would she want to revisit the plan to see if it needs modification or adjustment? How will she know if the plan needs to be modified?

Commit to the plan

■ Summarize the plan for the employee and ask if you missed anything.

■ Then ask if this is what she is going to do.

Later, after you have had this conversation, reflect on the process.

■ What did you notice?

■ What did you notice about your employee's readiness? How did you know she was ready? What did you hear or see?

■ What did you notice about your employee's ambivalence as you moved to planning? Did it resurface and, if so, how did you respond? If not, was there anything else you noticed?

■ Were there times when it was easier to listen and guide? What did you notice about these times?

■ How confident are you now in the employee's ability to carry out this plan and make this change?

CHAPTER 12

Planning with Your Organization

Unlike planning in MI with individuals, planning in organizations *is intended* to ensure that the leader is steering the company in the right direction, and to some extent is developed to *hold the whole organization accountable*. In other words, the plan is created for the organization rather than for the individual employee. The plan is typically known by everyone in the organization and is developed so that it is implemented in the best order and within a time frame that will most likely lead to success. Planning for organizational change is also developed in a shared decision-making format, in which leaders and employees have specific tasks. But before we plunge ahead, let us pause to consider a couple of questions.

IS THE ORGANIZATION READY TO PLAN?

As in the case of individuals, the first three questions are: Is the organization ready to plan? Do the staff want to plan with the leader? And how should the leader be involved in the planning? You can check whether you are hearing mobilizing change language (commitment language, activation, or taking steps) and determine whether your staff are ready, willing, and able to start planning. There are many ways that you can assess for change language with your organization. You might reflect to the organization, "We are really ready to do this"; "We feel that we have the knowledge we need to move forward." If the staff agree, you can then move to talking in more specifics about how to make the change. You may ask what is needed for the next step: "What would be helpful for us in continuing the planning process?" or "Would it be helpful for us to brainstorm about how to plan the change?"

When it comes to the specific changes, it is important to recognize that the staff members who work in the area where the change will take place are very likely to be the best ones to plan how to implement the change. In practice, this means that you want them to determine the steps needed to implement the change in their daily work routine. Your task is to help the staff think about what might need to be changed in their workflow and performance, and what might need to be modified in order to be successful. But you do not necessarily need to decide how the plan should be carried out; the staff are in the best position to develop the how.

When management participates in staff discussions of how to best organize, plan, and, in particular, carry out the specific tasks required of the staff, it tends *to limit* rather than stimulate staff discussion. When managers share their own ideas or focus on specific ideas in these discussions, they tend to steer toward the least promising ideas raised. This happens simply because the staff tend to believe that management's ideas are those that will win out in the end, no matter what the staff find best. If, instead, management or leaders let the staff work on their own during the proposal phase, *asking them* to bring a full proposal to the management team, the resultant ideas and proposals are far richer, more thoughtful, and easier to implement. This was an important lesson that we learned, and it taught us to carefully consider the roles that leaders and staff play in the planning processes.

It is also important to understand the importance of the leadership's role in the process. Although members of the staff are best at figuring out and planning the *how*, the leaders are needed to continuously communicate the overall goal and mission of the work, to offer support, secure resources, and ensure that deadlines are met. They need constantly to ensure that the process is moving ahead, to affirm and acknowledge the work that is being done, and to communicate the new process to the organization.

The leaders also need to keenly bear in mind that organizations—like individuals—may feel hesitant, even after a decision has been made and a plan is developed. People tend to bounce back and forth in confidence and determination as they move through the process. When your staff are trying to implement the change, ambivalence may arise again, which simply means you may need to listen again, and reflect and focus on cultivating change talk. In particular, the leaders need to remind the staff that during a normal process of change on the way to improvement, people typically go through a phase in which they perform worse than normal. This phase is often called *the valley of despair,* pictured in Figure 12.1.

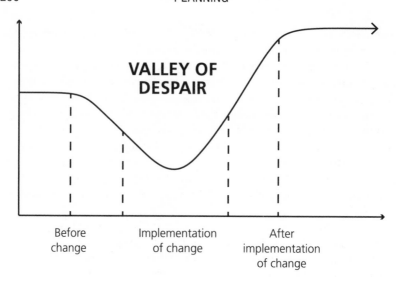

FIGURE 12.1. Valley of despair.

The valley of despair is the place where old, familiar routines are left behind, while the new and hopefully better routines are not yet fully actualized. In a change process, the staff pass through this phase to get to the other side, where there is the promise of higher performance. But this phase is often very frustrating and disappointing for them, because they know that they can do better than they currently are. When in the pit of the valley, they will easily lose faith and confidence in the change. We suggest that you share this insight with your staff so that they are aware that you know this uncomfortable phase will occur and are ready to support them through it. Consider for a moment how you might predict and factor in this process in preparing your employees, so they are clear that this transitional low point is understood, accepted, and embraced by you and the organization.

For instance, just before implementing a new therapy method, Marie, the head of an alcohol treatment facility, presented the picture of the valley of despair during her leadership team meeting and then at an all-staff meeting. She described what her expectations were during implementation and her anticipation that for a while the overall quality of treatment would decline. She told the staff that she and the leadership team took full responsibility for a lower level of performance. She said, "We know that when you are all learning these new methods, you will need to check manuals and focus on trying to remember everything and may not be as present with clients as you typically are. It takes time to learn and become familiar with a new approach. But once you have learned it and it has become your new way of approaching clients, we believe that the outcome of treatment will be better than it is today. It may take months, though, and in that period, you will probably get frustrated and feel that you did better before we started implementing the new therapy method. You will probably be right. But we ask you to continue, and we will back you up all the way."

The leaders need to support their staff during the period in which the staff may perform worse than they did before. They need to continue to support and encourage, and even directly take responsibility for the lower performance, because they know that this is part of the path to improvement. We find that being clear about the valley of despair phase helps minimize recurring ambivalence.

OPENNESS TO FAILURE

It is not only to be expected that the performance in the organizations falls a bit, before it improves, as we described with the valley of despair model; it is also to be expected that mistakes and failures will happen. Yet the good thing about failures and mistakes is that the organizations can learn from them as they strive in their process of change toward a better quality of services. But in order to learn from their failures, the staff and leaders need to be open about and to share and discuss them. However, a climate of trust is essential if you want your staff to share and learn from failures. Stephen Covey argues that trust is the glue that holds teams and organizations together—and there's plenty of research to back up this statement. *Fortune* magazine's research showed that companies with high levels of trust "beat the average annualized returns of the S&P 500 by a factor of three. . . . With trust, all things are possible—most importantly: continuous improvement and sustainable, measurable, tangible results in the marketplace" (Covey & Conant, 2016).

We have mentioned the importance of trust many times. But the only sustainable way to consolidate trust is by modeling it continually every day. But in addition to behaving in a trustworthy and honest way, you may also use specific tools to demonstrate that failures and feedback are stepping-stones for further learning and improvement. For instance, you can use a 360 leadership assessment of yourself to help communicate that you are also working on improving. This tool can help you manifest to the staff what you are hoping to improve on, what you want to hear from them about your overall performance, and how they might help provide feedback about your progress, especially if you slip up at times. As an example, Donna, the leader of a large social service agency, asked her staff to provide her with feedback on her leadership. She decided to share the results of the feedback with her leadership team and the entire organization. From the survey, she learned that her staff felt that she was often unavailable and did not seem open to listening when they were able to grab a moment of her time. Donna shared the scores and comments with her employees so they would see that she had received and read them all. She also created a response, in which she shared what she had learned from their feedback and what her goals were for the next year. She shared that she truly wanted to be available to them but often was overbooked and rushed, which led to her appearing not fully present and alert in conversations. She explained that since she was committed to being available to her staff, she had decided to set aside open times in her schedule each week (by posting the times on her office door) so that they would know she was available for open-door meetings. She also shared that she was going to work on being more present in all conversations moving forward, but worried that there might be days where she would be distracted or preoccupied about something coming up. She suggested that staff members who felt that she was not giving them her undivided attention should say, "I can see you have something else on your mind," which would help her refocus. She also asked them to reassess her progress on these two goals quarterly, saying she would send out a survey to gather that input.

When leaders decide to share feedback as Donna did, they strike a note that acknowledges that nobody is perfect, that everyone has areas that can be improved, and that they want the team to notice improvement but also to offer help when they are slipping back into old patterns.

WHAT IF THE STAFF WISH TO PERFORM A CHANGE THAT YOU DON'T FIND REASONABLE?

There are certainly times when the staff propose a plan to their leader that they have worked out completely on their own and that is ready to implement. The staff may, for instance, recognize that they need to change intake times so more clients can access services. They may already know how to shift schedules, who will work which shifts, and how the rest of the groups and sessions will be covered. When a detailed plan has been worked out, the leader needs to ask for clarification about "why" this change is important. How might this "why" align with or support the mission or values of the organization? *Why* should the organization do this? If the staff are committed to a change that is not, in fact, supporting the organizational goal, this is, of course, something that the leader should discuss with them. For instance, if a team decided to allow all team members to work 4 ten-hour days because this schedule would make them happier, and they believed they could cover the work, but the new schedule actually decreased access to care for clients, the leader may need to revisit the team's goal. In a case like this, the leader may argue against the change and may even have to say no. It is the leader's job to remind the staff of the organization's mission, goals, and values. However, even in this situation, the leader may—and should—praise the staff for their enthusiasm, creative thinking, and good intentions and encourage them to bring future ideas to her attention.

The "why" should always align with the organization's mission and values and should always be at least part of the reason that changes are considered. It is your organization's mission, values, and "why" that help you implement changes, even when change gets hard. Understanding this before moving to planning is critical.

WHAT IS GOOD ORGANIZATIONAL PLANNING?

Just as with individual employees, the planning process is important because it helps the organization work through the change steps and prepare ahead of time. The leader's job is to be clear about deadlines, to offer support, to secure time for the staff to prepare, and to help and guide them when needed. They may also help the staff think about the change process and what to expect and anticipate ahead of time. They might share how typical barriers can be overcome and may offer other practical advice along the way. For instance, they might connect with other sectors or groups that are needed to facilitate the process of planning and implementation. There are many ways to formulate a plan and, just as with individual plans, there are specific guidelines that may help.

Just as with plans for individuals, plans for organizations need to be *specific, rewarding,* and *open to revision. Specific* means that a plan is observable and measurable. This is critical to ensuring clarity of understanding throughout the many layers of the organization. If the plan is not specific, teams, employees, and leaders may be left confused. Specificity allows everyone to monitor how the plan is progressing and whether the expected gains are eventually achieved.

Specific, Observable, and Measurable

How can an organizational plan become specific, observable, and measurable? First of all, if a goal is not specific, you won't know whether you are making progress. For instance, if you and your staff say, "We would like to give our clients a higher quality of life," what does that mean? How will you know if you are getting there?

When leaders wish to set a specific goal for the organizational change, they can brainstorm with their staff by asking, "How will we know when we have reached the goal? What will be different?" The answer may, for instance, be "We will know that the goal is reached when we have achieved a 10% decrease in premature drop out from treatment"; or "We will know that the goal is reached when 80% of our clients have stopped heavy drinking 1 month after treatment start"; or "We will know that we have reached the goal when 60% of our clients see a doctor within 1 week after intake." In planning, the goal needs to be as specific as possible. You want everyone in your organization to have a clear view of what you are all working to achieve, and of whether you are making progress or need to revisit and revise the plan. Being specific about the goal is the first important step on the road to change.

Rewarding

The plan itself should be *rewarding* for the organization and hopefully for the staff too. *Rewarding* can mean more satisfied clients or more satisfied customers. But a plan can be rewarding for the staff only, if, for instance, a change in work performance means an undiminished level of service to their clients or customers, while also offering more flexibility and job satisfaction to the staff.

A rewarding plan can also involve celebrating milestones. Most often, this reward can be simply acknowledging the work and success that has already been achieved. The sense of reward is unique to each person, each team, and each unit. For many people, however, the feeling that they are doing a good job is rewarding in and of itself. Very often, a reward does not have to be big or expensive; it just needs to be felt as a reward by the person or the team. As a leader, you might simply ask what you can do or what the team can do to make the plan rewarding.

There is a lot of current literature on what is rewarding and motivating in work. We suggest that you read more on this topic if you are interested. Understanding how reward systems can hurt and help work performance is important to know but is outside the scope of this book.

Open to Revision

Like individual plans, organizational plans should be *open to revision*. Rarely does a first plan predict all the issues that will arise along the way. You should decide and announce the specific times for evaluating the progress of the plan. Leaders can use the *plan, do, study, act (PDSA) cycles of learning* used by quality departments in organizations as a model for evaluating plans and progress.

The PDSA model requires that leaders and staff ask three questions:

1. "What are we very specifically trying to accomplish [*aim*]?" The aim determines which specific outcome the organization is trying to change.
2. "How will the organization know that a change is an improvement [*measures*]?" Leaders and staff identify the appropriate measures to track success.
3. "What changes in services or routines can be made that will result in improvement [*changes*]?"

In the PDSA model, the key changes are first identified and described (the *plan*), then implemented in a cyclical fashion (the *do*). The changes are not only implemented, but also tested and evaluated (the *study*), as illustrated in Figure 12.2. The testing part is necessary, because it allows the organization to revise the plan if the testing demonstrates that neither the change nor the plan is working as expected (the *act*).

After careful planning, the staff, along with management, will implement the changes in work procedures, closely study the results of their changed routines, and look for insights about how to perform better. Finally, the staff and management will make the successful changes permanent or will modify the changes that need more work. This process can continue serially over time, and refinements can be added with each cycle. Sometimes structures in the organization automatically allow for such a cyclical review process, as in the vignette featuring Maria and her quality-assurance team.

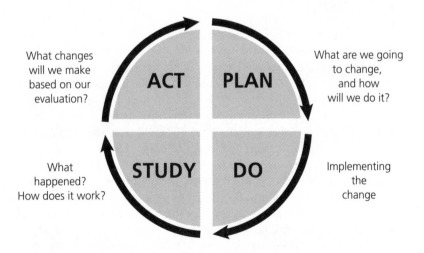

FIGURE 12.2. The PDSA (plan, do, study, act) model.

Standard data may differ from organization to organization, but in helping organizations devoted to health care, addictions, or social services, client outcome data (e.g., How many clients stopped drinking excessively 1 month after treatment began?; How many clients dropped out prematurely?; How many clients got a job during treatment?), are often the information needed to measure whether the organization has reached the goal. Sometimes you might collect other data, like process data (e.g., How many times are clients seen by a therapist?; How often does relapse occur during a phase of treatment?; In how many therapy sessions are the client's significant others involved?) to be able to assess if the plan is working, step by step. Monitoring of data rather than using subjective guessing and making assumptions prevents conflicts and discussions about *whether* the organization is implementing the actual desired change.

Achievable

Organizational goals should always be reasonable, but unlike individual plans, they do not have to be fully *achievable*. They just need to be compelling enough to help the staff feel that they are reaching for something that is making an impact and that matters. The leaders and the staff strive to deliver perfect services, even though that goal might not be possible. For instance, in the treatment of addictions to alcohol, organizations ultimately aim at offering treatment that helps 100% of their clients to never again drink in ways that create problems for them. When organizations monitor the outcome of services, both the leaders and staff know that they cannot reach the ultimate goal. They want to continually work to find a way to help all of their clients all of the time, but know they are likely to fall short. To help guide the organization to the ultimate goal, the leaders will want to describe a goal that they truly believe that they can almost reach. For instance, they might set the goal of ensuring that 75% of clients seeking treatment do not drink heavily 1 year after beginning treatment, and that 80% will stay in treatment until the client and treatment team agree on discharge. However, they know that, according to the current data, only 50% of clients reach that expectation. Having such specific goals allows the organization to determine if it is fulfilling its mission and if its goals seem reasonably achievable. Knowing the organization's current performance and what research shows is possible enables the leaders and staff to decide to aim for a 10% improvement over the current level by striving for an outcome in which 60% of clients are not drinking heavily 1 year after treatment and stay in treatment. It is important that the organization believes it can achieve the annual goal, even as it aspires to the ultimate goal of 100%. The staff may not find it easy, but they collectively should believe that it is achievable. Remember, plans can always be revisited and revised.

The Organization's Reasons for the Change

The *reasons* for change, just as with individuals, are the most important part of planning in organizational change. These reasons should always stem from the organizational mission and goals, and leaders need to reiterate them again and again. They are the overall "whys." It is important for leaders to remember that it is their task to continually remind everyone of these "whys" because they help you guide changes. Often the "whys" are discussed in management teams and are very clear to the leaders. However, when the message about needed change is finally delivered to the staff, the "why" is all too often reduced to a few sentences, if it is there at all. Instead, the message that the staff hear is about what is expected of them. If this is the case, there is a high risk that the staff start perceiving organizational change as change for its own sake, and not as driven by the organization's overall mission or values (Sinek, 2009). Making sure that the "why" is communicated is crucial when discussing, initiating, and implementing change; it can prevent failure, wasted work and resources, and a lack of trust in the leader.

Steps/Strategies

Although the staff may be the best at describing how organizational changes should be implemented, you may wish to help them incorporate *steps* into the plan. As is the case of individual change, in organizational change, too, the goals are often complex and are not reached quickly. Teams can be guided to incorporate specific steps into the plan that include designating who is responsible for each task, what specifically needs to be done, how the team will know when it is done, and the expected completion time. Leaders can help the teams by simply asking them to explain in detail how they will carry out this plan. When the steps are clear, you may help them write the plan down in a clear and consistent way and even suggest the use of project management software (e.g., Basecamp, Microsoft Project) to track and communicate progress.

Support and Continuous Engagement

It is important to be aware that the responsibility for describing and adopting goals as well as for supporting and overseeing improvements of organizational services cannot be delegated. What a leader measures and pays attention to is what the organization pays attention to as well.

The leaders need to constantly support the staff and focus their efforts on the changes that the organization has decided to implement. When they are actively engaged, the staff and, ultimately, the entire organization pays attention. If a leader stops caring about the implementation of the change, the staff and ultimately the entire organization stop caring, too.

But how do you support and pay attention to the implementation of change? It is both easy and difficult. The easy part is that you do so by constantly manifesting this change as your own priority. You can ensure that you always participate in change team meetings or other meetings in which the plan for change and its implementation are discussed. You can comment on the process in newsletters, during staff meetings, and in the minutes of management team meetings. Or you can give rewards or acknowledgments when specific milestones are reached. That part is easy. The not-so-easy part is making the process of support sustainable and focused over time.

We often compare the leader's role in the implementation of change with that of the circus artist who has plates spinning on high sticks. Like the artist, leaders are constantly aware of plates that are about to slow down and risk falling to the ground. To keep the plates from falling, they constantly run between the sticks, giving them a spin, again and again. It is the same with a leader's focus on the organizational goals. And just as with the artist, there is an upper limit as to how many plates you can keep going at the same time. As we pointed out in Chapter 8 on focusing with your organization, two or three priorities are the limit. Jim Collins (2001) reminds us, "If you have more than three priorities, you have no priorities."

SUMMARY

The planning process is important in organizations. Specific plans for *how to* perform the change should be developed by the staff since they know best how to make the changes happen. The leader is needed to set clear deadlines, secure resources for implementation, support the process, and induce optimism about the result. The leader should be aware that there may be a phase in which old routines have been left behind and the new routines are not yet fully secured and implemented. At that point, the leader will have to signal clearly to the staff that she takes responsibility for this temporary decline in quality, believing that before long it will be even higher than before. The leader also needs to ensure that the staff feel free to fail, and trust that the organization will support them through this process of improvement.

Organization Vignette

Under Marie's leadership, the audit team decided that the acute phase of treatment should be improved. Their main argument was that too many clients only came for one appointment, did not attend subsequent sessions, and therefore did not really benefit from full treatment. The team was ready, willing, and able to make these changes, so it was time to start planning. The team needed to work through how this goal could be achieved. First of all, the goal needed to be really specific.

MARIE: What should the goal be? How will we know that we have improved the acute phase of treatment? (*open-ended question*)

[After a brief discussion, everybody—both staff members and management—agreed that the organization should aim for a 25% decrease in early dropout. Early dropout was defined as dropout within the first 4 weeks of treatment.]

MARIE: (*asking the staff—and, in particular, the representative from the nursing staff, since the nurses make up the team responsible for acute treatment*) What do you think? Is 25% reduction a reasonable goal? (*asking for commitment*)

NURSE: Sure, we think it makes sense to strive for that. It will not be easy, but we will be pleased to try.

With this new specific target, a 25% reduction in early dropout, the audit team turned an unclear goal, the improvement of acute treatment, into a goal that was *clear, concrete, and achievable.* The clarity of the goal allowed the rest of the organization to know whether or not it had been achieved.

MARIE: How can we make the change process and the goal rewarding? (*open-ended question*)

The audit team members replied that being involved in the process of improvement was a reward in itself. They looked forward to implementing their ideas and seeing better outcomes in client care. They shared that they were keen to deliver good treatment, and it was frustrating for them to see so many clients only showing up for treatment once or twice. Marie thanked them, expressed her confidence that the staff would be able improve their routines, and added that she would like to celebrate at an all-staff meeting when the early dropout rate reached the first 5%-point decrease.

MARIE: Let's break down this goal into steps. What specific steps do we need to reach to achieve the 25% reduction? (*open-ended question*)

The audit team members discussed the matter and agreed that all therapists in the organization should improve their communication skills with new, ambivalent clients. They decided that the therapists should be trained in MI. In the audit team's minutes, Marie wrote that in order to prevent early dropout, the team believed that there needed to be a focus on improving communication skills among staff, MI skills in particular. Marie also added that the management team, together with the staff, would plan how and when the training should take place, and would have this plan completed within 2 months.

The team agreed that the next step would be to improve the structure of the first session with clients, that there should be no wait time for the first session, and that sessions needed to be conducted in a calm and quiet setting. The team decided to initiate a quality circle (a working group, consisting of staff only) to develop a proposal for how these changes could come about. It was decided that Marie would articulate the mission for the quality circle, describing the first session's goal and the tasks involved. The staff participating in the quality circle would then describe what procedures were necessary to perform in order to reach the goal for the acute treatment. The quality circle was given 60 days to develop the proposal and was asked to present it at the next audit team meeting.

The audit team also decided that the third step would be to collect data that measured whether the goal had been reached. These data elements included client satisfaction after the first session, client understanding of the detoxification process, and family members' understanding of the treatment process. Another quality circle was initiated to develop specific plans on how to incorporate data collection into daily routines. Again, it was decided that Marie would articulate the mission for this quality circle, too, describing the task and work procedures for data collection. This quality circle was also given 60 days to develop the plan and was asked to present it at the next audit team meeting.

Finally, the fourth step was to ensure continuous supervision and feedback to the staff, making sure that they received sufficient coaching and support to be able to acquire their new communication skills. The management had the responsibility for securing implementation of this step. It included ensuring both that sufficient time was allocated in the schedule to provide coaching and feedback and training for the supervisors and coaches to provide effective coaching.

The audit team decided to initiate more quality circles in their planning as a way of including as many employees as possible in the change process. The smaller working groups, consisting of the staff only, were given the task of developing specific plans for a sustainable structure for the acute treatment phase and instructions for documentation of the sessions. In other words, the staff were made responsible for developing plans on how to implement the changes into their daily schedules. The audit team, together with Marie, gave the quality circles clear instructions for their specific remits and specified on how their tasks fit into the larger change initiative. They were given descriptions of the specific tasks they were to accomplish, and a time frame by which to have their proposals ready to present to the audit team. Marie drafted the instructions for each quality circle and included them in the audit meeting's minutes. Before concluding the meetings, she would read the minutes aloud, allowing all members to provide comments. She ended by asking for each member's commitment to work toward achieving that part of the overall plan (secure commitment). Securing each member's commitment demonstrated to everyone that the quality circles' work was backed by all staff members of the audit team as well as by the management group.

Here is what the project plan looked like and what was shared with the rest of the organization in the meeting minutes:

Our Mission: To help clients solve their problems with alcohol and live a life of abstinence or controlled drinking.

Our Goal: At present, 30% of clients leave treatment within the first 3 months. Our goal is to reduce our current dropout rate by 25%.

Our Why (reasons): We believe that if we can improve the acute phase of treatment, we will be able to better engage clients in the following planned treatment courses and help them reduce their drinking.

Steps:

1. Quality circle to develop a process for the first appointment, with no wait time, in calm, welcoming surroundings.

2. Quality circle to develop a process to track new outcomes so as to monitor our progress—due to be presented in 60 days.

3. Quality circle to develop a structure and documentation for the acute treatment phase—due to be presented in 60 days.

4. Management team to develop a timetable and process for training and for providing feedback through coaching and supervision, enabling the staff to learn and implement new MI skills—due to be presented in 60 days.

Reward: We will celebrate at an all-staff meeting when we reach a 5% reduction of the current dropout rate.

Commitment: Each member of the quality circle, the audit team, and the management has agreed to this plan and goal.

A week after the audit team meeting, the quality circles started their work. The proposals proved to be both brilliantly conceived and easy to implement, having been formulated by the staff who knew the most about the specific work situations, and who, accordingly, enjoyed a high level of ownership and confidence in implementing the change.

This example is based on a true story from the alcohol treatment center where I (A. S. N.) was a CEO for many years. During the time that I was head of the organization, the quality circles consistently presented thoughtful plans and suggestions to the audit team, who almost always implemented the ideas right away. Once in a while, the quality circles would present interim considerations and perhaps express doubts about what to recommend. If this happened, the working group would invite the management to supply additional information, to help explore further, to offer advice, and to help the group get a clearer picture of the task. The managers were only consulted, however, if the quality circle expressly invited them to participate in a specific meeting; they were not permanent members of the circle. By empowering the entire staff to share their proposals, the organization benefited by seeing regular improvements that were easy to implement because they were grounded in the staff's experience. In addition, the staff felt respected and involved. Although I left the organization some years ago, the center still uses an audit team (with both staff and management representation) and quality circles (with staff representation only) to ensure that the leader listens to the organization (the staff) when considering or developing improvements and/or changes of performance in service delivery.

SELF-REFLECTIVE EXERCISE. PLAN WITH YOUR ORGANIZATION

You now have an understanding of your organization's ambivalence and a focus, and you also understand why this change is important and that your team believes in its ability to carry it out. You will continue the process with these in mind. You will continue to engage by reflecting understanding, gently guiding the conversation to the focus, and evoking as you move to planning.

If you are considering moving to the planning process, it should be based on the fact that you are hearing readiness (commitment language, taking steps, or activation) from the organization. Keep in mind that, while some groups might be ready, others might not. You might have consensus, or you might have to help a group decide what it is committing to do.

Continue the conversation with your team. The conversation can be free-flowing and the planning questions can be used as guides. Always

remember to continue the engaging process too by reflecting understanding.

Confirm readiness. You might feel that some groups are ready to
move forward and that others are not. You might have consensus, or you
might have to decide for the group. You can check on the team's readiness first to see

- Are we ready do this?
- What do you think our next steps should be?
- It sounds like some of us are ready to move forward and some are
  not.
    - Summarize what you have heard as to why this change is impor-
      tant, how it relates to the overall mission, and why the team believes
      the group is able to manage it.
    - You can also summarize that you notice that some are anxious
      that you should be careful about how you move forward.
- You can then let the team know what you have decided, why you
  have decided to move forward, and why the decision is important to
  the overall goal.
- You can ask the team to commit: Are each of you ready to do this
  and move forward?

Guide through the plan. Once your team is clear that the organization is
moving in this direction, and why, you can use the evoking conversation
to help guide the plan. Remember that if the change is very simple you
might not need all these details, but the more complex the change, the
more you and your employees might want to think about each part of the
planning process together.

Remember the goal is to have plans that are specific, rewarding, and
open to revision.

- Now that we have decided to make this change, what specifically are
  we wanting to change? How will we know that we have achieved it?
  How will others know that we have achieved it?
- Does that goal seem achievable, or does it feel like a real stretch?
  (If it feels like a real stretch, how might we modify the goal to still
  achieve what we want but in a way that's within our grasp?)
- You can summarize all the reasons you have heard about why the
  team, yourself included, want to make this change. You can remind
  the team that is important to keep these reasons in mind as you all
  continue. You might ask in what ways can we keep our "why" for
  making this change our focus as we move toward our goal.

- What specifically will we do, by when, and which staff members will be responsible for this task? For instance, which staff members should be involved in or take care of the detailed planning?

- How might we know that we are making progress as we continue to carry out our plan? What would be signs of success or milestones? How should we celebrate successes and progress?

- When will we revisit the plan to check if it needs any modification or adjustment? How will we know if the plan needs to be modified? How do we follow up on the planning tasks that we have delegated to staff?

Commit to the plan

- Summarize the plan for the group and ask if you missed anything.

- Then ask the group to commit to this plan. Are all of you ready to do this? Are each of you willing to move forward with this plan?

Later, after you have had this conversation, reflect on the process.

- What did you notice?

- How did you know that your team was ready? What did you hear or see?

- What did you notice about your team's ambivalence as you moved to planning? Did it resurface, and if so how did you respond? If not, what else did you notice?

- Were there times when it was easier to listen and guide? What did you notice about those times?

- How confident are you now in the team's/organization's ability to carry out this plan and make this change?

CHAPTER 13

How Can You Become a Better Listener?

I (C. M.) once asked my son how he was coming along with his homework. He replied, "I am almost done." I said, "That's great. What do you mean by you're 'almost done'?" He said, "Well, I know exactly what I need to do; now I just need to do it." That maybe sums up how you feel. We hope that you have found some of the ideas we shared in this book interesting and helpful, and are now thinking, How do I implement them? How do I bring them to life? The good news is that you probably already have some experience with this kind of learning. In learning every new skill, the process is the same. If you want to learn to play the piano, you learn a bit about chords, notes, and fingering. Then you simply practice and receive feedback. You often look to someone who plays the piano at least better than you do to provide the feedback. Or, if you want to learn to run a marathon, you likely read a bit about what it takes to run a marathon, learn ways to build to that level of performance, then run and look to others who run to provide tips, tricks, and practice routines.

The process is similar in learning MI. Typically, we tell people who want to learn MI that the ideal way to go about it is to attend a workshop, usually for 2 to 3 days, to learn the basics. Select a workshop in which you have time to practice with feedback, and then develop a practice or feedback plan. To be good at MI usually requires practice with feedback and not just a 2-day training.

People learn MI in many different ways. Some read MI books and practice on their own, looking to the employee response as their feedback. Or they might videotape their practice and seek out feedback online or through a videoconference. You might want to seek out ways to learn that work best for you with the time and the resources you have available. The good news is that there is no one way to learn MI. And deciding to begin, to listen, to understand, even if you don't learn all of the MI process, can lead to a better understanding of your organization and your employees. It can help you learn more effective ways to help them find solutions.

Let's look at some of the ways you could learn and practice MI. As you consider these ideas, you might ponder what would work best for you. You will want to think about how important it is to you to make these changes, what time you have to dedicate to learning MI, and what sort of team or support you have around you to help you as you learn this new skill. One thing to keep in mind when learning any new skill is that you are likely to stumble some, and may not even be very good at it at first. That is okay and part of the process. But it also means that you might want to give some thought first as to where you'd feel safe to stumble while learning. Where might you practice and feel free to not get it right or even mess up? Part of learning anything new is to feel vulnerable and diffident. It is important to create an environment or setting where you feel free to practice and are able to get feedback that is not only focused on what you are doing well and getting better at but also focused on what you might practice more and improve. We cannot decide for you where this arena might be, but we will give you some ideas of where you might look to find this practice arena for yourself.

In learning new competencies, we think it helpful to separate their elements into *knowledge, skills,* and *attitudes* (KSA). To perform any competency you need to acquire the relevant knowledge and skills and some quite specific attitudes. We will use these three dimensions to talk about the different ideas for learning MI in leadership.

KNOWLEDGE

Read Books

One way you might learn more about MI is by reading some of the many books on the topic. You can find a list of these books on the official MINT website (*www.motivationalinterviewing.org/books*). We recommend starting with the most recent book by the founders of MI, Miller and Rollnick (2013), entitled *Motivational Interviewing, Third Edition: Helping People Change.* There are a number of other books that focus on specific areas, such as MI in schools (Rollnick, Kaplan, & Rutschman, 2016), MI in health care (Rollnick, Miller, & Butler, 2007), or MI in social work (Hohman, 2015). You might decide to read one or several of these books to learn more about MI and how it is applied to your specific context. Once you have read more about what MI is, what the research has taught us about what works and what doesn't, and why MI helps people change, you may also want to read *Building Motivational Interviewing Skills, Second Edition: A Practitioner Workbook*, by David B. Rosengren (2018). In this workbook, Rosengren provides specific activities that you could use to practice MI and better understand its various elements.

As we mentioned earlier in Chapter 4, William Miller has also recently published a book on listening, *Listening Well: The Art of Empathic Understanding* (Miller, 2018). This book is an easy read and has practical exercises that improve the skill of empathic listening, which is an essential part of learning to incorporate MI into your leadership approach.

Attend Training

You may decide that you would like to attend a workshop or training in MI to help you better understand what MI is and how it works. There are many trainers and classes all over the world that teach MI. You can find some of them on the MINT website (*www.motivationalinterviewing.org/list-events*). You can also directly email trainers in your area and ask about their upcoming workshops. A list of trainers is available on the MINT website (*www.motivationalinterviewing.org/trainer-listing*). There are likely trainings near you.

What is important to know about training is that a workshop format is the best one for learning MI. In a workshop, a trainer will expose you to MI by modeling it for you, and then you get to practice it with feedback. This type of format will help you assess what areas you might want to focus your practice on to improve. Sometimes becoming attuned to an overall sense of the spirit of MI or the conception of change is the place to begin, before improving your skills. When selecting a workshop, we suggest that you investigate the trainer's background and experience. The most desirable option is a trainer who is proficient in MI since she is able both to demonstrate it and coach you in your practice. Some trainers may know MI only from books but not practice it themselves. Although they can describe MI, they may not be able to demonstrate it. We find that having a trainer who is able to model MI for you and coach you on your practice is important in learning how to actually practice MI, as opposed to just knowing what it is.

Typically, we would recommend that you take training from someone who provides MI in your work context. So, for instance, if you work in the smoking cessation field, having a trainer familiar with applying

MI to clients who smoke is ideal. However, because MI at the leadership level is relatively new, it is not likely you will find trainers who have this specific specialty. You can still attend a training to learn the basics of MI and then think about the guidance we have provided here about when and when not to apply MI. We have also started a Facebook group you are welcome to join, where you can share your own ideas of applying MI to leadership, and hear from others on how they are doing this as well. (You can find a link to the Facebook group on this book's website; see the box at the end of the table of contents.) There is also a new Facebook and LinkedIn group called MILO (Motivational Interviewing Leaders and Organizations). This page was started by several MINT members who are also researching and applying MI in businesses. They offer new opportunities for learning, as well as videos and resources for leaders interested in applying MI in organizations.

Increasingly, trainers are also finding ways to provide MI training online, where there are a few opportunities for this type of training. As busy business leaders, the chances that you will have 3 days to attend a training are few, so you might want to check out some of the online options. Typically, they present parts of MI in 1-hour formats and then provide ways for you to practice with feedback. Some trainings offer practice and feedback in coaching sessions after you have completed the online modules, which might be an option. Just as with reading books on MI, however, we do recommend that you think about online training as a way of gaining the knowledge to move forward, but keep in mind that you will also want some form of actual practice with feedback if it is not offered as part of the training.

SKILLS

Just as there are many ways to obtain the knowledge about MI, there are many ways to practice MI skills. The difference between knowing and doing is where practicing a skill is critical. Without reflecting on your actual performance, it is hard to know if you are improving or even actually doing MI. Leaders often believe that they have understood what their employees are saying when they haven't. Or they seem to believe that they have neither bias nor their own outcome in mind, when in fact they have, but hide it behind clever questions or reflections. They might also get stuck when trying to evoke reasons and ideas for change, not knowing where to go or what to try next. Leaders might not be able to evaluate their own practice clearly. We like to use the analogy of new dancers. When they practice a dance step, say, a graceful turn, in their own minds they are prima ballerinas. However, when they look in a wall-size mirror as they practice the same turn, it becomes very clear they have a long way to go before they can even contemplate trying out for a ballet company.

This sense of being a novice is likely to be your experience too, and having feedback along the way will help you develop your skills and improve your overall success in using MI to help guide your employees or organization toward change.

We often hear leaders say, "I already do that." You might be having the same thought. And in truth, they and you might well be practicing some parts of MI. You might know that you are focusing your attention, for instance. Or you might use open-ended questions, summaries, or reflections. It is rare, however, that leaders at first use all of the MI processes. If you feel that at least some of what you have just read sounds familiar, that is great. You are on your way. You can build on what you already know how to do and add the parts that are new.

You might start with where you think you are doing well already and develop a plan for getting feedback on this area first. You want to be sure that you actually are doing well in the area that you feel is one of your strengths. It may be that you are doing well, or it may be that you are not seeing your practice in an objective way. Having another person's feedback might help you to improve your practice with confidence.

Formats to Practice

Establish a Learning Community

You could form a group with other leaders interested in learning this approach. Read this book and practice each part together, giving each other feedback. You could meet for breakfast or lunch twice a month, either in person or over a videoconference. Our Facebook group can help support you in your learning. You might connect with other leaders in this group and set up a learning community. You could take one chapter a month, discuss the chapter's ideas, and practice the skills.

Find a Coach

You might consider finding a coach who will listen to your actual practice of MI and give you specific feedback. When looking for a coach, you will want to find someone who is proficient in MI and has helped others improve their use of MI. Ideally, it would be best to find a coach who speaks your language and practices MI in your field. For instance, if you are a leader who wants to use MI in leadership, you will want a coach who also uses MI in leadership. Because this is a new MI field, however, you may not be able to find anyone proficient in MI and leadership to start with. If that is that case, you can certainly work with someone who is proficient in MI and adapt MI to your leadership role, as we have discussed. You can also use our Facebook group to explore areas of uncertainty with the authors and other community members.

When selecting a potential coach, you might ask about whether her own MI practice has been evaluated. In the MI world, many practitioners have had their sessions coded, and this feedback gives some evidence of their proficiency. These coding instruments were developed primarily for research, but are now used in learning practice as well. They are designed to give learners feedback about their skills and an overall view of their proficiency. It is not the only measure that will tell you if someone is proficient; you might also know based on their experience or on recommendations or feedback from others. Just as in any profession, coaches will have different levels of MI proficiency. A good rule of thumb is that a coach needs to be at least a little better at MI than you are to begin with, but ideally will have a few years of using and helping others learn MI under her belt.

It is also important to know that coaching involves a relationship, and not every coach will be the right fit for you. A coaching approach might not be one with which you connect. A good relationship is key. So, you might also set up a beginning session to see if you and your coach connect and seem to work well together. The relationship you establish, the coach's ability to give you specific and helpful feedback, and his or her understanding and proficiency in MI are all considerations to take into account when selecting a coach.

Practice with Your Team

You might ask your team for feedback. Explain to the group that you are trying to learn something new and set aside time in your group or individual meetings for feedback. You could create a learning community with them and learn this approach together, setting up bimonthly meetings for practice and learning.

You might also simply pick someone on your team with whom you feel comfortable and with whom you could try out your skills. You could set aside practice time with your partner, asking him to bring up an issue he is facing, to practice what you have learned, and to ask for feedback at the end of your conversation. It would be ideal if you could tape the practice, so you could self-reflect on your own practice as well. Typically, you want to start your practice with the spirit of MI. How well are you thinking about and trying to practice being in a partnership or a collaboration, expressing empathy, accepting your partner's absolute worth, being nonjudgmental, evoking solutions or ideas from him and not providing your own solutions or ideas, and resisting your righting reflex to fix the problem? Once you feel some congruence with the spirit of MI, moving through the four processes is a good plan. You could also practice using OARS, seeing how well you do with staying with these four skills, while never letting go of the MI spirit. Here are some ideas for questions you might ask yourself and your practice partner:

- "How well did I do in understanding what you meant, not just in what you were saying?"
- "In what ways did you feel I was understanding you? In what ways did you feel I was not listening?"
- "What feedback would you give me about how I might listen to understand more?"
- "Were there times when you thought I was giving you advice or guiding the conversation toward my own point of view? If so, in what ways?"
- "In what ways did I demonstrate the desire to understand your views and your ideas?"

Once you feel that you are doing well with the engaging process, you could move on to asking questions about how well you are focusing, which might include:

- "How well did you think I understood the main focus, or target, you wanted to discuss?"
- "How well did I do on letting you guide the conversation, while at the same time keeping us focused on that target?"
- "In what ways might I have kept our focus clearer?"
- "What feedback do you have on how I might have developed a clearer focus with you and/or kept our conversation focused?"

You can then move on to your evoking practice.

For Your Partner

- "How well did I do in understanding the importance of this change for you? Are there other things you think I could have done to understand that more?"
- "How well did I do in understanding your belief in your ability to make this change? Are there other ways in which I could have understood that more?"
- "Where did you feel the ideas or solutions for this change came from? From you or from me? If they came from me, in what ways did they come from me?"

For You

- "What was your partner's reason for making the change? What is important to her about this change? How confident is she that she can change if she decides to?"
- "In what ways did you elicit or deepen her sense of importance or confidence about changing? In what ways could you have done more of that?"
- "How well did you do with understanding, but not expanding, sustain talk, or reasons to not move forward or change?"
- "If ideas or solutions to move forward toward change were in the conversation, where did these ideas come from [you or your practice partner]? What skills did you use to help bring these ideas forward?"

If your practice partner moved toward planning, you could reflect on that process as well. Remember, though, that MI does not have to include planning to be helpful. Often, new learners feel that they have to progress to planning to be successful and end up pushing the conversation forward faster than the employee is ready to go. But if the employee is ready and willing, and you are hearing mobilizing change talk (commitment language, activation, or taking steps) then moving to planning makes good sense.

For Your Practice Partner's Reflection

- "Did you feel you were ready to talk about a plan when we moved to planning? If not, what would have helped you be more ready?"
- "How well did I do in understanding whether you were ready to plan? What could I have done better?"
- "How well did I do in guiding you to think about a plan for success? What could I have done better to help you plan?"
- "How confident do you feel in your plan? If you are not confident, what could I have done better to help build your confidence in your plan?"

For Your Self-Reflection

- "Was your practice partner ready to move to planning? In what ways did you hear readiness [mobilizing change talk]?"
- "In what ways did you support planning and her thinking about the different elements of successful planning?"
- "How ready does your partner feel to take the first steps toward change?"
- "In what ways might you have helped more with preparing for action or taking steps?"

These are just a few of the possible questions you and your partner might consider. As you focus on your practice, it is likely there will be specific questions that are focused on your own areas of growth that you might want feedback on. You might also use some of the tools created for learning MI to help you think about your own practice and about areas in which you have improved and which areas you want to work on next. Worksheet 13.1 (at the end of this chapter) presents a guide on how to practice seeking and giving feedback on your skills. Appendix C (at the end of the book) provides a format for you to create your own learning plan. In addition, we have also included two self-reflective exercises (individual and organization focus) that runs through the whole book that you could use as well.

Notes on Feedback

When we are giving MI training, we often stop to talk about what makes feedback helpful before we move on to role plays and practice. Over the years, we have found that feedback is delivered in many ways and is in many cases not helpful. Sometimes a person is new to a skill, and the feedback partner only focuses on what the person did well. The partner fails to point out any areas for improvement and leaves him with nothing to work on moving forward. Similarly, sometimes the partner only gives feedback on all the ways in which the person fell short, and fail to focus at all on anything that was done well. Or the partner comes up with a long list of things the person did not do well, leaving him feeling overwhelmed. What is typically helpful is to ask the person practicing to self-evaluate first. You will be surprised when you do this at how often the learner says everything you were about to say. You can also tell where the learner is being hard on himself and not giving himself enough credit for improvement. We typically help the feedback partner to guide the self-evaluation and comment with her thoughts as she goes along. We find the format in Worksheet 13.1 to be helpful for self-evaluation. You can ask the person practicing the new skills the questions shown in the "Ask" column of Worksheet 13.1, and you can note what is reflected in the "Reflect" column.

Sometimes the feedback ends here because the learner and the feedback partner share the same views, and there is no need to add further comments. But there are other times when the learner and feedback partner may have different opinions, and the feedback partner has his own thoughts to share. In coaching or feedback, it is important that the self-reflection and the direct coaching feedback are present, so the learner can improve if needed. When I (C. M.), was learning to sing, my coach would often ask me how I felt or how I did. I would share my thoughts, which ranged from "that was horrible" to "I felt pretty good." I would then say, "I am going to keep working on X," which usually meant I was going to focus on the sound of a note or a note placement. He would almost always bring me back to the fundamentals. He would say, "No, I don't think that will get you the sound you want. I think you should work on breathing and opening your mouth with a relaxed jaw and a relaxed tongue." He was the expert on how to get me to sound the way I wanted to. He was guiding me to what I needed to focus on next. It is the same with coaching and feedback in MI. You want your feedback partner to help guide you, the learner, to what might be the most helpful next step. Learners may not always know what is best or might be on the wrong track. In training, we have worked with people who say things like, "I think I will devise better questions," when we can see that, if they reflected more, they would be able to engage better and move forward. Allowing them time to improve their questions would not be helpful.

We also train feedback partners to give specific feedback that is balanced. This means that they need to provide feedback that indicates what the learner is doing well and what the learner can improve. It is important to provide comments about what you notice the learner is doing well, even if it is simply to connect with the learner's intention. You might say, "I could tell you were really trying and really wanting to understand." If the only feedback a person gets when learning something new is that she is doing it wrong, she is likely to become frustrated and despondent. Highlighting what you've noticed she is trying to do better or what she is doing well helps her maintain confidence in continuing to practice. Equally important is being direct and clear on the areas of growth. When providing feedback on areas in which the learner can improve, we suggest that you limit it to two areas at most. The feedback should be specific. It can be about big areas, such as "I think it would be great if you could focus more on eliciting and not volunteering your own ideas, like you did when you said . . . ," or it can be more narrowly focused, as in "I think it would be helpful if you reflected more; you seem to ask questions rather than offer reflections." You also want to be sure the feedback is clear. Saying "I think you should listen more," is not clear. Saying something like "I think you tend to talk more than the employee; maybe you could try allowing silence or reflecting only when the employee has finished talking" is clear. After providing feedback, you always want the learner to reflect on what you shared and to share her thoughts about the feedback. The learner may agree with the feedback, may misunderstand, or may not believe she can or should do what you suggest. By providing space for the learner to share what she thinks about your feedback, you can help clarify what she is willing to try next. We suggest a format such as the following:

- "I noticed you also did _____ well."
- "I noticed you improved by _____."

- "One area you could focus on next time is _____."
- "What do you think about my feedback?"

It is important to focus the feedback on specific areas and build from there. Spirit is a good place to start with, suggesting that the feedback partner give feedback only on the leaner's attunement to the overall spirit. It is important not to focus yet on the learner's skills or on what she did, but on her intention. You can comment on what you noticed the learner did well and where you noticed that she was acting from her righting reflex.

As you or the learner continue to develop your skills, you can expand on feedback by including different elements one at a time. You might concentrate next on OARS, now focusing, now evoking skills, or responding to eliciting change talk. One way to help feedback partners give input is to have them use written formats. For instance, if you are practicing OARS, you might have the feedback partners write check marks for every time they hear an open-ended question, reflection, affirmation, or summary, and write down any specific examples of each one, such as a great reflection, that they felt were particularly good. Again, remind the feedback partner to provide feedback on what went well and what the learner might work to improve. These are just a few examples of questions you could use to guide effective feedback. As you tailor MI to your practice, it is likely you will have specific questions that are aimed at your own areas of growth that you might want feedback on. You might also use some of the feedback forms we have provided in the appendix.

Rosengren's (2018) *Building Motivational Interviewing Skills*, mentioned earlier, is also a great resource for learning different ways to practice. The collection of different exercises that Rosengren has put together can be used to help improve your practice.

ATTITUDE

The way we understand attitude, in association with competencies, is in terms of a person's overall openness or willingness to learn or acquire a given competency. For instance, if you were trying to improve your overall customer service competency, you might have the requisite knowledge. You understand what it takes to provide good customer service, because you might have read books or attended a training course on customer service. You might even have the appropriate skills. You can demonstrate, when asked, how to be helpful, positive, solution focused, and relational. You could even teach others to become more competent at customer service and model this skill. However, your overall attitude toward customer service might not be the right attitude. To be successful in customer service, your attitude likely needs to reflect that you believe that you owe the customer your respect, your undivided attention, your resourcefulness, and your creativity. If, on the other hand, your attitude toward customers is that you find them too difficult, demanding, and needy, you are likely not to be a good customer service provider. You have the necessary knowledge and skill, but your attitude will get in the way of your being excellent at customer service.

It is the same with any competency. When implementing MI in organizations, one roadblock that we regularly run into is the thinking of leaders or managers who do not believe MI will help them, even though they understand the research and can even role-play the skills. Their overall attitude is that change in employees and in organizations comes solely at the direction of the manager and not from collaboration with the staff. Such leaders do not believe that MI can be useful to them. If this is the case for you or for someone on your team, working through this assumption or attitude is an important first step. Ironically, MI may actually contribute to this attitude, because it may help you or the person to decide whether or not to use or learn MI.

Attitude is also revealed indirectly. It often shows up in leaders' belief systems, of which they may or may not be aware. For us, the hardest part of learning MI was trusting that the clients or employees could come up with their own solutions. We both regularly wanted to give advice. We are natural teachers and love teaching and sharing ideas and solutions. To be open to learning MI, we had to fight three things: our lack of trust that our employees could come up with the solutions themselves, our own need to show that we were smart, and our desire to be the teachers. We were lucky to have good coaches who would investigate our intentions when they noticed these tendencies in practice. Here is an example of a coaching conversation with one of us (C. M.).

> COACH: Tell me, right there (*when listening to the tape*) you gave that piece of information. How did that go?
>
> ME: Not as well as I hoped. They started explaining why that would not help.
>
> COACH: What did you hope would happen?
>
> ME: I thought if I shared my idea they would come up with their own or would use my idea.
>
> COACH: So you wanted to know their ideas and you tried to get that by sharing your own. What might it sound like if you let go of your idea and just got curious about theirs?

This type of feedback was typical, and the coach would point out, "This is not the first time you felt the need to provide your ideas or teach something." This was so helpful to me because I had no idea that what I was doing was counterproductive. I really thought I was being helpful. But when I was able to see what was getting in my way, and began trusting that my employees could come up with ideas themselves, their confidence grew and they started to improve in ways they had not done before.

Part of why feedback from coaches who are proficient in MI is helpful is because they have had to go through this process themselves. They have had to look at their own intentions and work through what they were aiming to do and what was actually happening. They likely had to shift their skills and approaches to be able to trust the process and guide their employees. A good coach also typically knows the common errors that learners make. They can tell when you are responding to your righting reflex, or when you are more focused on the problem than on the side of change.

If you are working on learning MI in a community, you might talk about your intentions and self-reflect together with your team about what you meant to do, and then ask your team or practice partners for their own reaction or response to your intention. What is nice about your employee's or practice partner's responses is that they are great feedback for determining if what you are doing is helpful or working, regardless of whether it even is MI.

If you are able to do so, working with a coach can be very helpful in identifying any attitudinal beliefs that are in your way. It is our conviction that while a leader's intentions are almost always good, her specific approach may not be effective. The righting reflex is a great example of having a good intention and an ineffective approach.

If you are not able to work with a coach, you might instead tape-record your practice, then draw three columns on a sheet of paper, and comment on yourself as you listen to your work. Listen through the whole tape once, noting down any time stamps that you want to return to. They might be points where you thought your practice went well and want to look at what you did more specifically to help reinforce it, or they might be areas where you felt stuck or did not do went well and you might want to reflect more on what you were trying to do and what you might do differently next time. Your column headings might read like those in Worksheet 13.2 (at the end of this chapter).

Learning to listen and to learn MI is an ongoing practice. Collectively, we have been using MI for over 20 years, and we still find that we are learning new things all the time. If you are interested in incorporating MI into your leadership approach, it is likely it will feel cumbersome at first, but with practice, over time, it will feel more comfortable and you will get better and better.

Learning MI often spills over into all aspects of your life. You start listening at home, in your community, and even at the grocery store differently. You also start noticing when you are not listening and when the conversations you are having are not productive, and might find that you shift to using your MI skills. MI takes some practice but in the end is worth it. What better way to show your employees that they matter than to learn how better to understand them and support their growth?

SUMMARY

There are many ways that lead to Rome, and there are many ways to learn MI. The most important message is that listening to what you do and having others also review and provide feedback on your actual practice is an important part of learning. When leaders observe and receive feedback on their actual use of MI, they begin to realize that they aren't always practicing it the way they should be. Learning MI together with others can be very helpful, both for receiving feedback and also for keeping the focus on continuing to learn and use MI in a busy work life.

Worksheet 13.1. MI Practice Feedback Worksheet

The following guide provides a conversation flow to help with giving feedback when observing MI practice.

Ask	Reflect
1. What did you think you did well? Anything else that you noticed you did well?	*Reflect what you hear, and agree that the person shared what is going well. Add anything you also noticed and thought went well. Do not agree with something that you did not think went well just because the person thought so.*
2. Where did you notice you improved or saw growth? Any other way that you noticed you improved?	*Reflect what you hear and also agree with any areas you noticed and saw as growth that the person mentioned as well.*
3. In looking back now, where if anywhere, would you have done something different or wish you had done something different?	*Reflect what you hear.*
4. What are the one or two areas you want to focus on for improvement?	*Reflect what you hear, and agree with any areas that you also think would benefit from further focus.*

Worksheet 13.2. MI Self-Reflection Feedback Worksheet

The following guide provides a format for you to use when self-reflecting on your own recorded MI practice.

What did the employee mean?	How did I respond?	What was my intention?

APPENDICES

APPENDIX A

Matrix: Who Is to Benefit?— Leader versus Employee

	Leader benefits from change.	Leader is not affected by change.	Leader benefits from the status quo.
Employee benefits from change.	MI may be appropriate—with due care taken. (*You have a bias and desire; ensure you are focused on employee benefit.*)	MI is appropriate.	MI may be appropriate—with due care taken. (*You have a bias and need to focus on employee benefit only.*)
Employee neither benefits nor loses from change.	MI is not appropriate. (*You are the only one who benefits, and you have a strong bias.*)	MI is appropriate.	MI may be appropriate—with due care taken. (*You have a bias and need to focus on what is best for the employee.*)
Employee loses from change.	MI is not appropriate.	MI is not appropriate.	MI may be appropriate—with due care taken. (*Be careful: you have a bias and could respond to your own wishes.*)

(continued)

Here are some examples:

	Leader benefits from change.	Leader is not affected by change.	Leader benefits from the status quo.
Employee benefits from change.	Anna is trying to decide if she should attend a training to improve her customer services skills. If Anna does decide to improve in this area, the leader also benefits, because a key performance indicator that the leader is measured against is customer satisfaction. **MI may be appropriate—with due care taken.** *(You have a bias and desire; ensure you are focused on employee benefit.)*	Fred is trying to decide if he wants to attend training in time management and organizational skills. If he improves in this area, it does not directly impact the leader, because the leader has no personal stake in Fred doing his work in a more organized or efficient manner. **MI is appropriate.**	Tina is considering a promotion and is not sure if she wants to apply for or believes she can do the new job. The new job is a new opportunity and comes with more benefits and money. The leader values this employee and does not want her to leave the team. If the employee does get the job, the leader is left with having to find a replacement and is worried the new employee might not be as good as Tina. **MI may be appropriate— with due care taken.** *(You have a bias and need to focus on employee benefit only.)*
Employee neither benefits nor loses from change.	If John, the leader, adds a new service line for existing clients, he will receive a bonus. The nurse, Lindsey, is asked to consider learning to do and add this new service. The change would not make Lindsey work more hours or harder during the work week, and she would not make more money from the change. **MI is not appropriate.** *(You are the only one who benefits, and you have a strong bias.)*	Mary is considering trying to add a new reporting and team structure to see if it helps her team improve its efficiency and effectiveness with clients. The team is performing well now, so Mary is not sure if this is a good change or if she should keep things as they are. Mary's supervisor is indifferent as well. **MI is appropriate.**	Josh is considering a lateral move within the organization. The new role has the same pay and similar responsibilities. He was asked by another leader to consider it, but is happy to stay where he is and is happy to move as well. Shelby, Josh's current supervisor, values Josh and does not want him to leave her team. If Josh does move, Shelby will have to find a replacement and is worried the replacement might not be as good as Josh. **MI may be appropriate— with due care taken.** *(You have a bias and need to focus on employee benefit only.)*

(continued)

	Leader benefits from change.	Leader is not affected by change.	Leader benefits from the status quo.
Employee loses from change.	Andrew, the division director, is evaluated against productivity measures and is asking Trish, a therapist, to consider increasing her workload and manage more cases. This increase does not help Trish in any way and just gives her more work to do. **MI is not appropriate.**	Amy is asked to take on a new project for another division that her supervisor, Jason, is indifferent about. Jason does not necessarily agree that it is a priority, but does not object if Amy wants to help the other division. Amy sees this as an additional burden to an already heavy workload and does not see a benefit to helping. **MI is not appropriate.**	Al is asked to move to a new position that has less responsibility and less pay. He wants to be a team player, but does not see this as valuable to him. His supervisor, Matt, values Al and does not want him to leave his team. If Al does move to the new job, Matt is left with having to find a replacement and worried the replacement might not be as good as Al. **MI may be appropriate— with due care taken.** (*Be careful: you have a bias and could respond to your own wishes.*)

APPENDIX B

Matrix: Who Is to Benefit?— Leader versus Organization

	Organization benefits from change.	Organization is not affected by either change or the status quo.	Organization benefits from the status quo.
Employee benefits from change.	MI may be appropriate. (*Use with caution, because your primary goal as a leader is to serve the organization. In the MI conversation, ensure you are focused on the employee benefit only.*)	MI is appropriate.	MI may be appropriate. (*Use with caution, because your primary goal as a leader is to serve the organization. In the MI conversation, ensure you are focused on the employee benefit only.*)
Employee neither benefits nor loses from change.	MI is appropriate.	MI is likely appropriate.	MI may be appropriate.
Employee loses from change.	MI is probably not appropriate.	MI is probably not appropriate.	MI may be appropriate.
Here are some examples:			

(*continued*)

	Organization benefits from change.	Organization is not affected by either change or the status quo.	Organization benefits from the status quo.
Employee benefits from change.	Tina is considering implementing a new screening training for the admissions department, and if it is implemented. it will mean higher quality care for the organization. **MI may be appropriate.** (*Use with caution, because your primary goal as a leader is to serve the organization. In the MI conversation, ensure you are focused on the employee benefit only.*)	James is considering applying for a clinic manager role that would increase his responsibilities and pay. The organization has many good candidates for this role. **MI is appropriate.**	Michele is considering modifying her work schedule to have more of a work–life balance, which would lead to less time at work and less willingness to take on new projects that do not fit into a 40-hour work week. The organization benefits from Michele's overtime now and her willingness to take on additional projects when asked. **MI may be appropriate.** (*Use with caution, because your primary goal as a leader is to serve the organization. In the MI conversation, ensure you are focused on the employee benefit only.*)
Employee neither benefits nor loses from change.	Erin, a clinical supervisor, is asked to attend and learn a new clinical supervision model. She does not specifically gain from this new approach and feels that her current supervision model is effective; however, she does not mind learning it either. The organization would benefit from having consistent and standardized supervision models across the organization. **MI is appropriate.**	Andrew, a clinical supervisor, is considering adding a new team to his existing group. He likes being a team player and does not see doing this as more work but does not specifically benefit from the increased responsibility. The organization benefits from his leadership and oversight and in not having to find another leader at an additional expense. **MI is likely appropriate.**	Judy, a child therapist, has been approached by a competitor and is considering a lateral move to that organization. She is not sure if she would be better off staying where she is or leaving. The roles, pay, and work are similar. Her current organization values Judy because she is able to manage a large caseload and provide high-quality therapy to her clients. If she does leave, the leader of the organization will be in the position of having to fill the position and will lose Judy's productivity for at least 3 months. **MI may be appropriate.**

(*continued*)

	Organization benefits from change.	Organization is not affected by either change or the status quo.	Organization benefits from the status quo.
Employee loses from change.	Lucy, a billing representative, has been asked by her organization to consider switching to a new electronic documentation system because it will help the organization better manage cross-system needs and communication. Lucy is comfortable with the system that is currently used, and does not see a benefit to using the new system in her job. She only sees the benefit for other departments, not for billing. **MI is probably not appropriate.**	The organization needs an employee to take on a training initiative, but is indifferent as to which employee is chosen. Casey is one of the people asked to consider taking on this project. Casey believes that if he takes the lead on this, it will overwhelm him and his department. **MI is probably not appropriate.**	Pamela has been asked by her former supervisor from another company to move to his department, because he liked working with Pamela and because the agency is in trouble and might lose its funding if changes are not made soon. This change would mean a temporary demotion for Pamela, but would help out her former supervisor and possibly save important community services. Pamela's current organization benefits from Pamela staying where she is, because she is a valued employee and manages current projects that have important objectives for the company and rapidly approaching deadlines. **MI may be appropriate.**

Motivational Interviewing Learning Plan

The following guide is designed to help you create your own MI learning plan.

Where am I and where do I want to be?

Overall MI Goals

- Internalize the spirit of MI.
- Increase the knowledge and use of basic MI skills and strategies.
- Be aware of different MI strategies for use with a variety of audiences.
- Recognize and utilize my strengths with MI.
- Pursue ongoing professional development in the use of MI.

What are my long-term goals for implementing MI in my practice?

(*continued*)

Why is MI training important to me?

What are my strengths in using MI? How can I use these strengths to build my skills?

What will it take for me to reach my goals in increasing my implementation of MI?

What am I ready, willing, and able to work on to continue skills building?

Where do I want to start? What is my short-term learning goal?

What options do I have to practice? How can I make more opportunities? How can I get feedback on my practice?

What kind of assistance do I need? How can I get it?

References

Aarons, G. A. (2006). Transformational and transactional leadership: Association with attitudes toward evidence-based practice. *Psychiatric Services*, 57(8), 1162–1169.

Aarons, G. A., Ehrhart, M. G., & Farahnak, L. R. (2014). The Implementation Leadership Scale (ILS): Development of a brief measure of unit level implementation leadership. *Implementation Science, 9*, 45.

Bandura, A. (1997). *Self-efficacy: The exercise of control*. New York: Freeman.

Bass, B. M., Avolio, B. J., Jung, D. I., & Berson, Y. (2003). Predicting unit performance by assessing transformational and transactional leadership. *Journal of Applied Psychology. 88*(2), 207–218.

Blanchard, K., & Miller, M. (2004). *The secret: What great leaders know and do*. San Francisco: Berrett-Koehler.

Boyatzis, R. E. (2006). Using tipping points of emotional intelligence and cognitive competencies to predict financial performance of leaders. *Psicothema, 18*(Suppl.), 124–131.

Brimhall, K. C., Fenwick, K., Farahnak, L. R., Hurlburt, M. S., Roesch, S. C., & Aarons, G. A. (2016). Leadership, organizational climate, and perceived burden of evidence-based practice in mental health services. *Administration and Policy in Mental Health and Mental Health Services Research, 43*(5), 629–639.

Brown, B. (2012). *Daring greatly: How the courage to be vulnerable transforms the way we live, love, parent, and lead*. New York: Gotham.

Brown, B. (2017). *Braving the wilderness: The quest for true belonging and the courage to stand alone*. New York: Random House.

Brown, B. (2018). *Dare to lead: Brave work. Tough conversations. Whole hearts*. New York: Random House.

Burke, B. L., Arkowitz, H., & Menchola, M. (2003). The efficacy of motivational interviewing: A meta-analysis of controlled clinical trials. *Journal of Consulting and Clinical Psychology, 71*(5), 843–861.

Collins, J. (2001). *Good to great*. New York: HarperCollins.

Colonello, V., Petrocchi, N., & Heinrichs, M. (2017). The psychobiological foundation of prosocial relationships: The role of oxytocin in daily social exchanges. In P. Gilbert (Ed.), *Compassion: Concepts, research and applications* (pp. 105–119). London: Routledge.

Covey, S. R. (1989). *The 7 habits of highly effective people: Restoring the character ethic.* New York: Free Press.

Covey, S. R., & Conant, D. (2016). The connection between employee trust and financial performance. *Harvard Business Review.* Retrieved from *https://hbr.org/2016/07/the-connection-between-employee-trust-and-financial-performance.*

D'Onfro, J. (2015). LinkedIn's CEO on the most important leadership lesson he's learned. Retrieved from *www.inc.com/business-insider/linkedin-s-jeff-weiner-on-the-most-valuable-lesson-hes-learned-as-ceo.html.*

DiClemente, C. C., & Velasquez, M. M. (2002). Motivational interviewing and the stages of change. In W. R. Miller & S. Rollnick, *Motivational interviewing: Preparing people for change* (2nd ed., pp. 201–216). New York: Guilford Press.

Drucker, P. (1967). *The effective executive.* New York: Harper & Row.

Ewest, T. (2017). *Prosocial leadership: Understanding the development of prosocial behavior within leaders and their organizational settings.* New York: Palgrave Ltd.

Gifford, W., Graham, I. D., Ehrhart, M. G., Davies, B. L., & Aarons, G. A. (2017) Ottawa model of implementation leadership and implementation leadership scale: Mapping concepts for developing and evaluating theory-based leadership interventions. *Journal of Healthcare Leadership, 9,* 15–23.

Gilbert, P., & Basran, J. (2019). The evolution of prosocial and antisocial competitive behavior and the emergence of prosocial and antisocial leadership styles. *Frontiers in Psychology, 10,* 610.

Gordon, T. (1970). *Parent effectiveness training.* New York: Wyden.

Green, A. E., Albanese, B. J., Cafri, G., & Aarons, G. A. (2014). Leadership, organizational climate, and working alliance in a children's mental health service system. *Community Mental Health Journal, 50*(7), 771–777.

Green, A. E., Albanese, B. J., Shapiro, N. M., & Aarons, G. A. (2014). The roles of individual and organizational factors in burnout among community-based mental health service providers. *Psychological Services, 11*(1), 41–49.

Greenhalgh, T., Robert, G., Macfarlane, F., Bate, P., & Kyriakidou, O. (2004). Diffusion of innovations in service organizations: Systematic review and recommendations. *The Milbank Quarterly, 82*(4), 581–629.

Guerrero, E. G., Padwa, H., Fenwick, K., Harris, L. M., & Aarons, G. A. (2016). Identifying and ranking implicit leadership strategies to promote evidence-based practice implementation in addiction health services. *Implementation Science, 11,* 69.

Harvard Extension School. (2019). Collaborative leadership: Building the organization of the future. Retrieved from *www.extension.harvard.edu/professional-development/programs/collaborative-leadership-building-organization-future.*

Hettema, J., Steele, J., & Miller, W. R. (2005). Motivational interviewing. *Annual Review of Clinical Psychology, 1,* 91–111.

Hickey, K. (2018). Why inner work is the ultimate retention strategy. Retrieved from *www.betterup.co/inner-work-ultimate-retention-strategy.*

Hohman, M. (2015). *Motivational interviewing in social work practice.* New York: Guilford Press.

Ibarra, H., & Hansen, M. T. (2011). Are you a collaborative leader? Retrieved from *https://hbr.org/2011/07/are-you-a-collaborative-leader.*

Judge T. A., Piccolo R. F. (2004). Transformational and transactional leadership: A meta-analytic test of their relative validity. *Journal of Applied Psychology, 89,* 755–768.

Leake, G. J., & King, A. S. (1997). Effect of counsellor expectations on alcoholic recovery. *Alcohol Health and Research World, 1*(3), 16–22.

Lencioni, P. (2002). *The five dysfunctions of a team: A leadership fable.* San Francisco: Jossey-Bass.

Lencioni, P. (2012). *The advantage: Why organizational health trumps everything else in business.* San Francisco: Jossey-Bass.

Levy Merrick, E., Garnick, D. W., Horgan, C. M., & Hodgkin, D. (2002). Quality measurement and accountability for substance abuse and mental health services in managed care organizations. *Medical Care, 40*(12), 1238–1248.

Lorenzi, P. (2004). Managing for the common good: Prosocial leadership. *Organizational Dynamics, 33*(3), 282–291.

Lundahl, B. W., Kunz, C., Brownell, C., Tollefson, D., & Burke, B. L. (2010). A meta-analysis of motivational interviewing: Twenty-five years of empirical studies. *Research on Social Work Practice, 20*(2), 137–160.

Kirkeby, O. F. (2004). *Det nye lederskab [The New Leadership].* Copenhagen: Børsens Forlag.

Madathil, R., Heck, N. C., & Schuldberg, D. (2014). Burnout in psychiatric nursing: Examining the interplay of autonomy, leadership style, and depressive symptoms. *Archives of Psychiatric Nursing, 28*(3), 160–166.

McLellan, A. T., Carise, D., & Kleber, H. D. (2003). Can the national addiction treatment infrastructure support the public's demand for quality care? *Journal of Substance Abuse Treatment, 25*(2), 117–121.

McLellan, A. T., McKay, J. R., Forman, R., Cacciola, J., & Kemp, J. (2005). Reconsidering the evaluation of addiction treatment: From retrospective follow-up to concurrent recovery monitoring. *Addiction, 100,* 447–458.

Mikulincer, M., & Shaver, P. (2007). *Attachment in adulthood: Structure, dynamics, and change.* New York: Guilford Press.

Miller, W. R. (1983). Motivational interviewing with problem drinkers. *Behavioral Psychotherapy, 11,* 147–172.

Miller, W. R. (2018). *Listening well: The art of empathic understanding.* Eugene, OR: Wipf & Stock.

Miller, W. R., Benefield, R. G., & Tonigan, J. S. (1993). Enhancing motivation for change in problem drinking: Controlled comparison of two therapist styles. *Journal of Consulting and Clinical Psychology, 61,* 455–461.

Miller, W. R., & Rollnick, S. (2013). *Motivational interviewing: Helping people change* (3rd ed.). New York: Guilford Press.

Moyers, T. B., & Miller, W. R. (2013). Is low therapist empathy toxic? *Psychology of Addictive Behaviors, 27*(3), 878–884.

Naar-King, S., & Suarez, M. (2010). *Motivational interviewing with adolescents and young adults.* New York: Guilford Press.

Nielsen, A. S., Nielsen, B. (2015). Implementation of a clinical pathway may improve alcohol treatment outcome. *Addiction Science & Clinical Practice, 10*(1), 7.

Øvretveit, J. (2009). *Leading improvement effectively: Review of research* [Pamphlet]. London: The Health Foundation. Retrieved from *www.health. org.uk/publications/leading-improvement-effectively*.

Pink, D. H. (2009). *Drive: The surprising truth about what motivates us.* New York: Riverhead Books.

Piotrowska, P. J., Stride, C. B., Croft, S. E., & Rowe, R. (2015). Socioeconomic status and antisocial behaviour among children and adolescents: A systematic review and meta-analysis. *Clinical Psychology Review, 35,* 47–55.

Pishgooie, A. H., Atashzadeh-Shoorideh, F., Falco-Pegueroles, A., & Lotfi, Z. (2018). Correlation between nursing managers' leadership styles and nurses' job stress and anticipated turnover. *Journal of Nursing Management, 27,* 527–534.

Powell, D. J., & Brodsky, A. (2004). *Clinical supervision in alcohol and drug abuse counseling: Principles, models, methods* (rev. ed.). San Francisco: Jossey-Bass.

Quinn, R. E. (2004). *Building the bridge as you walk on it: A guide to leading change.* San Francisco: Jossey-Bass.

Reinke, W. M., Herman, K. C., & Sprick, R. (2011). *Motivational interviewing for effective classroom management.* New York: Guilford Press.

Rogers, E. M. (1995). *Diffusion of innovations* (4th ed.). New York: Free Press.

Rollnick, S., Kaplan, S. G., & Rutschman, R. (2016). *Motivational interviewing in schools: Conversations to improve behavior and learning.* New York: Guilford Press.

Rollnick, S., Miller, W. R., & Butler, C. C. (2007). *Motivational interviewing in health care: Helping patients change behavior.* New York: Guilford Press.

Rosengren, D. B. (2018). *Building motivational interviewing skills: A practitioner workbook* (2nd ed.). New York: Guilford Press.

Rosenthal, R., & Jacobson, L. (1992). *Pygmalion in the classroom: Teacher expectation and pupils' intellectual development* (newly expanded ed.). Bancyfelin, Carmarthen, Wales: Crown House.

Rubak, S., Sandbæk, A., Lauritzen, T., & Christensen, B. (2005). Motivational interviewing: A systematic review and meta-analysis. *British Journal of General Practice, 55*(513), 305–312.

Sfantou, D. F., Laliotis, A., Patelarou, A. E., Sifaki-Pistolla, D., Matalliotakis, M., & Patelarou, E. (2017). Importance of leadership style towards quality of care measures in healthcare settings: A systematic review. *Healthcare, 5*(4), 73.

Sinek, S. (2009). *Start with why: How great leaders inspire everyone to take action.* New York: Penguin Group.

Stinson, J. D., & Clark, M. D. (2017). *Motivational interviewing with offenders: Engagement, rehabilitation, and reentry.* New York: Guilford Press.

Swensen, S., Pugh, M., McMullan, C., & Kabcenell, A. (2013). *High-impact leadership: Improve care, improve the health of populations, and reduce costs* (IHI White Paper). Cambridge, MA: Institute for Healthcare Improvement. Retrieved from *ihi.org*.

Wagner, C. C., & Ingersoll, K. S. (2012). *Motivational interviewing in groups.* New York: Guilford Press.

Witkiewitz, K., Hartzler, B., & Donovan, D. (2010). Matching motivation enhancement treatment to client motivation: Re-examining the project MATCH motivation matching hypothesis. *Addiction, 105,* 1403–1413.

Index